Faith and Practice

OTHER BOOKS BY BISHOP WILSON

The Divine Commission
What a Churchman Ought to Know
The Promises of Christ
Outline Series

Faith and Practice

By the Right Reverend
FRANK E. WILSON, D.D., S.T.D.

MOREHOUSE PUBLISHING
WILTON, CONNECTICUT

ISBN: 0-8192-1082-X

Printed in the United States of America
by
BSC Litho, Harrisburg, PA

PUBLISHER'S FOREWORD

Since its original publication in 1939, Bishop Wilson's *Faith and Practice* has been recognized as a basic classic of the teaching, worship, and life of the Episcopal Church. It is safe to say that more than a quarter of a million readers have derived accurate information, inspiration, and enjoyment from its reading.

Now, on the occasion of renewal of the original copyright, the publisher has gone over it with care to revise it and bring it up to date. It is remarkable how little change has been required. The author was one of the most forward-looking Churchmen of his day, a leader in the movement to renew the Church and to encourage the social and ecumenical concerns that were then stirring. He anticipated many subsequent developments in these and other areas. Thus relatively little change has been necessary, and the book should continue to serve a new generation of Church people and inquirers as faithfully as in the past.

The original edition was affectionately dedicated by the author to the clergy of the diocese of Eau Claire, whose Bishop and Shepherd he was. The publisher ventures now to re-dedicate it to the memory of Frank E. Wilson, whose faithful witness continues long after his entrance into Eternal Life.

C. P. M.

CONTENTS

8 *Contents*

PREFACE

I LISTENED one day to rather a dull speech in which the orator urged that we forget all this business of doctrine and theology, and go out to help our fellowmen. At the end of it, a college president approached me and said:

"The students walk across our campus delighting in the flowers and shrubs which beautify the grounds. Few of them ever realize how the gardeners toil day after day, digging and planting, and weeding and watering. But if the underground work were neglected, there would be no flowers to admire."

True enough. The fruits of Christian living are beautiful to behold, but if the stability of the Faith were not maintained, the fruits would soon wither away.

This book presumes to do a little digging among the roots and to uncover some of the whys and wherefores of the Christian convictions which blossom more or less luxuriantly in the garden of the Lord. My readers may determine whether the writer is much of a gardener, but at least he knows that flowers do not just happen, and he believes that many of those who look to Christ would like to join him in this bit of spade work.

Suggestions have come both to the publisher and myself that the Outline books should be combined and issued in one volume. This has not seemed advisable to either of us. Instead, we are producing this résumé of Christian doctrine in which is incorporated some of the material already published in the Outlines—notably the chapters on the Holy Scriptures, Prayer, and the Sacraments. Most of the book is entirely new.

May God nourish the seed sown in these pages and give such increase as shall please Him.

F. E. W.

The Epiphany, 1939.

Faith and Practice

I

WHAT'S IT ALL ABOUT?

MILLIONS of dollars for education! It is a common newspaper headline. Year after year towns, villages, cities, and states appropriate huge sums of money from the public funds for schools, colleges, and universities. These are augmented by gifts and bequests from generously-minded individuals until the totals reach impressive figures. Physical property and equipment for educational purposes represent enormous investments; endowments run into hundreds of millions of dollars, and the current operating expenses of the American educational system call for literally billions of dollars annually. From twenty-five to thirty million young people are the beneficiaries. It is one of the world's largest and most expensive projects.

To all this the public reaction is invariably favorable. Ask the average man-in-the-street and he is likely to respond— "Of course, it has to be done. Anything that makes for the increase of knowledge is to be commended."

How many of these men-in-the-street have ever thought it out to any logical conclusion? Glibly they assume that the increase of knowledge is a desirable achievement. But why? What is the good of all this knowledge anyhow? Where does it get us? What does it do for us? Are we any better off with it than we would be without it?

Several answers will be promptly forthcoming. Someone quickly replies—"Certainly. Knowledge makes for greater happiness and, therefore, the more we can have of it, the happier we will be." But does it? How often does knowledge only serve to stimulate discontent? Look about in your own acquaintance, select specific individuals with whom you are on intimate terms, and ask yourself whether it is really true that those who know the most are necessarily happier than those who know less. Possibly there is something in the old adage that "ignorance is bliss." If so, then why not leave people to be happy in their ignorance?

Comes a more thoughtful answer. The intellectual life is higher than the physical life, and it is obvious that we ought to expend our strongest energies for that which is best. We say so, because we have taught ourselves to think so. In what way is the intellectual superior to any other side of human life? Modern psychology reminds us that the brain has two functions, one intellectual and the other emotional. Diligent research in this field has made it plain that if you develop the intellectual (which means knowledge) to the neglect of the emotional (which means feeling) you will succeed in producing a large crop of high-class criminals.

Still another answer goes a step further. It says that, after all, mind controls matter. The man with knowledge always dominates the man with mere brute strength. Therefore knowledge is more powerful and of a higher order. But we may not be so sure about that either. Pit the muscular man against the intellectual man and the muscular man is quite likely to get what he wants.

Of course, you say, that may be so in certain individual cases, but not when you take the long view. The world of knowledge is always supreme over the world of physical power. Look and see. Men of brains are the ones who make and control the destinies of human life.

Then my thoughts revert to that most interesting science of archeology. Modern archeologists have done wonders in digging up the ruins of ancient civilizations. They have deciphered the hidden meanings of ancient inscriptions and have laid bare whole periods of forgotten history. These discoveries are a magnificent triumph of modern knowledge. But these very victories over the past reveal to us plainly that people of the olden times knew much more than we once gave them credit for. These early civilizations are paraded before us with achievements which we can scarcely parallel today. Just outside the city of Rome stand the famous ruins of the Baths of Caracalla, dating back to the early years of the third century. An English woman took a party of us to see them. She pointed out the various parts of the great structure as it must have appeared in the days of Imperial Rome—here was the entrance and there was the disrobing room, here were the hot baths and there were the cold baths, here was the library, and there was the club room. Then she turned to us and asked—"Can any of you figure out how the water was transferred from the cold chamber to the hot chamber?" We all gaped stupidly in silence. She explained that she always asked that question, sometimes of experienced engineers in the parties she was conducting, and no one was ever able to give a satisfactory answer. The builders of that old ruin had used some principle of hydraulics which is now a mystery.

There are many "lost arts" which the ancients knew but which have not been re-discovered in modern times. The science of archeology proves that knowledge is not an exclusively modern product but that the ancients had it in large quantities. Yet what became of all that knowledge of an earlier day? It was broken, overwhelmed, destroyed, buried under the savage attacks of ignorant barbaric tribes. The modern knowledge which lays bare ancient knowledge thereby proves conclusively that knowledge itself is not necessarily supreme. If it were, the ancient knowledge would have survived. As a matter of fact, it succumbed to brute force. What reason have we to think that the treasured knowledge of our own enlightened time has any better chance of surviving than that of long ago?

Perhaps the pessimistic Old Testament preacher was right when he said, "In much wisdom is much grief: and he that increaseth knowledge increaseth sorrow."[1] He was right from his point of view. But one must remember that the preacher in Ecclesiastes was contemplating the vanity of the pursuit of earthly interests. If you read Ecclesiastes alone, you will get the blues. Read it with its New Testament supplement and you will see how the vanities of this world dissolve into the realities of eternity. Knowledge begins to acquire true value only in the light of eternal life. Apart from eternity knowledge becomes mere curiosity.

If you are preparing here for an eternal destiny, then of

[1] *Ecclesiastes 1:18.*

course, you will make the best possible use of your intelligence. The more you can learn of this world, the better you will be able to use it in the perfecting of that Christian character which carries beyond this world into the realm of eternity. Take, then, another text from the sayings of our Lord to qualify the doleful observations of Ecclesiastes—"This is life eternal, that they might know Thee, the only true God, and Jesus Christ, whom Thou hast sent."[2] There you begin to get a sound reason for the accumulation of human knowledge. God gives it validity by making it a contributing factor in the preparation for eternal life. Knowledge divorced from God is a practical absurdity and a spiritual impertinence. When Agassiz, the great scientist, was performing an experiment, he always bowed his head in a moment of silence because, he explained, "I am about to ask God a question."

All of this should mean something to us Americans with our comprehensive system of compulsory education, our enormous school population, and the cataracts of money we pour out every year in support of the program. If it is merely for the pursuit of this world's knowledge, then we are chasing expensive rainbows. For the plainest thing about this world's knowledge is that one day it will vanish.

At this very point may be found the solution of the fictitious conflict between science and religion. Properly speaking there is no such conflict at all because they are both meant to collaborate in a common purpose. The Christian religion sets the course toward that larger life which follows the completion of our human experience. Science provides some of

[2] *St. John 17:3.*

the instruments with which we prepare ourselves for that greater future. The Christian is placed in the world to use it, and he needs to use all of it by the most intelligent methods he can devise. Every scientific discovery is therefore an asset in his onward march to eternity. The more we can learn of natural laws, the better equipped we shall be to pass out of the natural world into that which is over-natural. For this life is a training school for more life to come. Such a purpose dignifies science far beyond any mechanical interpretation which ignores man's spiritual qualities. Religion has nothing to fear from science. Science has no cause to shun religion. If in times past religion has sometimes been timidly suspicious of scientific achievement, it is equally true that science has sometimes misconstrued religion and disparaged a straw man of its own invention. Fortunately a better day has come and such occasions of friction are rapidly disappearing while each learns to esteem the other more highly.

Even so one still meets, here and there, the superficial rejoinder that after all we know something about this world while we know little or nothing about any other; therefore the sensible course is to devote ourselves to what is here and decline to be concerned with any possible hereafter. If that were really the case, there is only one logical conclusion. Moral values promptly become extinct. Mercy, sympathy, self-control, good-will—all these become so many sentimental oddities. The practical mode of life is to seize all you can before someone else beats you to it. Gather the rose-buds while they are fresh because soon we will all be dead, sunk in an oblivion of endless nothingness.

The trouble is, there is something within us which shouts

an emphatic No! Try as we will to be hard, and merciless, and indifferent to the claims of others, we cannot escape the innate conviction that there is a real difference between right and wrong. The worst men have their tender moments when they simply cannot be entirely selfish. The more thoughtful materialist will say it is because of future generations. We must maintain ideals, practice self-control, adhere to certain moral principles in order to make the world better for our children. We are beneficiaries of our fathers and we are thereby under obligation to improve what we have received for the sake of those who come after us. That is our future life. We must cultivate a long-range perspective and consider our descendants for whom we are literally responsible.

But there again our reason emerges into unreason. There is something appealing in the idea of self-sacrifice for the benefit of those who come after us until we are brought up abruptly to face the fact that someday nobody will be coming. It is all well enough to labor for future generations, but what about the time when there will be no future generations? Let us go in for a really long-range perspective. The day arrives when this world comes to an end. Just when or how is a matter of no consequence. It may be next week or a million years hence. Some scientists think the earth will eventually be absorbed into the sun and vanish in vapor. Others suggest that it is more likely to cool off and become a dead world incapable of sustaining life. Either way the conclusion is the same. Some day this world ends and there will be no future generations. Then what becomes of our care-fully-guarded ideals and principles? What is the good of our labors and sacrifices if finally they all end in nothing? We are simply pyramiding futilities.

Christ's way is more credible to our intelligence and more creditable to our efforts. We may die but we shall not perish. "God hath given to us eternal life."[3] The best efforts we can put forth here will never be lost because there is a hereafter. Human life is not a temporary illusion. It has a meaning which outstrips time. That is why the faith and practice of a Churchman becomes of paramount importance. The Christian Gospel offers a way of life in this world which finds its bloom in the world-to-come. How we live now determines how we shall be prepared to live then. If this be not true, there is no sense in submitting to the injustices, trials, and indignities which our daily experience visits upon us. We might better call the whole thing off, turn out the light, and be decently obliterated. But "now is Christ risen from the dead,"[4] and "thanks be to God, which giveth us the victory through our Lord Jesus Christ."[5]

[3] *I John 5:11.*
[4] *I Corinthians 15:20.*
[5] *I Corinthians 15:57.*

II

BELIEF IN GOD

NOTHING can ever be proved absolutely. Everything in this world is related to everything else. Therefore if you are to understand anything completely you must be able to understand everything. For the same reason, to prove any one thing absolutely means that you must be able to prove everything. That is rather a large order for human intelligence.

Nevertheless, when we tell one another that we can prove this and that, our statements do really have a meaning. We do not say that we have complete proof for anything, but that we have enough for working purposes. It is not absolute evidence that convinces us, but a *preponderance of evidence* that one thing is more true and accurate than another.

It is important to keep this distinction in mind when we are considering religious matters. There is a good deal of loose popular clatter to the effect that religious convictions rest upon wishes and imagination while legal, logical, and scientific conclusions are based on demonstrable facts. The latter, we are told, constitute proof while the former is not much more than charitable conjecture.

Yet it is a matter of common knowledge that many things

are known to be true which can never be legally proved. Conversely, the court records are full of instances where something has been legally proved which turns out later to be entirely false.

Similarly our systems of logic are of human contrivance and are therefore bound to be vulnerable. For example, there is the classical bit of logic taken from the Psalms of David:

> David said, "All men are liars";
> Therefore, David, being a man, was a liar;
> Therefore, what David said is not true;
> Therefore all men are not liars.

Of course, it is nonsense but it is logical.

Scientific proof is generally considered more dependable and, on the whole, it is. But there also the footing may become slippery. The recently promulgated theory of relativity and the whole scope of the "New Physics" show clearly that many points which were considered scientifically established a generation ago are called in serious question today.

So when someone bluntly demands that we should prove the existence of God, we reply—what do you mean by proof? In the first place there are different kinds of proof. You don't prove a material fact in the same way that you prove a mathematical formula. You may demonstrate to your own satisfaction that a stone is hard by feeling it, but you do not convince yourself that two and two make four by touching the numbers. Evidence for the existence of God is of a different quality than either of these, and you must not expect to prove God by some laboratory experiment. And in the next place, nothing can be proved absolutely, leaving no possible question unanswered. But we do believe we can produce a *preponderance of reasonable evidence* that God does exist. If you say that this is a call upon faith and merely begs the question, we reply that the proof of anything begins with a call upon faith. In the cleanest scientific experiment you must start by assuming that you have a mind which will work and that there is reliability and uniformity in the laws of nature. At the outset you cannot be sure of either of these points, but you must assume they are true if you are to make any beginning at all.

Well, then, let's see about God. I start with myself and the world in which I live. Where did we come from? We are the product of preceding ages. But where did these preceding ages come from? They are the result of still earlier ages. But there must have been something before them and something else still further back. So we continue to retreat into a past ever more dim and distant until our reason explodes and our minds stop ticking. Somewhere we must come to a pause and say—here is the origin of things. There must be a First Cause. Otherwise common sense collapses and all our thinking loses its validity for want of an anchor. We would be like a man reaching off into thin air for a foothold and ending up in a crash of nothingness. Of course, you can't explain it but you can't explain anything else without it. The alternative is to try to live in a delirium of unreason. That First Cause we call God—the Creator—the Source of all things— and our very existence demands Him, unless we prefer to question our own existence. In that case, we might as well fold up and sink out of sight.

Then I begin to study the world in which I live. The first

thing I discover is that my world is intelligible. It can be understood and my mind is capable of understanding it. Obviously the world must have been put together with some plan and sequence or there would be nothing intelligible in it for me to discover. But an intelligible world necessitates an Intelligence back of it with which my own intelligence corresponds. Suppose I study the operation of my automobile and learn how the various gears, and rods, and shafts perform their functions. Nobody needs to tell me that they work the way they do because they were made to work that way. Well, then, someone made them. Try if you will to tell me that my carburetor just happened to fall in the right place, that my wires by pure chance dropped on the spark plugs, that my wheels casually rolled themselves up and landed on the axles. I would very quickly form my opinion of your mental condition. Because I am able to understand the mechanism of that car proves conclusively that someone of similar understanding made it to be understood. My world is much more complicated and my comprehension of it grows much more slowly, but every step teaches me with increasing clarity that it is understandable, and that there must be an Intelligence which has produced it and continues to govern it. Otherwise my own intelligence is nullified. That Supreme Intelligence we call God.

As I continue to study my world I learn that there is a purpose in this creation. It is subject to certain laws and obedient to certain controls. I am able to grasp enough of all this to know that I must reckon with these laws if I am to keep on living. As I adapt myself to them and coöperate with them, I find new and wonderful results forthcoming.

By splicing these laws together with a purpose I can ride in railroad trains and fly in airplanes. I have not made these laws of steam power and aeronautics. I have simply discovered them and coöperated with them. But they have always been there. The steam engine and the airplane were perfectly possible a thousand years ago but the men of that day didn't know it. The marvels of a thousand years hence are quite possible today but we don't yet know how to get at them.

These purposes are inherent in the laws of the universe. They are there all the time whether we uncover them today or tomorrow. Now laws do not arise by spontaneous combustion. They come from a Lawgiver. And if there is a purpose to be discovered in those laws, nobody but the Lawgiver could have put the purpose in them. Constantly we find these purposes emerging as we coöperate with the laws, and the greater our coöperation, the greater the purpose. All of which points to the natural conclusion that there must be a dominating purpose of which all of these lesser ones are minor manifestations, and that whenever the time comes that mankind fully coöperates with all the laws of the Lawgiver, that final purpose will be achieved.

This Lawgiver we call God, and the purpose implanted in His laws we call the Divine Will. The state of life in which His purpose is fulfilled we call the Kingdom or Realm of God. So we pray, "Thy Kingdom come, Thy will be done." There you find real progress with an end to be attained. Otherwise life becomes a hodge-podge of disjointed impulses and a lawless nightmare of idiotic fantasies. There must be a Lawgiver with a purpose for His laws.

Here we are likely to be confronted with that horrid thing

called Evolution. Doesn't it seriously undercut any idea of a God with a design and purpose for His creation? The answer is—no. After all, the theory of evolution is a theory which may or may not be true, but if it is true it actually reinforces the idea. The principle of evolution simply states that on its physical side higher forms of life have emerged from lower forms by graded steps, some of which we have been able tentatively to identify. The process as we know it is frequently punctuated with blind spots but, on the whole it is a reasonable explanation. All it says is that the Creator began with elementary forms of life in which were resident the possibilities of development. In accordance with the Creator's own laws that development has taken place. The design and the purpose are strengthened by the theory and, incidentally, it is thoroughly consonant with the creation picture given in the first chapters of Genesis.

Occasionally popular clamor is raised over the assertion that evolution teaches how man is descended from the monkeys. Really it teaches no such thing. The theory is that human life began in a very simple form which gradually developed into something more complex. In the course of development some lines moved upward and some down. Remember that evolution does not necessarily mean advancement to a higher state—it may also indicate deterioration to a lower condition. Human life would mark the upward swing while the apes might illustrate a degraded development on the same evolutionary principle. When some students find certain similarities between humans and apes, they are suggesting that both may have had a common ancestry which is a very different thing from saying that one may be descended from the other. In any case, such conjectures are incidental to the broad theory of evolution itself.

As I consider myself and my world there is another factor which I may not overlook—namely, the sense of moral responsibility. Usually we assemble all such evidences under the general name of "conscience." There is a moral sense which is universal in mankind. It prompts us to do things because we *ought* to do them whether we want to or not. At different times and among different peoples this inner impulse expresses itself in a variety of moral codes and customs, but the variations only emphasize the universal presence of the impulse itself.

All people are conscious of a distinction between right and wrong. It is quite true that what was considered right once may be considered entirely otherwise now, but that simply means growth and advancement in the response to conscience. The distinction between right and wrong, the consciousness of moral responsibility is there, inbred in us, a normal factor in human nature. Neither can it be said that this is an artificially cultivated reaction to the conventional standards of our day because conscience often forces us to go diametrically opposite to current public opinion. The philosopher Kant called it the "categorical imperative," and was so deeply impressed that he counted it the most compelling evidence of the existence of a Supreme Moral Arbiter. The universal presence of moral consciousness among men implies a moral principle embedded in the very constitution of human life. It is another law which demands a Lawgiver. That Moral Arbiter we call God—the Decider, the Referee, the Umpire, the Judge of human conduct. Every time I say

"I ought" I am predicating a Reason for doing something which I might not want to do at all. Otherwise I am an impractical sentimentalist for abandoning the standards of teeth and talons which should properly keep me selfishly ferocious in all my behavior.

Add to these considerations the further fact that men have always held some sort of belief in a Supreme Being. It is not surprising that religion has often assumed grotesque aspects and that the gods of primitive races have been obnoxious monstrosities in the light of modern learning. The soul of man has mounted by painful stages just as his body and his mind. The important fact is that men have always sought God. It is inconceivable that there should be such an instinct for God unless there were a God to be found. Otherwise human life would be irrational and human experience would be a fictitious dream.

No one of these points mentioned above can be called a "proof" of the existence of God. But if you add them up, the cumulative effect of them is very impressive. If proof means the *preponderance of evidence*, it is difficult to escape an affirmative answer. "Is such-and-such a place inhabited?" "Yes." "How do you know? Did you see people there?" "I found the ground cleared and the land under cultivation, a house built with smoke rising from the chimney and curtains in the windows, newly-washed garments hanging on a line, tools scattered here and there, live stock feeding in a meadow, and I heard someone call as I passed by. No, I saw no person and I got no affidavit of occupancy, but the preponderance of evidence proves to me that the place must be inhabited." Most people would agree that it is harder to explain away the evidence for God than to accept it. Evidence that God does not exist is practically nil. All things considered, it is less strain on our credulity to believe that God is than to believe that He isn't.

Some people can never be convinced of anything contrary to their own prejudices. Once on a railroad train I fell into conversation with an opinionated growler who held forth on the charity racket, insisting that all the money raised for charity was so much graft for the hypocrites who professed an interest in the needy. Finally I said: "I have been a director on our local charity board for fifteen years and I know its operations inside-out. What you say is perfect nonsense—unless, perhaps you believe I am piling up my own bank-roll out of it." To which he replied, "I wouldn't be at all surprised." Such a man would never be convinced of God unless some personal catastrophe crushed through his ugly shell of self-righteousness. Sometimes that happens.

What, then, does this preponderance of evidence indicate? It indicates God the Source of all creative power, ever present sustaining His creation, the Supreme Intelligence, the Moral Guide, and the final Answer to human searching (in theological language—omnipotent, omnipresent, omniscient). Put this all together and it says one thing more—Personality. For when we speak of a person we mean a being possessed of reason, intelligence, self-consciousness, a sense of moral responsibility.

The evidence is overwhelmingly in favor of a Personal God, and now we want to know Him. That brings us to Revelation.

III

REVELATION

Man is a combination of many things. If he consisted entirely of mind, the solution of human problems would be greatly simplified. But that does not happen to be the case. Undoubtedly one of the chief causes of confusion in the realm of religious experience arises out of the tendency to treat Man purely as a reasoning creature when we know very well he is much more than that. He is also the embodiment of instincts, intuitions, emotions, will—feelings and impulses—ideals and aspirations. Knowing all this, how can we still insist that Man's every action must be judged only at the bar of reason? Religion as a determining factor in the emotions and will as well as the intellect cannot be submitted to such an inadequate test. It is scarcely in order to declare that spiritual elements which human reason may not be able to digest shall promptly be ruled out as unreasonable. It is too much like saying that a baby is inhuman because he creeps on all fours. Religion may be reasonable without being absorbed in reason.

Now the Christian religion deals with all of human life. Certainly it appeals to a man's reason but it does more than that. It also touches his emotions, draws upon his instincts, and stimulates his will. The scope of it includes reason but surpasses it. Let us emphasize this point. We are quite likely to accept something as true if we can wrap our minds around it and to declare something else untrue if it is beyond our intellectual comprehension. To reach such a conclusion is to use only part of our natural equipment. Is truth really dependent upon our mental abilities? How often does one say —"I know something is so but I can't tell you just why." We have no more right to declare a thing untrue because it escapes our reason than we have to declare a thing invisible because it is beyond our sight. We may not be able to see it but it may still be capable of being seen. Our intuitions and our feelings may be able to reach points which our minds may be unable to penetrate, but our conclusions may be no less valid because of that. The appeal to reason is wholesome and necessary, but it is not the only appeal in the broad field of human experience.

It is not easy for us to grasp this because we of the modern age have been so deeply inoculated with a spirit of unquestioning confidence in scientific achievement. We must remember that science is descriptive. It does not explain things —it describes what it finds. By experiment the scientist learns that the same elements under similar conditions always act the same way. That's good science. When the materialist adds—therefore, the whole world is one great machine driven by blind force—he is not at all scientific. He has stepped quite outside the field of science and has used his imagination. The Christian welcomes the scientist's facts, but denies the conclusions of the materialist on other grounds entirely.

It sounds very wise and very practical for one to say— "Of course, you can't expect me to accept something which I do not understand." Very well—then you will refuse to listen to the radio, you will decline to answer the telephone, you will stay out of elevators, you will refrain from riding in railroad trains, automobiles, or airplanes, you will deny yourself any medical treatment, and you will send away most of the food prepared for your meals. Show me the person who understands all of these daily accessories of modern life which we accept and use without question! Oh, but you say, somebody understands these things and we find they actually work. So also says the Christian. Christ understands God fully, and plenty of devout followers of Christ have had a good usable knowledge of Him. We lay hold of their experience and we also find it works.

Must it be true that the only things that really happen are those which we can understand? In that case there could have been no eclipses of the sun and moon a thousand years ago when people were ignorant of what an eclipse might be. There could have been no tidal waves or earthquakes. Pompeii could not have been actually destroyed by a volcanic eruption. Certainly there never could have been a Gulf Stream at that time because our ancestors had not yet discovered it and they could not have explained it if they had discovered it. The answer comes that today we do understand such happenings and therefore they might well have occurred despite the prevalent ignorance of those earlier times. Well—how can we tell how much our descendants a thousand years hence may be able to understand? It is quite likely that they will be far more enlightened than we are, and various matters which we might be tempted to rule out today may be simple of explanation for them. All of which warns us that we should be properly cautious about discounting those occurrences which are commonly called

MIRACLES.

Let's have done with the idea that miracles contradict science, that they fly in the face of reason, or that they violate the natural law. They do nothing of the kind. Science leaves plenty of room for the possibility of miracles. Reason simply acknowledges that they are occurrences outside its normal field of operation, and natural law always has to recognize that there may well be other laws beyond its own orbit.

Suppose I roll over a stone from the top of a hill. By natural law that stone is due to keep going until it reaches the bottom. Suddenly it stops half way down. What has happened? Let us say that it has run against a tree and there it stays. No laws have been broken. Two different laws have come together at a given point and have produced a different result. (We shall have more to say about this in the chapter on Prayer). Such an incident is easy to understand because two laws of the same kind have coincided.

Let us suppose again. This time it is a boy who falls in the water and is drowning. At the risk of his own life a man leaps in, drags the boy free of the inexorable law that humans can't breathe water, and saves his life. What has happened? It is more than the physical act of pulling the boy from the water. The force of will-power made the man take the risk and his will was actuated by a consciousness of responsibility, by the claim of friendship, or perhaps by parental love if he happened to be the boy's father. In a word, personality has entered the picture and because of it the results must be different. Personality is not something which may be weighed and measured, but it is a factor which may not be disregarded. If, then, it is possible for a human person to intervene and change the natural course of events, why should it seem strange for the Divine Person to intervene at times in the affairs of His own creation—not to disrupt it but to direct and control it?

Two kinds of corruption have made people somewhat skeptical of miracles in any form. One is the irrational flight of imagination eager to discover a miracle where it does not exist. Some people have an appetite for the bizarre. The simplest coincidence appears to them as a marvel. Their persistent exaggerations irritate their more sensible friends and invite disbelief in any supernatural occurrence. Some of these neurotics are deeply religious persons but they do damage to Christ by their hysterical credulity. When everything is a miracle, nothing can be miraculous.

The other corruption is, of course, the faking of supernatural powers. Those who trade in human weaknesses are not averse to carrying their deceptions into the very holy-of-holies. Religious charlatans always make life hard for the honest Christian. Sooner or later they are bound to be exposed but in the meantime they shatter the faith of those who have trusted them. The faking of miracles has aroused suspicion of anything that might be called miraculous.

Yet—let us consider our Saviour's miracles. Some of them are not as strange as they appeared to be once. By modern methods of treatment we can now cure some of the same diseases which He cured in the days of His ministry. Is it so hard to believe that what we can do gradually with our limited powers, He could do instantaneously with His divine power? Some of His cures may have been merely a foreshortening of similar cures which can be wrought by our clumsier methods today. Possibly when we know enough we may be able to explain many others of His miracles which are still incomprehensible to us now. Life is full of unaccountable happenings. Some people are possessed of capacities far more sensitive than the average. Often they astonish themselves by exhibiting abilities which they themselves are unable to explain. Our Lord's human life is unique in the annals of history. Such a life might well have been responsive to spiritual impulses beyond our broadest imagination.

Our Lord never performed any miracles in order to show off. At the beginning of His ministry He refused to dazzle the public with a spectacular exhibition, saying, "Thou shalt not tempt the Lord thy God."[1] He declined to perform wonders where faith was lacking and people were merely curious.[2] He never used His extraordinary powers for His own benefit—not even on the cross when the scoffers challenged Him to save Himself from death.[3] His miracles were signs and symbols called forth to authenticate His teaching for a people who expected unusual things from God. In the early years of the Church's life extraordinary events continued to occur, and instances have not failed to appear now and then down through the ages. Rationalize all you please

[1] *St. Matthew 4:7.*
[2] *St. Matthew 16:4.*
[3] *St. Mark 15:30.*

and there still remain many happenings, too well attested for doubting, which are far beyond the range of human comprehension.

Why should there have to be miracles anyhow? Would it not have been much simpler if the Christian faith could have been held within the bounds of that which was quite understandable and thus avoid all these difficult questionings? It might have been simpler—and it would have been deadly. Would anyone be willing that human progress should have come to a blank halt at the beginning of the Christian era? If Christ were to proclaim a Gospel which would be valid for an indefinite future, it was plainly necessary that He should incorporate into it elements which were above the reach of the people of His own day. Otherwise His Gospel would have been a temporary flash of human progress or would have come to a standstill rather than leave Him far behind. We might suggest three practical reasons for the presence of miracles in the Christian faith:

1. In order to illustrate the unique character of our Lord. From a Person who claimed spiritual authority in His own right, it would be expected that some unusual evidences of that authority would be forthcoming.

2. To encourage expectation of greater things to come. We need something to anticipate. We can't keep grubbing along at the same old level and expect to rise to any heights. We need a lift, something to reach for, something to stretch our spiritual muscles.

3. To jar our complacency. We easily settle into the routine of ordinary living and allow our sensibilities to be dulled by commonplaces. We forget that there may be anything

beyond the daily round of eating, sleeping and doing the regular chores of life. A wise God knows it is good for us if He occasionally breaks through to disturb our lazy equanimity. Now and then we need to be startled. In material matters, what would become of inventive genius if we lived on the stupid assumption that the pattern of life was complete and all that remained for us to do was to manicure it diligently and keep it in proper order? The same might be said of spiritual life. We would be dead on our feet if we were not spurred on by some extraordinary spiritual manifestations once in a while.

Surely there is no good reason for believing that the natural order as we know it in this world is the ultimate ceiling of all existence. Conscious as we are of the limitations under which we must struggle, we can scarcely escape the conclusion that there ought to be and must be a higher order of life unshackled by human handicaps. Indeed the logic of the situation demands it. We contemplate the ascending levels of vegetable life, animal life, and human life, and in simple reason we cannot stop there. We could not convince ourselves that human life is the top of everything. We are too well acquainted with its inevitable restrictions. There simply must be a higher order. We know that animal life runs the gamut of vegetable life—and more. We know that human life can reach down into animal life but also reaches much further in many other directions. Why, then, should it not be quite reasonable that there should be a still higher order which can penetrate human life without being confined within it? That means something above the natural —and that means supernatural. There is no sense in shrinking from the term. The separation between the two may not be nearly as impregnable as we often think it to be. God *is* a God of law and order, but we believe that the law of creation itself provides for a breaking-through of the supernatural into the natural order when circumstances may require it. God does not act capriciously—neither is He constrained within the narrow limits of human wisdom.

In the very nature of things miracles are possible. Well-attested events have occurred and do occur which cannot be adequately described by any other term. A personal God implies the probability of miraculous happenings. The Christian religion bears witness to the actual experience of such happenings. It is not afraid to face the supernatural because it believes that God has a right to speak to us in any way that will best suit His purposes.

REVELATION

A small child is a very helpless creature. If he is to survive the hazards of infancy he must be fed, clothed, protected, and generally cared for by his parents out of their mature experience. Later all of this early care must be supplemented by the instruction and training of his teachers who pass on to him the accumulated store of knowledge that belongs to the race. No child can be left to find his own way without some degree of help. Because his parents and teachers love him and feel a sense of responsibility for his welfare, they are morally bound to give him more than his natural inheritance would automatically provide.

Two considerations enter into the rearing of a child. In the first place, his parents cannot expect him to be an exact replica of themselves. He must develop his own individuality, discover and exercise his own talents, acquire his own experience, and construct his own character. On the other hand, he must receive guidance in doing all this. Now and then his parents and teachers must interfere with the course of his natural instincts—not by blocking them but by directing them with suggestions, restraints, encouragements, warnings and corrections. A proper balance in these two factors produces an educated person.

That, in a word, is the story of revelation. God has created human life for a purpose. He has equipped men and women with reason, emotion, will-power, and a sense of moral responsibility in order that they may work out a complete human life in response to His divine will. If He is to be true to the principle of His own creation, He must allow them to develop their own resources and work out their own destiny. But because He is the Father of all mankind, He cannot leave them to do it alone. Obviously if they are to accomplish His will, they must be taught what His will is. The whole history of the human race tells of Man's persistent striving to find God and his untiring efforts to know Him. It is absurd to think that He could have invested mankind with this capacity and this yearning without being prepared to meet them at least half way by revealing Himself to them. Not to do so would be plainly unfair—it would be expecting the impossible. Certainly a Heavenly Father must be as considerate of His children as a human father is of his. The human father knows he must offer a helping hand. The Heavenly Father can do no less.

God educates His children upward by revealing Himself

to them. This He may do in many different ways. So far as the individual is concerned, any life that is attuned to God may hear Him frequently. Perhaps it may be through the channel of conscience or perhaps some other way. There are people who are peculiarly sensitive to spiritual impulses. For them the veil between the seen and the unseen, between the natural and the supernatural, is extremely thin. We call them mystics. We don't know why they are as they are any more than we know why some people are better mathematicians than others. Their spiritual perception is keener than the average just as some people have sharper eyesight or more acute hearing. They respond with unusual readiness to anything that comes from God.

On the other hand are those of coarser fiber whose souls may be tough and calloused. Year after year they may go their irreligious way utterly indifferent to any spiritual impressions. Then something happens and this man who has habitually ignored God suddenly does an about-face and becomes a different creature. Thereafter God's guidance is the most real thing in his life. We say that he has been converted which simply means that he has "turned around." Really another miracle has occurred. God has broken through and revealed Himself.

Most of us belong to neither one of these classes. We are ordinary people. For us the great bulk of life consists of a series of commonplace events. Very seldom does anything startling or spectacular happen to us. Too many people assume that the supernatural is too unusual ever to meet them in the simple course of their prosaic existence. It is significant to remember that God called Gideon to the leadership of

Israel while he was doing his ordinary work on the threshing floor.[4] David was tending the sheep when God spoke to him through Samuel.[5] The word of the Lord came to Amos while he was performing his duties as a herdsman.[6] Whatever the star of Bethlehem may have been, God sent His message to the Wise Men through that channel by which they, as students of the stars, could best understand Him.[7] Christ called St. Peter and St. John while they were pursuing their daily occupation as fishermen.[8] All of which should tell us that divine promptings may come to us in very ordinary ways. How often have you felt an inner compulsion to do something which you must do though you may not be able to tell exactly why? On the other hand some of these calls of God come with strange accompaniments, which simply means that God does not need to work always in the same way.

This, however, is scarcely enough. We are all familiar with the personal vagaries of different men and women and we need something more substantial to stand in support of individual experiences. We look for more comprehensive evidences of revelation and we find them in the long sweep of human history. This we call "progressive revelation." Men as a whole are able to absorb about so much at various stages of their development. We find God leading them gradually, step by step, through ascending levels of spiritual progress. That is why religion has taken off from simple beginnings

4 *Judges 6:11.*
5 *I Samuel 16:1–13.*
6 *Amos 1:1.*
7 *St. Matthew 2:1–15.*
8 *St. Matthew 4:18–22.*

and has passed through many phases of spiritual progress. Every religion which represents an honest effort to know God contains some revelation of Him. The Hebrew people proved to be peculiarly responsive. They showed a "genius for religion" as the Greeks did for art and the Romans for organization. It is quite logical that they should have been God's "chosen people" for they chose God more fully than any others of the ancient races. But they also had to climb, as the Old Testament record clearly discloses. There is a wide difference in the religious conception of the period of the Judges and that of the times of the prophets. And always they were looking forward to the fulfilment of their expectations. They called it the "Messianic hope"—the unflagging anticipation of the coming of the Messiah who should satisfy their gropings after God and complete His revelation. "God, who at sundry times and in divers manners spake in time past unto the fathers by the prophets, hath in these last days spoken unto us by his Son."[9]

So Christians believe Jesus Christ to be God's supreme revelation of Himself. All earlier revelation is preparatory to Christ and all subsequent revelation is corroboration of Him. Christianity does not say that all other religions are wrong. It simply says they are inadequate. The best in all of them has been gathered up into Christ. He is the spiritual focus of all revelation. Therefore it is not surprising to find religious ideas of non-Christian origin incorporated in the Christian Gospel. Christ did not come to give religion to a world which had no religion. He came to fulfil the spiritual aspira-

[9] *Hebrews 1:1-2.*

tions of all of them—more especially those of the Hebrews because they had already outstripped all the others.

The Christian claim for spiritual supremacy justifies itself *first* on the grounds of the intrinsic merits of the Gospel. It is consistent within itself and it offers the most satisfactory answer to the whole question of life both here and hereafter. *Second,* it is historically sound. Christianity centers on the person of Jesus Christ. It is not a collection of doctrines, but loyalty to a Person who at one time lived on this earth and injected a new spiritual content into the stream of human life. *Third*, on its results. It has proved its adaptability to man as man, without respect of race, color, or condition. It has done more than any other to elevate character, to inspire love, mercy, self-sacrifice and all the highest virtues, to stimulate progress and the attainment of better things in this life as a preparation for the life-to-come. The Bible is the record of this. For that reason it is unique among books. It has no magical properties but it attains a standing all its own because it portrays and presents Christ—implicitly in the Old Testament and explicitly in the New Testament. Christ Himself is the Word of God—that is, the personal expression of God. The Bible tells of Him and we therefore call it God's Word. It is the record of the progressive revelation which reaches its summit in Christ.

Christianity depends on Jesus Christ. Without Him there is no Christian religion. He is His own Gospel and we, as Christians, stake everything on Him. The final answer to all questions touching the integrity of our Christian faith is found in the appeal to Christ. We know Him not only in the reading of the Bible but also through the continuous witness of the Church. As the Bible is the written record of Christ, so is the Church the living witness to Christ, and thereby becomes another channel of revelation.

By nature we are blind creatures groping for the God, who, we know instinctively, must be there. By revelation He opens our eyes and manifests Himself to us. Necessarily the whole process is mingled with mystery because it is the work of God rather than of human manufacture. But life itself is a mystery. It raises more questions with God left out than with Him included. If a religion of revelation leaves many questions still unanswered, it simply means that man still has a long way to go. And who will question that?

The important consideration is not how far we have gone, but whether we are going in the right direction.

IV

THE HOLY SCRIPTURES

THE BIBLE is the record of the revelation of God. God does not reveal Himself exclusively through a book. He reveals Himself in many ways, but chiefly through people and supremely in our Lord Jesus Christ. Books are made by men. God did not make the Bible—men wrote it. Therefore, when we say that the Bible is an inspired book, we do not mean to suggest that it is the result of divine dictation and, for that reason, exempt from the possibility of human blunders. We mean that the men who did the writing were actively seeking God's will, inscribing accounts of God's dealing with human life, and that the spiritual reliability of these accounts was tested over long periods of time by the people for whom they were written. Only in a secondary way can the Bible itself be called a revelation of God. It is the record of His revelation which culminated in the Person of Jesus Christ.

The Bible is important because of Christ—not the other way around. Christ did not come to deliver a book. He came to live a Life. The New Testament contains an account of that Life and a commentary on it. The Old Testament is a record of the preparation for it.

During the time of our Lord's ministry there was no such thing as the Bible as we know it today. There were certain sacred writings now incorporated in our Old Testament, but the contents of the Old Testament were not properly defined for sixty years after our Lord's resurrection. The New Testament did not begin to be written until twenty years after the conclusion of His earthly life, and its contents were not settled until more than three centuries later. During all this time the Church was busy carrying on His work. The Church, therefore, is not dependent upon the Bible. It is the Bible that is dependent upon the Church, because, when all is said and done, it was the Church that made the Bible. That is the reason why the only sensible way to interpret the Bible is by reference to the Church which made it. We must keep the order straight. First Christ—then the Church—then the Bible.

We usually speak of the Bible as a book. More properly it is a collection of books, written at different times, by different people, under very different circumstances, and often for quite different purposes. The Old Testament period covers something like two thousand years. The record deals with the religious development of people who were advancing, not only through stages of civilization, but also advancing in the knowledge and understanding of God. The earlier accounts come chiefly in the form of stories of a simple nomadic life (as in Genesis), followed by somewhat more definite records of an agricultural period (as in Judges). This in turn is followed by something approaching more formal history in an organized kingdom (as in I and II Kings). Finally, after the fall of the kingdom and the period of exile, we have the literary record coming out of a more cultural life down to the time of Christ (as in Ezra and the later prophets).

Naturally the earlier writings include certain crudities which were attendant upon a less developed state of social life but which were gradually outgrown. It is quite true that the adventurous life of David was flavored with primitive conceptions of an angry God wreaking vengeance here and there when His will was thwarted. But in the next five hundred years such conceptions gave way to the loftier idea of God yearning over His people such as we find in Hosea and the Second Isaiah.

The Bible needs to be read with discrimination. Our Lord Himself sets us the example over and over again in the Sermon on the Mount. "Ye have heard that it hath been said, Thou shalt love thy neighbour, and hate thine enemy" (this is the old standard of Moses), "But I say unto you, Love your enemies."[1] Similarly our Lord sweeps aside the law of retaliation of an earlier day, "Eye for eye, tooth for tooth,"[2] and instructs His listeners in the better way of returning good for evil. It is simply hopeless to think of opening the Bible at any point, expecting there to find detailed directions as to what one should do in the twentieth century. Sometimes you will find straight contradictions, as in those instances when our Lord said, "*But,* I say unto you—." The beauty of the Bible is its sheer honesty. It refuses to gloss over the crudities and inadequacies of the early stages of religious development. But all the way through runs the golden thread of persistent search after God and the constant presence of

[1] *St. Matthew 5:43-44.*
[2] *Exodus 21:24.*

eternal truths, however incompletely realized—all leading up to fulfilment in the Gospel of Christ.

Every now and then someone comes forth with the brilliant idea that we ought to have a new Bible, retaining the finer parts of the old Bible and adding selections from later writers like Milton, Shakespeare, Tennyson and others. One practical difficulty of such an undertaking is that no two persons could ever be found who would agree on just what selections were to be incorporated in the book. It would inevitably boil down to a series of innocuous expressions of religious sentiment which could never hurt anyone. Such an inoffensive religion would be about as useful as a dry rain. Moreover, an artificial editing of this kind would mean the manufacture of a new religion. But the religion of the Christian is already settled in Jesus Christ. His faith is not in a book, but in a Person. The Bible is a mosaic presenting the picture of Christ set off by its Old Testament background.

Additions or subtractions are not helpful to the picture. This is not to say that you must gaze with similar devotion at every stone in the mosaic, or that you are to count them all of equal significance. You can be a very good Christian if you never read some parts of the Bible, but all are needed for the complete picture, just as all the records are needed in the county Court House for the history of any community. You would not go back and read the list of marriage licenses out of loyalty to your home town, but the record of them should be preserved. Neither do you need to read the lists of Joshua's warriors or of David's mighty men for spiritual refreshment.

There are three ways of approaching the Bible—literally, symbolically, and historically. No one of these ways is wrong. On the contrary, all of them are right, but no one of them is necessarily right for every portion of the Bible. Holy Scripture contains many different kinds of writing. Some of it is poetry, some is narration, some is prophecy. To approach all of them in the same way would be simple foolishness.

Suppose someone were to take a selection of well-known poems, a history of the United States, and a collection of wise proverbs, and bind them all together in a single volume. An enthusiastic reader holds up that volume and says, "I believe literally everything in this book." Someone reads him one of the proverbs—"A rolling stone gathers no moss." The first man enthusiastically declares, "Quite so. I must go right out on the hillside and fasten every stone so it can never do any rolling." "But," says the second reader, "that is a symbolical proverb. In fact, the whole book is symbolical. None of it can be taken literally." Whereupon the first reader turns to the account of the battle of Bull Run. But the second reader smiles indulgently and says—"That is not history. It never really happened. I assure you, this book is purely symbolical. The very name of this battle tells you it is only a parable of ranch life indicating the beginning of competition in the cattle business."

Absurd as it may seem, some people treat the Bible like that. One of these takes the story of Jonah and solemnly declares on God's authority that a man once lived three days in the belly of a fish. An intelligent study of this story shows quite clearly that it is a parable of personal responsibility, the sea being the customary symbol of trouble, the fish being the symbol of the spirit of distress, and the moral of the story teaching that one who evades a clear responsibility is bound to fall into trouble out of which he may learn to do his duty.

Or, perhaps, a very critical reader seizes upon St. Peter and St. Paul, declaring that they are not real men at all, but were types of Jewish and Gentile Christianity in conflict. The historical evidence for those apostles is as convincing as the evidence for Julius Cæsar or Constantine the Great.

The truth is that some parts of the Bible are to be taken literally, others symbolically, and still others historically. When our Lord said, "Go and baptize," He meant precisely what the words convey, a definite thing to be done. This is made perfectly clear by the fact that the Church proceeded at once to do exactly what our Lord had said. But when the author of the book of Daniel described the strange animal with sprouting horns, there can be little question that he was writing symbolically about the rise and fall of successive kingdoms. When the Old Testament chronicler wrote his account of the Chaldean conquest of Judah, with all its horrors and atrocities, he was writing plain history—a record of something that actually happened without any suggestion that, because it appears in the Bible, anyone will ever be justified in doing the same thing again.

Occasionally one finds a passage where all three of these points of view converge. For instance, "This do in remembrance of Me."[3] It is a literal command, so recognized by His disciples, telling the Church to preserve and perpetuate a specific sacrament. It is also symbolical because it typifies the sacrifice of our Lord, giving Himself to His people for spiritual strengthening. And it is historical as well, for our Lord

[3] *St. Luke 22:19.*

actually did administer bread and wine to the apostles at a certain time and in a certain place.

THE OLD TESTAMENT

The Old Testament was written in the Hebrew language. The first of such writings dates from about the ninth century before Christ. Up to that time the history of the race had been handed down by word of mouth from generation to generation in song and story, quite in the same way as the early history of any other race. These songs and stories were firmly fixed in the minds of the people, and were recited in their homes, around campfires, and on festival occasions. About the year B.C. 1000, some collections of them began to be assembled such as the *Book of the Wars of the Lord* and the *Book of Jasher*.[4] From similar sources came longer poems like the *Song of Moses*[5] and the *Song of Deborah*.[6] These collections mark the beginning of what we now call the Old Testament.

The contents of the Old Testament were gradually assembled but it was by no means a steady process. Down to the time of our Lord it was still an open question as to precisely what books should comprise the Canon (that is, the authorized list of contents).

THE APOCRYPHA

The word "Apocrypha" means "hidden" and was originally applied to a large number of writings at the beginning of the Christian era which presented religious mysteries

[4] *Numbers 21:14–20; Joshua 10:12–13.*
[5] *Exodus 15.*
[6] *Judges 5.*

under a mass of symbolical expressions. As applied to those books which we now call the books of the Apocrypha, the term (according to St. Augustine) refers to their hidden origin.

Nobody knows exactly who wrote them, but they had a very wide circulation among the Jews at the time of our Lord's ministry. As explained above, the Hebrew canon of Holy Scripture had not at that time been definitely fixed, and there was much difference of opinion in the rabbinical schools as to whether any or all of these books should be included in the Sacred Writings. When the Council of Jamnia (A.D. 90) settled the question of the contents of the Hebrew Bible, these fourteen books were all excluded. Meantime, however, the Septuagint (the Greek translation of the Old Testament writings) was being produced by the liberal-minded Jews of Alexandria, and the Septuagint included the Apocryphal books.

In the first Christian centuries, various collections of the Sacred Writings were in use, some containing certain of the Apocryphal books and some containing others. Straight down to the Reformation the Apocrypha was included in the official Christian Bible through all of Christendom.

The reformers of the sixteenth century pursued a different course. Finding their exclusive authority in the Holy Scriptures, they carefully examined the question as to the relative standing of these two sets of writings. They recognized a distinction but refused to abolish the Apocrypha which had been an integral part of the Christian Bible for so many centuries. In the first complete edition of Luther's Bible (A.D. 1534), the Apocrypha was included as a supplement to the

Old Testament with the notation that they were books "which are not held equal to the sacred Scriptures, and nevertheless are useful and good to read." Neither were they discarded in the English Bible but were retained as a separate section between the Testaments, and in the Sixth Article of Religion it was specified that the Church reads them "for example of life and instruction of manners; but yet doth it not apply them to establish any doctrine."

Protestant sentiment, however, has run more and more to a disparagement of the Apocrypha. About a hundred years ago (in 1827), the British and Foreign Bible Society, over vigorous protest, decided to omit it entirely from their printings of the Bible. Since that time, most English copies of the Authorized or Revised Versions have circulated without the Apocrypha until many readers of the Bible today scarcely know that the books exist. This seems very unfortunate. For fifteen hundred years the Christian world cherished the Apocrypha in its Bibles. It is a fair question to ask what right any person or group of persons has to drop out fourteen books from the Bible which the Christian world used for fifteen centuries and which most of the Christian world still uses today?

THE NEW TESTAMENT

It is important to remember that our Lord wrote nothing. It is also important to remember that for many years after the Church was launched on its career there were no Christian writings at all such as we have now in the New Testament. There was no need for them at the beginning. Our Lord was called "Rabbi" and plainly followed rabbinical

methods in instructing His Apostles. These consisted in
reiterating to a small, intimate group brief summaries of His
teachings which were carefully learned word for word. To
these memorized "Sayings" were added eye-witness accounts of things which the Apostles had seen Him do. All
this formed the substance of apostolic teaching—"all that
Jesus began both to do and teach."[7] From place to place the
Apostles traveled, repeating their story and teaching others
as they themselves had learned.

These oral accounts of the Messiah circulated through
Jewish communities all over the ancient world. Year after
year pilgrims from everywhere came up to the Holy City
for the annual feasts and sought further instruction. In Jerusalem the Apostles met these inquirers in groups—much as
the boy Jesus sat "in the midst of the doctors"—and taught
them to memorize the Sayings of Christ, His parables and
oral accounts of His deeds. Such official teaching was carried
away to all quarters and comprised the *Christian Tradition*
referred to by St. Paul—"hold the traditions which ye have
been taught."[8]

Then conditions began to change. The number of inquirers became so numerous that it was increasingly difficult
to care for them by the group method. These brief, concise
instructions began to be written down so they could be carried home by the pilgrims. Also the growing Church
brought more and more non-Jews into the fold who knew
only Greek and who were unaccustomed to the rabbinical
teaching by word of mouth. The Gentiles wanted it in writ-

[7] *Acts 1:1.*
[8] *I Thessalonians 2:15.*

ten form. So the Sayings of our Lord, or the "Logia," came into existence.

Then something else happened. St. Paul introduced a new style of letter-writing. In his missionary activity he went from city to city preaching and teaching the "tradition" and organizing congregations of Christians. But he was always under pressure to seek out new fields, and there were enemies on his track only too eager to tear down what he had erected as soon as he moved on to another place. St. Paul soon felt the necessity of following up his work by correspondence. He conceived the idea of writing letters ("epistles") addressed, not to an individual person, but to a congregation for public reading. A few personal letters that he wrote have been preserved, but most of them were sent to entire congregations, often with instructions to send copies to neighboring congregations. These letters were not intended to introduce Christ to people who had no knowledge of Him. They were written to reinforce the teaching the Apostle had already given, to answer questions and to deal with local problems of spiritual discipline and Christian behavior. St. Paul's epistles always presupposed a knowledge of the Gospel on the part of his readers. Any attempt to understand them is hopeless unless this fact is kept quite clear.

It was about the year A.D. 50 that St. Paul sent his first letter to the Thessalonians, which is the earliest Christian writing to come down to us. Other epistles followed. It is significant to note that all of these epistles had been composed before the first of the four Gospels was committed to writing. When some critics insist that the simple Jesus of the Gospels was subsequently distorted by St. Paul's subtle theology, it is well to remember that his epistles were all in circulation before any of the Gospels appeared. And it is not likely that the Church would have put its seal on Gospel records which were in conflict with the prevailing teaching about Christ—eventually gathering both into the canon of Holy Scripture.

From the very beginning, the Apostles were the accredited teachers. They had been His chosen companions, they had seen Him in action, and they had been trained by Him personally to fill the rôle of leaders. Those books which were written by Apostles, or by those who were close enough to the Apostles to give an accurate statement of apostolic teaching, were accredited by common consent and incorporated in the New Testament canon.

This is the Bible which continues year after year to be the best seller in the book market. It has been carried all over the world. It has been translated into a thousand languages and dialects. It has brought comfort, consolation, and enlightenment to countless numbers of people for the past nineteen centuries. No book has ever been under such persistent, critical scrutiny as this Book. It has been studied by the best minds of the ages—sometimes sympathetically, and often in a spirit of hostility. But through it all the Bible has come with flying colors, all the better authenticated because of the searching study to which it has been subjected. No intelligent person can afford to be ignorant of it. No Christian person can escape a sense of reverence for it.

V

THE HOLY TRINITY

SOMEWHERE G. K. Chesterton has written—"It is the saint who tries to get his head into the heavens; it is the atheist who tries to get the heavens into his head; and it is his head that splits."

As has already been said in a previous chapter, we cannot explain God because our heads are too little and our brains too feeble to accommodate Him. Nevertheless, if we are to do any orderly living we must have some orderly thinking behind it. Likewise if we are to pursue the will of God, we must organize our thoughts of God or we will never make any constructive progress. That is what we mean by theology —organizing our thoughts about God. We may never be entirely successful, but we can never stop trying.

One of our great difficulties is that we must use words to express ourselves. Since words are a human invention, it is scarcely to be expected that they can ever adequately describe God. Yet they are the only tools at our disposal. Even though we use them with the utmost care we are often confused by the changing shades of meaning which accompany the growth of any living language. Particularly is this true of the English tongue. In our Prayer Book the collect for the

Seventeenth Sunday after Trinity says, "Lord, we pray Thee that Thy grace may always prevent and follow us." Two or three centuries ago the word "prevent" meant to "go before," and it was quite in order to pray that God's grace might go before us and follow us, surrounding us with His gracious Presence. But in the course of time "prevent" has come to mean "to stop" or "to interfere with," which is not at all what the prayer intends to say. Yet when we have become accustomed to certain forms of devotional expression, it is not easy to change the language.

Or take a word like "rest." It has several meanings. It means to relax, and it also means to set something down. A negro servant always used to say, "Can I rest your hat?" But this word also means that upon which something is placed, like a book rest. And besides these meanings it also means the "remainder" or that which is left over. When we say a person has gone to his rest, it is a gentle way of indicating that he has died. And so on.

Many centuries ago Christians began to formulate their faith and struggled hard to find words which would be reasonably expressive. The terms they hit upon acquired a certain technical significance, but in the ordinary growth of language many of those same terms took on other meanings in common conversation. Thus we often have to do a little explaining because we cannot rearrange the whole language of theology every time popular usage adds something to the meaning of a word here and there. This is true in the case of the Church's doctrine of the Holy Trinity.

When the word "person" is used in casual speech, it at ones suggests a separate, distinct, individual human being.

Therefore the trinitarian formula, "three Persons in One God," is quite likely to imply to the average mind three Gods somehow or other combined into one Deity. But that is precisely what the Trinity does not mean. The unity of God (monotheism) is the very heart of all Christian teaching. The words "person" and "substance" were very carefully chosen to indicate that which was united in the unity. "Substance" refers to the essential Being of God which is always one. "Person" does not mean a separate being but a distinct Self. There are three Selfs in one Being—or three Persons in one God. For want of better names we call them Father, Son, and Holy Ghost (or Holy Spirit, which means the same thing), and we differentiate their operations as we attribute creation to the Father, redemption to the Son, and sanctification to the Holy Spirit.

Now, of course, this is raising us into a very thin atmosphere where we are likely to become bewildered. Remember, we are attempting to describe God and our little minds are not altogether efficient instruments for such a task. We can get some insight through analogies, though we recognize that no analogy can go all the way. In my own life I consist of three selfs. I am the subject, object, and umpire of my own actions. When I have a problem to solve, I talk it over with myself and eventually pass judgment on the conversation. Sometimes I say my better self has won the argument. I am a three-fold human being—yet I am only one.

Here is a table which is a material unit. It is made up of length, breadth, and height. Each one is that particular table, yet the table itself requires all three of them.

Or consider the sunlight. It consists of the source of light, the rays which come from the source, and the illumination which is produced. It is not sunshine without all three of them, but each one is distinct from the other two.

Take the well-known combination of hydrogen and oxygen which we call H_2O. Here it may be found as water, over there it may be ice, and in another place it will be steam. They are all different, but in essence they are exactly the same.

The root, the trunk, the branch are all one wood. The fountain, the stream, the river are all one water. The past, the present, the future are all that mysterious thing which we call time.

Neither any one of such analogies nor all of them taken together can give anything like an exhaustive description of the Holy Trinity but they are at least suggestive. They point the way toward what God must mean to us and check it in with our common experience of life. For our whole conception of God has been a development through the centuries from lower to higher levels as we have advanced in our appreciation of His revelation of Himself. In primitive times people thought of many different gods, which meant polytheism. Then they began to think of one Supreme God while still allowing for the possible existence of other gods, which is what we call monolatry. From that it was a simple step to monotheism—faith in one God beside whom there can be no other. Finally came the unfolding of the One God in three Persons, which is the Holy Trinity.

This is the progressive advancement which one finds in a study of the Holy Scriptures. Traces may be discovered of all these various stages with hints of God's three-fold Being appearing here and there and gradually rising above all others. The New Testament is full of allusions in thoroughly personal terms to God the Father, to Jesus Christ as His divine Son, and to the sanctifying activity of the Holy Spirit. Yet the whole Christian record is solidly committed to the essential unity of the One God. In several places this is summed up in very definite trinitarian statements. Our Lord's "Great Commission" at the close of St. Matthew's Gospel says emphatically—"Go ye therefore, and teach all nations, baptizing them in the name of the Father, and of the Son, and of the Holy Ghost."[1] In our Lord's last discourse as related by St. John we read—"But the Comforter, which is the Holy Ghost, whom the Father will send in My name, He shall teach you all things."[2] The final benediction in St. Paul's second Epistle to the Corinthians shows clearly what his teaching must have been—"The grace of the Lord Jesus Christ, and the love of God, and the communion of the Holy Ghost, be with you all. Amen."[3] And the opening salutation in the first Epistle of St. Peter is to the same effect—"Elect according to the foreknowledge of God the Father, through sanctification of the Spirit, unto obedience and sprinkling of the blood of Jesus Christ."[4] And the practice of the early Church bears this out, for we find in the earliest records (dating from about the end of the first century) that Christians were following literally the injunction given in St. Matthew's Gospel to baptize converts in the triune Name of the Father, the Son, and the Holy Ghost. The subsequent

[1] *St. Matthew 28:19.*
[2] *St. John 14:26.*
[3] *II Corinthians 13:14.*
[4] *I Peter 1:2.*

history of the Church leaves no question as to the steady teaching of the Holy Trinity in all parts of Christendom.

People who would like to reduce the Christian religion to a handy system of ethics will be sure to ask why this needs to be so. Admittedly the doctrine of the Holy Trinity is beyond our intellectual grasp, and why should we be loaded down with an intellectual puzzle when a simple faith in the One God might answer all of our needs? The quickest reply is to say that our needs may not be so easily supplied. The divinity of our Lord and the active operation of the Holy Spirit must somehow be fitted in with our faith in the One God if the integrity of the Gospel is to be preserved at all. Certain very practical considerations on these two points will be discussed in later chapters, but just here we would touch on two useful reasons for a doctrine which no one would be likely to manufacture out of his own imagination.

1. In recent years much study has been devoted to the question of personality and we know more about it than we used to. What we have been learning fits neatly into the doctrine of the Holy Trinity which was defined long before anyone ever thought of modern psychology. God must be personal if he is to have any significance to us. You can't have faith in an idea, you can't worship a principle, you can't love an abstraction. The whole of human life is built around the personal equation. It would indeed be a puzzle to conceive of a Creator of a thoroughly personalized human life who was not Himself possessed of personal qualities. That would be too much like thinking of an author who could not read or a singer without a voice. Our imaginations would expire under such a strain.

Well—the study of personality shows clearly enough that a person cannot exist alone. The very qualities which make a person demand another person to complete them. Love means nothing unless there is someone to love. The will must have an object upon which to express itself. Reason must have something to reason about. A completely isolated person would soon cease to be a person.

But God must be complete in Himself. If He were dependent upon something outside of Himself, He would be a finite being and therefore less than God. Hence there must be a personal relationship within the being of God and quite independent of His own creation. Infinite love requires an infinite object of love. Therefore we say that the Father eternally loves the Son, and the Spirit is the bond of affection between them. There is something social about God or He could not be a Person—in which case we would have no basis for knowing anything about Him anyway. So if we are puzzled with the idea of the Trinity, we must face an even greater puzzle without it. And we can't escape all puzzlement when we are thinking of God.

2. The doctrine of the Holy Trinity assembles within itself the best that is to be found in non-Christian faiths in their search after God. Mohammedanism, for instance, looks to God as the all-powerful Creator and the supreme Governor of the universe. Brahmanism and other oriental faiths conceive of God as ever-present and practically identified with His creation—forms of pantheism. Pagan cults expect God to be concerned with all the various interests of human life, and have separate gods for different things. There are phases of truth in all of them. The Holy Trinity says—yes, God is

supreme, He is also present in His creation, and He is definitely interested in all human affairs. All of this is expressed in the Three Persons in One God—the Father, the Son, and the Holy Spirit. He is creating, sustaining, and energizing—or to put it in theological language, He is transcendent, immanent, and pervasive.

All searchings after God converge upon Jesus Christ. He is the fulfilment of all religions, and He reveals God to us in trinity. His teaching has come down to us in precept and instruction, in narrative and parable. The Church has endeavored to gather them all together in the concentrated doctrine of the Holy Trinity, not only as a summarized expression of His teachings, but as a protection to the full content of what He taught. We find that it coincides with our own experience, meets our spiritual needs, elevates our conception of God Himself, and expands our religious horizon.

Therefore, "I believe in One God the Father Almighty . . . And in one Lord Jesus Christ . . . Being of one substance with the Father . . . And . . . in the Holy Ghost . . . Who with the Father and the Son together is worshipped and glorified."

VI

CREEDS AND DOCTRINE

IN CHRISTIAN teaching faith always has to do with persons. It is not a matter of wishful thinking; neither is it an amiable ability to swallow things whole. Faith means the capacity for confidence in a Person.

Sometimes people say they have faith in a government. They do not really mean that. They mean they have faith in the persons who administer a government. You do not have faith in an automobile, or a fire extinguisher, or a vacuum cleaner. You have faith in the people who make such things and believe they will turn out a satisfactory product. Faith belongs to persons, not to things.

It is important to keep this straight in our Christian minds. When we stand up in church and recite the Creed, we often say "that is my faith." Whereupon someone draws the conclusion that the Christian faith consists in the proper recitation of an ancient formula. The Creed is not your faith—it is an expression of your faith. Your faith is in God, not in any combination of words, however venerable they may be. In a derivative sense you may speak of "the faith once delivered to the saints," meaning thereby that body of doctrine which expresses the foundation upon which your faith rests. But your faith is always in a Person.

Faith represents an attitude of life. It is far more than verbal assent to any proposition. The good old doctrine of justification by faith does not mean that you win your soul's salvation by speaking up affirmatively in a loud voice. Your life may belie your words, in which case your statement of faith is vitiated. Justification by faith means that your hope of divine approval is justified by the fact that your life is definitely facing Christ in the path of Christian progress. You may declare it in words, but as Studdert Kennedy once put it, what you actually do is to "bet your life on God."

I tell you that I have faith in a friend, I believe in him, I trust him. You ask why. I say it is because I know his family. I know something of his training. I am familiar with what he has done, his previous record, his reputation, what he stands for and what other people think of him. All this is the basis of my faith in him.

That is what the Church has done with our Lord Jesus Christ. At the outset the Church proclaimed her faith in Him. Why? Because, said the Church, we know His Heavenly Father, we know how Christ Himself was born into the world, how He lived a sinless life, how He did nothing but good, suffered, and died, and rose again. We know His personal representative, the Holy Spirit, and we have His matchless teachings supported by His peerless character. That is the Church's creed—the expression of our Christian faith.

Why is a creed necessary? Why must we have doctrine anyhow? May we not swing our lives toward God, fasten our faith on Him, and let it go at that without bothering our heads over formal statements as to what it all means? There are two answers to such questions. In the first place, our minds are an important part of us and we must use them. Because faith means an attitude of life, it covers all the elements of which we are made—will, instinct, feelings, reason. We must not only love God but we must think about Him, and if we are to think intelligently we must organize our thoughts. Christian doctrine is (as we have said before) organized thinking about God.

But the Creeds themselves grow out of the second answer. Very early in Christian history certain persons began to twist the Gospel to suit their own ideas and strayed away from the apostolic tradition. Some of them said that Christ was divine but not really human. Others declared that He was a very fine man but not necessarily divine. Still others took a half-and-half position, selecting only those portions of the Gospel record which happened to fit their particular contentions. In order to protect the integrity of the Gospel the Church found it necessary to state the case in exact terms which could not be misconstrued. For example there was a queer idea propounded that our Lord did not really die—that being divine He could not die, and that the Crucifixion was not an actual event. In repudiation of any such extraordinary garbling of the facts and to clarify its own position, the Church wrote it into the Apostles' Creed in such plain terms that it could never be misunderstood—He "was crucified, dead, and buried; He descended into hell." Suppose the Church had been content merely with saying that Christ really was crucified. The distorters might have replied that they fully agreed, but that the Crucifixion did not bring death to Him as we all have to face it. Then anybody could have made it mean anything he liked and the reality of our Saviour's death would

have been held in serious question. So the Church bore down
on it, stating it in four ways in order that no one might mix
the meaning.

You see, it is not sufficient to say, "I believe in God." It
makes a difference what kind of God you believe in. As the
Archbishop of York has well said—"We tend to become
like that which we worship."[1] People who worship an in-
dulgent deity, too good-natured ever to reprove them for
wrong-doing, are sure to discount sin and become self-satis-
fied, self-centered, and self-righteous. Those who worship
a vague spirit of Goodness soon become spiritually shallow,
sentimental, and deficient in the sense of personal responsibility. On the other hand, those who may worship an exact-
ing Judge gradually turn critical themselves, censorious and
unsympathetic with the frailties of their neighbors. It can
scarcely be otherwise. Cast your best thoughts and aspirations toward an unworthy object and the same unworthy
characteristics will be stimulated in your own life. It is far
from satisfying when people say they are religious. We want
to know what kind of religion they have. Adherents of a
bad religion are often excused on the ground that they are
very much in earnest. The simple truth is that the more earnest they are for a bad religion, the worse their case becomes.

For this reason the early Christians were in conscience
bound to defend Christ against misrepresentation and to protect the very character of God. The whole question of Christian living hung on that issue—because "we tend to become
like that which we worship." Therefore when prospective

---

[1] *William Temple, "Personal Religion and Life of Fellowship," Longmans, Green
& Co., N. Y., pp. 1-2. The entire passage is most pertinent.*

converts presented themselves for Holy Baptism, they were expected to declare their faith. At first it was sufficient that they should make some such statement as, "I believe that Jesus Christ is the Son of God."[2] Then occasions arose when certain Gospel truths in support of this declaration were misconstrued and the required statement of faith was correspondingly expanded. Thus the Apostles' Creed began to grow as a baptismal symbol. Nobody ever sat down and composed it out of his own imagination. It was hammered out on the anvil of Christian experience to preserve the fulness of the Christian revelation. The Apostles were the accredited teachers of the Gospel who passed judgment on the authenticity of the instruction given by any other teachers. As they gradually slipped out of the picture by death, it became desirable to have a brief summary of their teaching as a declaration of faith to be used by converts at baptism. Thus early in the second century, just after the apostolic age, simple baptismal creeds began to appear. There was the Creed of Antioch, the Creed of Jerusalem, the old Roman Creed, and others differing slightly in form but all serving the same purpose. They were seldom written down because in those days of persecution it was dangerous to have too many records available to persecutors. Often these simple statements were used by Christians as passwords to identify themselves one to another. Out of these several creeds the Apostles' Creed finally emerged and was generally accepted.

In the time of Constantine (A.D. 312) Christianity came out into the open and the period of persecution ended. Almost immediately a queer distortion of Christian teaching

[2] *Acts 8:37.*

appeared in Alexandria, in Egypt, under the name of Arianism. It accepted the current baptismal creeds, but twisted the meaning of them to such an extent that the apostolic tradition was fairly submerged. The difficulty became so acute that a General Council of the Church was called at Nicaea in A.D. 325 to settle the question. There the Church repudiated Arianism and put forth a conciliar creed so carefully phrased that misinterpretation would be virtually impossible. It was based on the earlier Creed of Caesarea. Another corruption of Christian teaching caused the Council of Constantinople to revise it in a few particulars. It has been commonly known as the Nicene Creed and was promptly accepted throughout Christendom as the authoritative summary of the Christian Gospel.

These two are what we mean by the "historic Creeds."[3] They have stood the test of many centuries of Christian experience. They are the only statements of faith adopted universally by the undivided Church. Everything in them is taken from the Holy Scriptures, and they consist chiefly of plain facts regarding our Lord Jesus Christ with little or no theological interpretation. Theology grows, changes, develops as human knowledge increases. But there must be something to develop. The creeds are the raw material on which theology works. In the past four centuries a number of other confessions of faith have been launched upon the Christian world in the breaking away of various denominational

[3] *The Athanasian Creed is really a doctrinal hymn intended to reflect the special teaching of St. Athanasius, but not prepared by him. It appeared in the fifth century, and was used for instruction of congregations in the south of France. To some extent it found entrance into public worship in much the same way as the* Te Deum. *It is an instructive historical document on a footing quite different from that of the historic Creeds.*

bodies until many people in a confusion of mind have protested against any creeds at all. But there is really a difference. The historic Creeds are not the creeds of a nation or of a separated body of Christians. They are the products of the universal Church living in unity and speaking in unison. "The Nicene Creed aims at promoting unity, the later confessions at justifying division; the former states only what is essential, the latter descend into detail and include a large number of disputable and highly contentious propositions."[4]

Obviously there must be a recognized framework of Christian teaching if Christianity is to possess any substantial character at all. To become a Christian, or to be a follower of Christ, or to believe in the Gospel means nothing until something explicit is offered to show what such an act of allegiance covers. If I say that I believe in Napoleon Bonaparte, what do I mean? Do I mean that I am convinced he was truly an historical person, or that I approve of his military policy, or that I sanction his rather questionable personal life? Such a statement means nothing until something is specified about it. To say that you believe in Christianity but not in creeds is like saying you believe in education but not in schools, or that you believe in justice but not in laws, or that you believe in mathematics but not in the multiplication tables. Christianity is a way of life and it must have a road to travel with directions, landmarks, and recognized points of progress.

After all, what do the historic Creeds include? Briefly they consist of the following:

[4] *Charles Harris, "Creeds or No Creeds," E. P. Dutton & Co., N. Y., p. 251.*

Creation Of All Things by God.
The Incarnation.
The Crucifixion.
The Resurrection.
The Ascension.
The Final Judgment.
The Holy Ghost.
The Church.
Holy Baptism.
Eternal Life.

Expunge any one of these from the Christian faith and you have a mutilated Gospel which is not Christianity.

The historic Creeds are a protection to the integrity of the Gospel. They are a unifying bond extending throughout the Christian world. They preserve the continuity of the Christian religion. They maintain a standard by which all developments of Christian doctrine may be tested. They are a compass for Christian travelers and an anchor against spiritual drifting. They serve as a constitution for the Church and a check upon changing by-laws and disciplinary regulations. They make for stability of purpose in the Church as a whole, and the recitation of them is a powerful aid in fortifying the faith of every individual Christian.

The public recitation of the Creeds often raises a question which in some instances is a matter of conscience and in other cases an alibi. How can one stand in a congregation and go on record as believing these articles of faith when some of them are beyond one's ability to understand and about which one's belief is certainly dubious? How can I say, "I believe" when I am not sure whether I do or not? The difficulty here lies in a misconception of the purpose of the Creed. It is not

a contract especially drawn up for each individual worshipper. It is a statement of the Church's faith in which the
individual shares as a member of the Body of Christ. To hesitate over it is like a man questioning his family relationship
because he cannot understand some of his father's peculiari-
ties. No one can say he completely understands every item
mentioned in the Creed, but that need not prevent him from
reciting it in unison with his fellow-worshippers. There are
plenty of things about the human body which the physician
does not understand. Yet he does not wait until he is sure
about everything before treating his patient. He must treat
his patient as a whole person even though some parts of him
he may not understand. Those unanswered questions he
holds in suspension while he goes about his healing business.
So the individual Christian may have questions in his mind
which he cannot resolve, but he holds them in suspension
while he says the Creed with the rest of the Church. He is
not announcing to the wide world that he knows all about
it. He is pledging his allegiance to Christ and stating his adherence to the Church which teaches that faith.

If we think of ourselves as isolated persons dealing with
God separately, we shall always be in intellectual trouble.
When we learn to consider ourselves as parts of a corporate
society, we shall see how the Creed serves the Body of which
we are members. The members come and go, but the Body
lives on in order to produce and nourish new members.

VII

THE INCARNATION

WORDS, in the usage of Holy Scripture, are more than so many vocal noises. They belong to the person who utters them and are part of him. They are imbued with a certain power and reality, as though bearing part of the very personality of the speaker. When "the word of the Lord" came to the Old Testament prophets, it meant that divine authority including something of God's vital energy reposed in it. Thus in our Lord's parable of the Sower, "the seed is the word of God,"[1] possessed of a living spark which grows on its own power. Said our Lord, "The words that I speak unto you, they are spirit and they are life";[2] "now ye are clean through the word which I have spoken unto you";[3] and He warns us that "every idle word that men shall speak, they shall give account thereof in the day of judgment."[4]

Upon this background the prologue of St. John's Gospel was written: "In the beginning was the Word, and the Word was with God, and the Word was God . . . and the Word was made flesh, and dwelt among us."[5] Briefly, that

[1] *St. Luke 8:11.*
[2] *St. John 6:63.*
[3] *St. John 15:3.*
[4] *St. Matthew 12:36.*
[5] *St John 1: 1–14.*

74

tells the story of the Incarnation. Jesus Christ has been God since the beginning of all things. At a certain point in human history He assumed human nature and for a brief time lived as Man among men. He was not a man who was in some mysterious way endued with divine properties. He was God who for a short time and for a special purpose took upon himself human properties. The Christian Gospel is not something which originates with man and reaches up to God. It is something which comes from God and descends upon men. If Christ were no more than a divinely inspired man, He would be only a beautiful example of what God can do with one responsive life. We would look and wonder and be helpless. But the Incarnation tells us that God became Man, that He injected a new spiritual power into human nature in which we may share by union with Christ. He is Representative Man. Through that One Man God does something for all men. As St. Paul puts it, "Have this mind in you, which was also in Christ Jesus: who, existing in the form of God, counted not the being on an equality with God a thing to be grasped, but emptied Himself, taking the form of a servant, being made in the likeness of men."[6]

Always men and women have been in search of personal contact with God. But how could it ever be accomplished? Man is a small speck in creation. God is the supreme power over an enormous universe. The gulf is too great. How could a man see God and live? In electricity, if you connect up a small machine with a huge dynamo, the excessive electrical energy will blow out the little machine and reduce it to ruin. Therefore a means has been devised by which the power may

6 *Philippians 2:5-7 (Revised Version).*

be stepped down through a transformer and be adjusted to the capacity of the feeble machine so that it will help rather than destroy. In some such way we might say that Christ is a transformer of God's divine life, adjusting it to our human capacity of reception. I know the objections to such an analogy but at least it is suggestive.

The Incarnation is the central fact of the Christian faith. Without it Christianity falls to the ground. That is why Christians have proclaimed it, defended it, fought and died for it since the very beginning of Christian history. In the days of the Roman empire the pagans had no particular objection to adding another god to their Pantheon, and the Christians might have escaped persecution and martyrdom if they had been willing to accept such a broad-minded invitation. But they steadfastly refused. To them Christ was God as no other could possibly be called divine. They rejected all compromises and took the consequences. After the pagan persecution was lifted, crowds of pagans flooded into the Christian fold, and it was not long before questionable teaching about the person of Christ began to appear. On this point the Church took an unequivocal position, realizing that a reduced Christ meant the eventual dissolution of the whole Christian Gospel. In four great Councils the Church declared itself on four denials of the truth of the Incarnation. The first was a denial that Christ was truly God. The second denied that He was truly human. The third attempted to divide His single personality. The fourth confused His human and divine natures. The Church's doctrine was summed up at the Council of Chalcedon in the year A.D. 451 by declaring that:

Christ is truly God;
He is perfectly Man;
He is one Person;
He has two natures.

In theological language Christ is one divine Person possessed of both divine and human natures, "truly, perfectly, indissolubly, and without confusion." Many deviations from this historic teaching have occurred since those early days, but they all fall under one or another of these heads. In other words, the Church covered the ground fifteen centuries ago and settled its convictions permanently. On that footing it has weathered the storms of the ages and still moves forward with undiluted faith in the Divine Saviour.

To some impatient souls all this may seem quite theoretical and highly speculative. What's the good of all these fine distinctions anyhow? So long as we live wholesome Christian lives, what does it matter whether or not we have any consistent doctrine of the Incarnation? The point is that faith and practice go together, and a wholesome Christian life is the fruit of a sound Christian faith. Oh, yes, I know you will occasionally find a person living a very good life who has never bothered his head about any kind of faith at all. But where did he get his standard of good living? How did he come by his Christian ideals? He has borrowed them from the Church which has preserved and proclaimed them through the loyalty of those who really did concern themselves with the underlying faith. Break down the support of sound doctrine and Christ becomes a patch-work figure meaning a thousand different things to a thousand different people, with the authenticity of His Gospel dissolved and the moral principles of the Christian life thinned into sentimental vaporings. Why should you exert yourself to live like a Christian? Is it because you like the flavor of it? Or because you consider it conventionally correct? Or because you think it is the best working policy? Slippery reasons, all of them. Why should you try to live like a Christian? Because Christ said so with divine authority. There is a reason that will really stand up. What you do not believe is a matter of no great moment. What you do believe is of supreme importance. It supplies a substantial background for your daily living. When a man says, "I don't believe in Christ but I try to live a good life," I reply, "That's worse for you than it is for Christ and puts a question mark against all of your good living." But if a man says, "I do indeed believe in Christ and try to live His way," I reply, "That's fine for both of you and gives some reality to your good living." The doctrine of the Incarnation is more than a speculative theory. What we think of Christ is truly important.

THE DIVINITY OF CHRIST

For practical purposes we may approach the question of the deity of our Lord from four angles:

1. *His own human life.* It clamors for explanation because of its superlative difference from any other life that has ever been lived. "The character of Jesus forbids His possible classification with men." His sinlessness, His loyalty, His compassion, His assurance, His insight into human nature, His grasp of eternal values—they are beyond natural imagination. His matchless teaching and His complete exemplification of that

teaching are without any parallel. In all the record of human history this one Life stands unique. It calls for an explanation different from that of any other life.

2. *What He thought of Himself.* On His own authority He set aside requirements of the Law which to the Jews were of divine origin and supplanted them with His own commandments. He accepted worship and adoration from His followers such as belong only to God. In clear, bold statements He identified Himself with the Heavenly Father—"I and my Father are one,"[7] "no man knoweth the Son, but the Father; neither knoweth any man the Father, save the Son, and he to whomsoever the Son will reveal him."[8] When He asked the Apostles who they considered Him to be, St. Peter made his famous declaration, "Thou art the Christ, the Son of the living God"—for which our Lord blessed St. Peter and assured him that the Heavenly Father had taught him to say it.[9] To a blind man whom he had healed our Lord asked, "Dost thou believe on the Son of God?" The man replied, "Who is he, Lord, that I might believe on Him?" "And Jesus said unto him, Thou hast both seen Him, and it is He that talketh with thee."[10] At the time of His trial the High Priest placed Him under solemn oath and demanded, "Art thou the Christ, the Son of the Blessed?" To which our Saviour replied categorically, "I am; and ye shall see the Son of man sitting on the right hand of power, and coming in the clouds of heaven."[11]

There was no doubt as to what He meant, for His accusers

[7] *St. John 10:30.*
[8] *St. Matthew 11:27.*
[9] *St. Matthew 16:16-17.*
[10] *St. John 9:35-37.*
[11] *St. Mark 14:61-62.*

immediately carried Him off to Pilate and charged Him with blasphemy, just as on an earlier occasion His enemies had sought to destroy Him for "making Himself equal with God."[12] The records are full of it. There can be only one of three answers—either He was a fraud, or He was deluded, or He spoke the truth. No one can study the accounts of His life and harbor for a moment the idea that He would deliberately engage in deceit. Neither can anyone consider His clear thinking, His soundness of judgment, and the wholesome sanity of His teaching and, in the face of these, reach a conclusion that He was a victim of hallucinations. The alternative is to believe that He must have been speaking the truth.

3. *What others thought of Him.* "I believe that Jesus Christ is the Son of God," said the Ethiopian after St. Philip had taught it to him in preparation for baptism.[13] St. Paul writes to the Romans about Jesus Christ, "declared to be the Son of God with power."[14] To the Colossians he says, "in Him dwelleth all the fulness of the Godhead bodily."[15] St. Peter speaks repeatedly of "the Lord and Saviour Jesus Christ."[16] St. John is emphatic about it—"Whosoever shall confess that Jesus is the Son of God, God dwelleth in him, and he in God."[17] These are a few samples. It must be remembered that these men were Jews, members of a race which had suffered everything in defense of their faith in the One God. For them to attribute divine properties to any other than the

[12] *St. John 5:18.*
[13] *Acts 8:37.*
[14] *Romans 1:4.*
[15] *Colossians 2:9.*
[16] *II Peter 2:20.*
[17] *I John 4:15.*

God of their Fathers would have been an inconceivable reversal of all their history and training—unless they were completely convinced of its absolute truth. They might have been imbeciles or they might have been emotionally unreliable, but the record contradicts both possibilities. They were solid, practical men—workers in a well-established fishing industry like St. Peter and St. John, or business men like St. Matthew, or a physician like St. Luke. As for St. Paul, he was possessed of one of the keenest analytical intellects of his day. And they all staked their lives on their faith. There is no way to account for it except on the assumption that they thoroughly believed it beyond any possibility of careless language.

4. *Christian experience.* Writings of the early Church Fathers have been preserved for us since the days almost immediately following the Apostles. They are unanimous about it. The Christian community worshipped Christ as God from the very beginning—both Jewish converts with all their monotheistic traditions and Gentile converts for whom it might have been easier. They battled for the integrity of our Lord's deity through the long succession of General Councils of the Church. As the Gospel spread, this conviction took fast hold of all ranks of people and of widely different races. In every age the best minds of the day have worshipped and adored Him while the common people have given their lives to Him as to God. Countless lives have been revolutionized by faith in His divine mission while throngs of people have offered themselves and everything they had to Him as their God and Saviour. In no other cause has such a stream of sacrifice been laid at the feet of Deity. No other

influence has so deeply affected society the whole world over at various stages of civilization. Perhaps they were all mistaken. Possibly they were all guilty of a colossal blunder. In that case the best and finest in the last twenty centuries must have been predicated on a fiction—which is a little too much for any reasonable mind to accept.

THE VIRGIN BIRTH

"The Virgin Birth" is not the same as the "Immaculate Conception." They are two distinct doctrines but are often popularly confused. The Virgin Birth means that our Lord was born of a human mother by an act of God without the agency of a human father. The Immaculate Conception means that our Lord's mother, the Blessed Virgin Mary, was herself conceived and born without any taint of original sin. This last doctrine was not known among the early Christians. It grew up during the Middle Ages and remained a matter of pious opinion until A.D. 1854 when it was declared to be an article of faith in the Roman Catholic Church.

The Virgin Birth, however, is another matter. From the very beginning it has always been an integral part of the Christian tradition. Two accounts of it appear in the recorded Gospels,[18] that of St. Luke deriving from St. Mary herself, and that of St. Matthew coming from our Lord's foster-father, St. Joseph. There is no time when it has not been part and parcel of Christian teaching, and there is no ground for questioning it except on the assumption that such things do not happen. As a matter of fact such a birth from a single parent is not as contrary to nature as it might seem. Instances

[18] *St. Matthew 1-2; St. Luke 1-2.*

of it do occur among certain insects such as the bees. Nevertheless, it is quite true that it is not known among human beings.

That is an important point. If our Lord were merely a human being, we might expect that He must have been born in the usual way. But when God becomes incarnate, we might well expect something different. We do not believe in the Incarnation because of the Virgin Birth of our Lord. We believe in the Incarnation on other grounds—and then we find that the Virgin Birth is a fitting method for accomplishing it.

Sometimes it has been contended that the old pagan mythology refers to great heroes as born of virgins and that the Virgin Birth of our Lord is a legend carried over from these old stories. They have been examined carefully by the best of scholars, and there is no parallel which can begin to justify such a contention. The Jews did not anticipate that the Messiah would be born of a Virgin. Both the Jewish and Gentile Christians despised paganism and fought bitterly against any pagan encroachments on their Gospel. They would have been horrified at the thought of incorporating a pagan legend into the Gospel which meant life itself to them.

Any birth is a mystery. It is no matter of wonder that the birth of our Lord was more mysterious because He was, and is, an exceptional Person. It would answer nothing to dismiss the Virgin Birth as a miracle unless Christ Himself is also dismissed. Once we recognize our Lord's divine character, His human birth is a miracle anyhow. The purely natural birth of a sinless life would be not only a physical miracle but a moral miracle as well. In view of the record which is inherently honest, in view of the age-old faith of the Church in the Virgin Birth, and in view of the added difficulties of any other explanation, it would seem that we are well warranted in sharing the statement of the historic Creed that He was "conceived of the Holy Ghost, born of the Virgin Mary."

A point in theology is worthy of mention. The Incarnation is an act of God. If it means that God took a single human life, naturally produced, and raised it to a unique dignity, then that one life was benefited and the human race received a beautiful example of something. But if Christianity has any vital significance to the rest of us, it means that God was interested in the race, not in a single individual. God did not elevate one person who was already created. He, as an eternally existing Person, took human nature upon Himself, thereby projecting His divine presence into the whole stream of human life. Thus in the incarnation of Jesus Christ God's redeeming power becomes available to all of us, and all mankind is benefited. This union of divine and human natures in the one Person logically calls for the joint action of God and a human being. This is precisely what happened in the Virgin Birth of our Lord. It fits serenely in the Christian picture.

The doctrine of the Incarnation has also certain practical consequences. It precipitates the Christian Gospel out of the world of theory into the realm of persons. This makes it true to our own experience because, after all, we live in personal terms. We talk about ideas and ideals, but our dealings are with one another, person to person. Try as we will to be objective and impersonal, we cannot escape the personal element, simply because we are built that way. Personal life is the one thing that is common to all of us. Through no other channel could God reach us so effectually. Christianity is not the religion of a book, or of a philosophy, but of a Person. You don't believe in a system—you believe in Christ. The simplest human being can be loyal to a Person where he would be lost in a maze of subtle theories, however convincing they might be. Back of Christ we may build our philosophy and our theology, but it is He who gives substance to all of it.

Moreover, the Incarnation brings God and man to a point of sympathetic understanding. God is no longer a divine Ruler located far off in the distant heavens. He has become one of us. God's love and mercy are no longer academic qualities. He has lived our life, faced our troubles, met our temptations. In all our sorrows, failures, and tribulations— God knows and God understands because He has been there too. When we approach God in need of help, we do not come to a coldly righteous Divine Principle, but to a Friend and Companion who has struggled with life as we know it and "was in all points tempted like as we are."[19] Once I called on a young man in a hospital who was choking and wretched with a bad quinzy. He was miserable and frightened until I said, "I know just how you feel—I've had it myself." Whereupon he smiled, gratefully received the ministrations of the Church and got well. So when our troubles get us down, God says, "I know all about it—I have been there too." You can go to a God like that with assurance of a sympathetic reception. Without the Incarnation divine

[19] *Hebrews 4:15.*

sympathy would be largely a fiction. Is it any wonder that hospitals are peculiarly Christian institutions, that the care of the sick, the feeble, the helpless, the aged is a Christian contribution to a world of hard knocks? It is a better world to live in because God became incarnate in Jesus Christ our Lord.

Finally, because of the Incarnation, Christianity is always progressive. It looks not to the past but to the future. You do not reverence a dead Hero. You worship a Living Lord. Christ is not back yonder—He is up ahead leading the way. Christians do not mourn the passing of a Golden Age when the Master once lived among men. They anticipate the coming of a glorious future when Christ shall come into His own. Because of the Incarnation He is "Jesus Christ the same yesterday, and to day, and for ever."[20]

[20] *Hebrews 13:8.*

VIII

THE ATONEMENT

THE SECRET of living in the natural world consists in adaptation to environment. People who live in a cold climate must develop a natural resistance to the low temperature, while those who live in the tropics must acquire a similar resistance to the beating sun. Should a man wish to descend into the unnatural environment of deep water, he will provide himself with the artificial accommodation of a diving suit by which he can stand the change for a time. Take a fish out of the water and he dies quickly. That's the difference between a rational man and a fish which lives by instinct. But in either case, adaptation to environment is the crucial question.

Well, man has also a spiritual environment—which is God. His soul thrives or shrinks as he accommodates himself to God's presence. The eye does not create light. It is the light rays beating on the sensitive optical membrane which produce a response and man sees. Likewise the ears do not create sound and the lungs do not make air. They respond to external forces acting upon them. So does God act upon the soul of man and as he responds, his consciousness of God becomes stronger and his spiritual faculties become more acute. Man is made to respond to God.

Sin is the refusal or the failure to respond to God. Notice —it may be either one. Many people would shrink from denying God but are quite complacent about ignoring Him. But indifference to God is likely to be just as disastrous as the wilful rejection of Him. "It is as possible to destroy one's life by starving as by poisoning it."[1] The essence of sin is selfishness—an unwillingness to go to the trouble of making a response to God. Sometimes it is selfishly convenient to capitalize the preference of the moment and demand our own way. But when we insist on having our own way, we are sure to precipitate difficulties both with God and with one another. A vivid recollection of my youth is of a hysterical woman rushing about the house and screaming, "I must have my own way." One scarcely needs to add that it was not long before that home was a total wreck. It is because someone insists on having his own way that quarrels and discords arise, that wars and strife are fomented, that crime and cruelty corrupt our society. God wills harmony, righteousness, peace, and love. When we fail to respond to that Divine Will, we are committing sin against God.

Down at the bottom sin is a matter of choice. Originally God created man fully equipped for a perfect response to the Divine Will. But that response had to be free. A forced response always loses its validity. Therefore man was given free-will in order that he might serve God because he wanted to and not because he had to. Man chose his own way rather than God's way, and so sin entered into the world with all its

[1] *Paul B. Bull, "Instructions on the Atonement," Morehouse-Barlow Co., N. Y., p. 8.*

corrupting influence. We may struggle all we please with social maladjustments, racial antipathies, and international animosities but we are dealing with effects rather than causes. Behind all of them lies a spiritual dislocation where the final answer must be found. Clean up the social problems and more of them will arise. Wash out the spiritual perversion and the social problems will take care of themselves.

Somehow something had to be done about this question of sin. God had decreed a righteous creation and He could not be finally thwarted. God might have commanded men to be good and it would have been done. But in the process He would have violated His own gift of free-will. The correction had to come by the way of human choice. But how could warped human nature make such a choice? Man had to be reconciled to God but man had blunted his powers of reconciliation. What to do?

"God was in Christ reconciling the world unto Himself."[2] The response had to come from man but man was incapable of making it. Only God could do it as it had to be done. Therefore God became Man in the incarnation of our Lord Jesus Christ. What man could not do for himself, God did for him in the person of our Saviour. "He hath made Him to be sin for us who knew no sin; that we might be made the righteousness of God in Him."[3] His life was a perfect offering to the Heavenly Father, sealed by His death on the cross. He surmounted the obstacle of human sin, and as we become identified with Him we are relieved of our own spiritual disabilities which cannot exist in union with Christ. It is not

[2] *II Corinthians 5:19.*
[3] *II Corinthians 5:21.*

merely that He set us an example. As we have seen, the Incarnation means that God took human nature (not a single
human life) upon Himself. The race is drawn up to God and
what He did for all of us is made applicable to each one of
us. "He died for all, that they which live should not hence-
forth live unto themselves, but unto Him which died for
them, and rose again."[4] "As He joins Himself to the whole
race of man in the Incarnation, so He joins Himself to separate individuals in the Sacraments."[5] This is what we mean
by redemption—a buying-back. "The Son of Man came not
to be ministered unto, but to minister, and to give His life a
ransom for many."[6]

E. G. Selwyn has told the following story about the island
of Formosa when it was still part of the Chinese empire. A
Chinese named Goho was appointed governor of the island.
From time immemorial it had been the custom for the For-
mosans to offer a human sacrifice once a year. Previous gov-
ernors had humored them, providing some condemned
criminal for the annual atrocity. Goho could not bring himself to do it. He persuaded the people to substitute a pig or a
goat for the human victim. For a few years all went well.
Then came one of those strange reversals of sentiment and
the people began to clamor for the old-time human sacrifice.
They threatened to seize their own victim in spite of the governor's orders and Goho could not restrain them. Finally he
gave in. "Go," he said, "to the forest tomorrow morning
at nine o'clock, and at such and such a place you will find a

---

[4] *II Corinthians 5:15.*
[5] *Darwell Stone, "Outline of Christian Dogma," Longmans, Green & Co., N. Y.,
p. 94.*
[6] *St. Matthew 20:28.*

man tied, wearing a red robe, and a red hat, and a scarlet cloth over his face. Strike; for he is your victim." Eagerly the natives went to the appointed place and found a man sacrificially clothed, tied to a tree. Quickly knives were raised and the blood-lust was satisfied. As the scarlet cloth fell away from the face of the murdered victim, they recognized him. It was Goho. From that day there have been no more human sacrifices. Instead, the people celebrate annually a solemn thanksgiving on the anniversary of Goho's death.[7]

It is a striking instance of vicarious sacrifice—self-giving for the sake of others. If it is effective when man does it for man, how much more efficacious must it be when God does it for mankind. The singular character of the Christian religion lies in the fact that vicarious sacrifice stands at the center of it. "Feed the Church of God, which He hath purchased with His own blood."[8] "In whom we have redemption through His blood, the forgiveness of sins."[9] "Christ also hath once suffered for sins, the just for the unjust, that He might bring us to God."[10] Sin is selfishness, and the best antidote is the self-giving of vicarious sacrifice. The motive, of course, is love. Love is a propulsive force which gives and continues to give without counting costs. In this respect it is distinctly different from that modern flair for "service" as a profitable investment. "He profits most who serves best" is a slogan of modern business. Whatever virtue there may be in such a policy, it is definitely sub-Christian. Ours is a Gospel of sacrifice, not merely of service. Any equalizing of

[7] *Report of Anglo-Catholic Congress of 1927, pp. 91–92.*
[8] *Acts 20:28.*
[9] *Ephesians 1:7.*
[10] *I Peter 3:18.*

the results rests with God who, through our Lord Jesus Christ, gave Himself for us.

All this has sometimes been tied up to a doctrine of "substitution." We owe God our best. Insofar as we have failed to give Him our best we are in debt to Him. We can never discharge the debt because we can never do more than our best, and we owe that to Him anyhow. So Christ, who never failed of the best, does it for us, substituting Himself in our stead. There is an element of truth in this but it needs safeguarding. It does not relieve us from all responsibility. The effect of His sacrifice is available to us only as we identify ourselves with Him, follow His way of life, and keep ourselves receptive to His gifts of grace. That is why the Sacraments naturally follow on the Incarnation and the Atonement. They are the channels through which His spiritual benefits reach us.

Two points need to be remembered: (1) The cross is the symbol of Christian redemption and marks the climax of our Lord's sacrificial offering. But His death cannot be separated from His life. When He said, "I lay down my life," He meant more than the isolated fact of the Crucifixion. He meant the whole offering of daily obedience to the Heavenly Father. For purposes of study we may separate His life into a series of events and consider each one by itself, but no single happening must be torn from its context. The Sermon on the Mount is as much a part of the Atonement as the passion in Gethsemane. To concentrate His work of redemption exclusively on Calvary comes too close to the realm of magic. His life was the offering, which was completed in His death, and our reconciliation with God depends on both

(2) On the stage of history the Atonement occurred at a particular time, but its divine significance rests in eternity. This is something to be remembered in all our thought about God. He sees through the vista of eternity but we, because we are human, must have things presented to us in time. God's entrance into human life colors the whole stream of it—not merely that portion which, according to our human reckoning, comes after a certain date. Chronology is a human contrivance but God sees life as a whole. "One day is with the Lord as a thousand years,"[11] and our Saviour's sacrifice is that of "the Lamb slain from the foundation of the world."[12]

Father Bull has put it this way: "A person sitting on the top of a perfectly conical mountain sees at one glance a long procession of persons winding their way up to the summit. All, the first and the last, those who are highest and those who are lowest down, are present to him in one moment. But to those who are moving in the procession, there is a necessary sequence. Some are going before, some following after; some are out of sight, hidden by the turn of the road; some can be seen above or below them, winding their way up the same path, and then they disappear from sight, to reappear again.

"So the Procession of the Ages, the past, the present, and the future, winds its way up the Mount of God. To themselves they follow or precede one another; to God they are all present in the eternal 'Now' . . . Looked at as a whole, we see that the Atonement is the eternal Purpose of God. As

[11] *II Peter 3:8.*
[12] *Revelation 13:8.*

soon as sin becomes a possibility, redemption becomes a purpose."[13] The reason we are limited in our ability to comprehend the full meaning of the Atonement is that we are still part of the procession.

No doubt that is why the Church has never attempted to formulate a doctrine of Atonement. It is so sweeping in its application and its implication that we would scarcely know where to begin and where to end. We find the fact embedded in the Gospel and we experience the effects in our Christian living. Redemption is the atmosphere in which Christians live. It is the theme-song of the faith. No ordinary word is capable of expressing what it means, so we have manufactured a special word. "Atonement" does not derive from any usual language roots. It is simply the combination of "at" and "one"—the at-one-ment, the bringing together of God and man by the redeeming love of God, by the reconciliation of human obstinacy, through the one full, perfect, and sufficient sacrificial offering of our Lord Jesus Christ.

At the time of the French Revolution it was decided that Christianity should be abolished in favor of the reign of Reason. Some sprightly and thoroughly modern philosophers of the day devised a new religion which was stripped of everything supernatural, burdened with no touch of mystery, and completely rational. But their synthetic product received no response from the people. One of the clever inventors complained to the cynical Talleyrand that no one was interested in his new religion. Whereupon Talleyrand replied: "There is just one way to do it; you must lead a

[13] *Paul B. Bull, "Instructions on the Atonement," Morehouse-Barlow Co., N.Y., p. 36-37.*

sinless life; you must get yourself crucified; and on the third day you must rise from the dead. Then perhaps you can found a religion which will compete with the Christian faith."

We might add—that he didn't do it.

IX

RESURRECTION AND ASCENSION

ONE DAY a distressed mother walked into my office to talk about her young son, an unusually bright and precocious child. "I'm completely baffled," she said. "The other day I showed the boy a picture of the Crucifixion and told him the story. He asked 'Was He the Son of God?' I replied that He was. 'Was God His Heavenly Father?' I said 'Yes.' The boy thought it over for a moment and then burst out, 'I don't believe it. No father would ever let that happen to his son.' Now," the mother went on, "what am I to tell him? I can't let him grow up with such ideas in his mind."

"Why," I asked, "did you not tell him about the Resurrection?"

"Oh!" she exclaimed, "I never thought of that."

How can Christian people ever fail to think of the Resurrection? The New Testament is full of it. It was the central point of apostolic teaching. When the Christian community assembled to choose another Apostle in place of Judas Iscariot, the one requirement was that he should be a "witness with us of the resurrection."[1] The age-old Jewish tradition of the seventh-day Sabbath gave way to the first day of the week

[1] *Acts 1:22.*

as the Christian Lord's Day because it was the Resurrection Day. And for twenty centuries Easter Day has been the "Queen of Feasts" in the regular round of the Christian Year. How could anyone ever forget it?

Over and over again during His teaching of the Apostles our Lord foretold His resurrection. After the Transfiguration He said, "Tell the vision to no man, until the Son of man be risen again from the dead."[2] On His last journey to Jerusalem He said, "The Son of Man shall be delivered unto the chief priests, and unto the scribes; and they shall condemn Him to death . . . and the third day He shall rise again."[3] On the way to Gethsemane He promised the Apostles, "after I am risen again, I will go before you into Galilee."[4] Such warnings were too much for them and they were not prepared for the Resurrection when it did happen. But every Gospel tells the story of it, each one adding some details of its own.

On Good Friday the weary and heart-broken disciples were thinking only of providing reverent burial for the mutilated body of their Master. For them everything was over but a precious memory. When, on Easter morning, rumors began to circulate that the Lord had appeared to this one and that one, consternation and unbelief ran riot. Gradually they were convinced in spite of themselves. The sealed and guarded tomb was actually found to be empty, and by evening all the Apostles had seen Him except Thomas. The incredulity of that one Apostle has gained him the title of the "Doubting Thomas" from that day to this. Yet even he was finally

[2] *St. Matthew 17:9.*
[3] *St. Mark 10:33–34.*
[4] *St. Matthew 26:32.*

convinced when our Saviour appeared the following week and called him to touch the very wounds in the Sacred Body. Over a period of forty days our Lord came to them at different times both in Judea and in Galilee, giving them final instructions as to what He expected of them. It was no case of the wish being father to the thought, for those Apostles proved hard to convince.

Eventually they were so sure of what had happened that they took their lives in their hands to tell it far and wide. The first public sermon preached for the Church found its climax in the Resurrection.[5] St. Paul risked the contempt of the sophisticated Athenians by boldly proclaiming that God "hath given assurance unto all men, in that He hath raised Him from the dead."[6] The same Apostle reminded the Corinthian converts of the Christian tradition which he had already taught them and which was the accepted teaching of the Church, centering on the Resurrection of our Lord, from which he launched forth on his classic discussion of a general resurrection for all.[7] Straight through the New Testament the references are too numerous to tabulate. The recurrent emphasis is unmistakable as summarized in St. Paul's crisp ultimatum: "if Christ be not risen, then is our preaching vain, and your faith is also vain."[8]

In the Incarnation God took human nature upon Himself in the person of Jesus Christ as Representative Man upon the stage of human history. In His sacrificial offering Jesus made atonement for all mankind upon the stage of human history.

[5] *Acts 2.*
[6] *Acts 17:31.*
[7] *I Corinthians 15.*
[8] *I Corinthians 15:14.*

But human history will one day cease while God's work must continue. Therefore the completed work of Christ had to be raised into the realm of eternity without losing its anchorage in human experience. It could not stop at the grave. The inevitable goal of the Incarnation is the Resurrection. Our Lord accomplished redemption in a human life with a human body. But that redemption is an eternal achievement. To conserve, in God's eternity, this union of human and divine nothing could suffice but the resurrection of the sacrificed human nature of our Lord in order that the Sacred Humanity might be eternally presented to the Heavenly Father. Otherwise the whole mission of Christ would be merely an historical episode at a given date—interesting to us in retrospect but impotent as a means of reconciling man to God. Christianity might then be a piece of speculative philosophy but scarcely a vital religion.

This is not to say that by some species of legerdemain a carnal Body was somehow wafted up into the heavenly places. St. Paul reminds us that "flesh and blood cannot inherit the Kingdom of God" but that "there is a natural body, and there is a spiritual body."[9] We are carried beyond the reach of our ordinary experiences and cannot tell just what happened or how. The same Body that was buried in the tomb emerged from the tomb but was raised as a glorified Body free of carnal restraints. We may not be able to describe it, but our modern knowledge of the composition of matter facilitates the possibility of a spiritual force transmuting a physical body into something different without being contradictory.

[9] *I Corinthians 15:50, 44.*

There are three ways of looking at the Resurrection—as an hallucination, as a deception, or as a fact.

The hallucination idea has been pretty well exploded. The record is very clear that nobody anticipated the Resurrection and there was no antecedent atmosphere to accommodate unwarranted visions. The Apostles were not of the neurotic temperament that goes in for such things. They were solid, sensible men, thoroughly imbued with Jewish traditions, and often slow to grasp what our Lord was teaching them. There are no grounds for the hallucination idea except the wish to have it so.

That the Resurrection was one grand deception is clearly out of character not only with our Lord Himself but with everything we know about the Apostles. They didn't do such things. But if they had attempted it, they could easily have been refuted. Within a few weeks after the event, the Apostles were publicly preaching the Resurrection. If they had been perpetrating a hoax, there were crowds of hostile eye-witnesses who could have called them to account in short order. On the contrary, it is interesting to note that with all the questions raised about various points in the Christian teaching, no controversy appears concerning the Resurrection. Opponents were angry about it but seem to have been in no position to dispute it.

There are few facts in ancient history as well authenticated as that of the Resurrection. Person after person testified to it both singly and in groups, even "five hundred brethren at once."[10] The disciples were prepared to stake their lives on it—and did so. The Church built its faith around the Risen

[10] *I Corinthians 15:6.*

Lord, and the triumphant vitality of Christian progress can be accounted for by no other fact.

The logical supplement to the Resurrection was, of course,

THE ASCENSION.

The two go together in rounding out the conclusion of our Lord's redemptive work. The Ascension simply means that Christ returned whence He came—a fitting conclusion to His earthly ministry.

It is true that twenty centuries ago people thought of the earth as a flat surface over which the sky was arched like a great bowl. But it is not true that they localized God above the bowl where He was waiting for our Lord to return to Him. As early as the fourth century St. Jerome ridiculed such an idea.[11] Our Lord returned to the heavenly realm which is spiritual, not spatial. Anything inspiring or encouraging is always upward. Anything depressing or discouraging is always downward. When we are joyful and optimistic, we say that we are uplifted, that our spirits rise. On the other hand if we are dejected and unhappy, we say that our spirits are low, that we are downcast or down-hearted. Well—our Lord had been successful, He had achieved the purpose of His Incarnation, He was returning in triumph. Therefore, when He bid farewell to the disciples, He left them—upward. He was not traveling to a place. He was marking the end of His earthly experience. "The customary way of speaking of the Ascension as a 'going up' to heaven no more implies that heaven is locally above the earth, than the expression 'going

[11] *Charles Harris, "Creeds or No Creeds," E. P. Dutton & Co., N. Y., pp. 75-80.*

up to London' implies the belief that London is the highest place in England."[12]

We have the record of it in two of the Gospels and in the Acts of the Apostles.[13] In a certain period and in a certain locality Christ had lived, taught, and died among men. His divine mission had to be localized in order to make it humanly intelligible. But it was also necessary that His followers should understand the universality and timelessness of His Kingdom and of His Gospel. God was not exclusively concerned with a single generation of Jews who lived in a spot called Palestine at a particular date. He was concerned with the human race in all places and of all ages. His gift of salvation had to be made in human terms, which meant a time and a place. Then it had to be perpetuated in heavenly terms above time or place. Our Lord is not only an historical figure but a universal Saviour. In His ministry He was present with a small number of people for a few years. Through His Resurrection and Ascension He becomes available to all people for all time. He might have told this to the Apostles and they might or might not have understood it. By demonstrating it to them in the Ascension He made it unmistakable and unforgettable.

To the Apostles the Resurrection and the Ascension were thundering events. They changed the whole complexion of the future. Christians were not to be memorializers of a dear departed Friend. They were to be followers of a living Lord. With the passing of centuries there has been a tendency to

[12] *Ibid., p. 279.*
[13] *St. Mark 16:19; St. Luke 24:51; Acts 1:3–8–11.*

tame and domesticate Christ, but every year Easter and Ascension Day break through the spiritual crust of half-loyalties and remind us that we belong to "Christ, who is our life." Christians are not bogged down by the venerable antiquity of their religion, they are stimulated by its living qualities. On the Resurrection morning the women met our Lord newly risen. Through them He sent word to the Apostles to meet Him in Galilee, promising that He would go before them. Then came the Ascension, and Christ has been "going before them" ever since. The Christian life is an adventure but there are no risks in it which He does not share. If Christ were merely an example of bygone days, Christianity might well be synonymous with spiritual indolence. But the Resurrection forbids any such thing. He does not invite us into a spiritual hothouse, but out into the wind and weather of life where souls grow strong with effort and exercise—because He goes before us.

We do not ask that His Life should be reverently remembered. We pray, "Thy Kingdom come."

When you recall the strong personal devotion of the disciples for our Lord, does it not seem strange that they never erected a monument for Him on Mount Calvary? You never hear of the Apostles calling a convention at the scene of the Crucifixion or holding memorial services around the tomb of St. Joseph of Arimathea. The Resurrection attended to that. They were following Christ and He was no longer there. His monument is the Cross, but it is the Cross on ten thousand altars where His Life is constantly given to the faithful.

"He goeth before you." You don't know just where He will take you but you know He will be there. You can't predict the future but you can predict Christ. His appeal is not to your timidity but to your faith and courage. He is risen—and because He lives, we shall live also.

X

THE HOLY SPIRIT

LET US take a few illustrations. In the Scriptural story of Creation a picture is painted of God bringing the world into being. "And the Spirit of God moved upon the face of the waters. And God said, Let there be light: and there was light."[1]

The time came in the history of Israel when the Hebrew people were carried away into Babylon. Ezekiel stood forth among them as the prophet of the captivity to stiffen their loyalty and encourage their hopes. The prophet tells how the "Spirit lifted me up," how he met the people on the bank of the river Chebar to instruct them, how "the Spirit entered into me" and so on.[2]

At the opening of our Lord's ministry He found St. John Baptist baptizing people as a sign of repentance. In order to support the Baptist and to show His own community of spiritual interest with the people, Jesus also came for baptism. "And, lo, the heavens were opened unto Him, and He saw the Spirit of God descending like a dove, and lighting upon Him."[3]

[1] *Genesis 1:2–3.*
[2] *Ezekiel 3:14, 24.*
[3] *St. Matthew 3:16.*

On the feast of Pentecost following our Lord's ascension
something happened to the Apostles. They were gathered
together in the upper room in Jerusalem when a compelling
impulse stirred them. The best way they could describe it
was to say it was like a "rushing mighty wind" and like
"cloven tongues like as of fire." Whereupon they "were all
filled with the Holy Ghost," and boldly set out to bear that
witness to Christ which the Church has continued ever
since.[4]

The aged Apostle St. John had been banished to the island
of Patmos in one of the early persecutions of the Christians.
There he wrote a symbolical treatise on the sufferings, fortitude, and ultimate triumph of the Church, which is sometimes called the Apocalypse and sometimes the Revelation of
St. John the Divine. It is the last book in the Bible. In describing how it came to him he says, "I was in the Spirit on
the Lord's day."[5]

These are typical instances of what runs steadily through
the Bible from end to end. References to the Spirit of God,
the Holy Spirit, or the Holy Ghost (they all mean the same
thing) are far too numerous to tabulate. They imply a divine
personal Force acting upon God's creation. Sometimes, as in
the Creation story itself, it is God active in nature—the ever-
sustaining Divine Presence which not only created the universe but sustains and vivifies it. Sometimes it is God inspiring
or guiding men and women, as in the cases of the prophets
and other great leaders who were human instruments in the
hands of God. Throughout our Lord's ministry the associa-

[4] *Acts 2:2–4.*
[5] *Revelation 1:10.*

tion between Himself and the Holy Spirit was constant and complete. The Church, as the Representative of Christ on earth, was taught and led by the Holy Spirit and conveyed the Spirit of God to its members through the sacramental channels provided. Those who wrote the Christian record did so "in the Spirit," and thus gave us what we call the "inspired" Scriptures.

The Holy Spirit means God in action. The best way we can distinguish Him is in the trinitarian language of Three Persons in One God—the Father, Son, and Holy Spirit—which is admittedly inadequate because God is so much greater than any human language. But it does in some measure account for the facts as we attempt to correlate them. God is One and works as one. No single Person of the Holy Trinity works apart from the others but there are diversities of operations which may be more or less segregated. In the Heavenly Father we see God governing and directing His universe—while in the Holy Spirit we see God moving intimately in the lives of men and women to supply spiritual needs and stimulate spiritual motives. They are not two Gods at work but two personal activities of the One God. The Church is the particular sphere of the Holy Spirit, and the Sacraments are His particular means of operation.

This is not to say that the Spirit of God may be confined within any limits of the natural or human world. When we were discussing the Incarnation, we saw how Christian teaching has always understood that our Blessed Lord has existed from eternity as the Son of God, but that He became incarnate in human life at a certain time and a certain place for the sake of us humans who are conditioned by time and space. Well, in a somewhat similar way the Holy Spirit has always been operative, but at a given time and place His presence was particularly concentrated in the Church in order to meet our human needs. Said our Lord to the Apostles, "ye shall receive power after that the Holy Ghost is come upon you."[6] And on the day of Pentecost "they were all filled with the Holy Ghost."[7] So we speak of the Christian era as "the dispensation of the Spirit"—not that He was absent before or otherwise, but that since that day of Pentecost His presence has possessed peculiar characteristics.

If I go out in the sunshine, I am surrounded with light. If I hold a burning-glass over an inflammable object, I can focus the rays of light to a point of extreme brilliance and concentrated heat which may even produce a flame. I have not detracted from the generally prevailing light, but I have created a sphere of concentrated brilliance wherein special results can be achieved. So is the Spirit of God always present. Christ provides a focus through which that Divine Power is concentrated within a sphere called His Church, where the Spirit operates to a special purpose. Nothing has been detracted from His prevailing presence, but a point of contact has been established for us human beings because we need points of contact with God. Outside that sphere He can and does operate, but God has opened for us a normal avenue of approach which is plainly for our benefit.

All this is gathered up in the last paragraph of the Nicene Creed when we say, "I believe in the Holy Ghost, the Lord, and Giver of Life, Who proceedeth from the Father and the

[6] *Acts 1:8.*
[7] *Acts 2:4.*

Son; Who with the Father and the Son together is worshipped and glorified; Who spake by the prophets: and I believe one Catholic and Apostolic Church."

The night before His crucifixion our Lord had a long talk with the Apostles. He told them some important things about the Holy Spirit. "I will pray the Father, and He shall give you another Comforter, that He may abide with you for ever; even the Spirit of truth."[8] The word which we have translated "Comforter" is the Greek word "Paraclete." It means an advocate, a helper, one who pleads our cause and stands up for us. Three centuries ago, when the Authorized Version of the Bible was prepared, the word Comforter had a somewhat different meaning than the word now conveys. It comes from the same root as our word "fortitude" and had a much stronger significance than the gentle, soothing effect which we associate with "comfort" today. It means the Strengthener, the Inspirer, the Helper, the Instructor. All of these are functions of the Holy Ghost, the Comforter.

Said our Lord, "the Comforter, which is the Holy Ghost, whom the Father will send in my name, He shall teach you all things, and bring all things to your remembrance, whatsoever I have said unto you."[9] And again, "I have yet many things to say unto you, but ye cannot bear them now. Howbeit when He, the Spirit of truth, is come, He will guide you into all truth."[10] Our Lord had laid down the principles of His kingdom for all time but it was hardly to be expected that the Apostles could grasp them all at once. In the long history of the Church which lay ahead many difficult and

[8] *St. John 14:16.*
[9] *St. John 14:26.*
[10] *St. John 16:12–13.*

unforeseen problems would arise to which His principles would have to be applied. For these the guidance of God would be necessary and it would be supplied by the Holy Spirit who, through the Church, would progressively interpret Christ in a changing world. Our Lord's work would not be complete until He carried it back to the Heavenly Father as a finished product. Therefore it was necessary that He should leave them, but it was also necessary that they should not be abandoned to flounder in a sea of uncertainty. The need would be met by the special gift of the Holy Spirit who would do for them what our Lord Himself had been doing. "It is expedient for you that I go away: for if I go not away, the Comforter will not come unto you; but if I depart, I will send Him unto you."[11]

On the one hand the Holy Spirit would offer support and guidance to the faithful, and on the other hand He would "reprove (or convince) the world of sin, and of righteousness, and of judgment."[12] That is, He would convince the world of its sinful state, He would show the world what righteousness means as exemplified in the finished work of Christ, and He would demonstrate that the judgment and conquest of evil is to be found in Christ.

With all that in mind, it is not difficult to see what our Lord meant by His statement about "sin against the Holy Ghost" which has been the plaything of many a fanatical, self-constituted interpreter of Holy Scripture. "All manner of sin and blasphemy shall be forgiven unto men: but the blasphemy against the Holy Ghost shall not be forgiven unto

[11] *St. John 16:7.*
[12] *St. John 16:8.*

men."[13] The forgiveness of God is always available to those who recognize, confess, and repent of their sins. Naturally God's forgiveness is blocked if repentance is absent—He cannot forgive us in spite of ourselves. But repentance is due to the prompting of the Holy Spirit working within us. Therefore the denial of the Holy Spirit automatically places us outside the realm of God's forgiveness. "Blasphemy against the Holy Ghost" is continual, wilful refusal of God, and of course, it is unforgivable just as the refusal to eat is bound to result in starvation.

The Holy Spirit is the agent of God's grace in all the Sacraments but He has always been particularly identified with the Laying on of Hands, or Confirmation. "Then laid they their hands on them, and they received the Holy Ghost."[14] In Christian symbolism the number seven is the perfect number. Therefore in the prayer of Invocation in the Confirmation service the seven-fold gift of the Spirit is asked for those being confirmed.[15] We ask for:

1. *Wisdom,* to aid us in our search for God.
2. *Understanding,* to lead us to the knowledge of the truth.
3. *Counsel,* to help us discern right from wrong.
4. *Ghostly strength,* to support us in doing right.
5. *Knowledge,* to teach us the will of God.
6. *True Godliness,* to help us lead good lives.
7. *Holy Fear,* or respect and reverence for God.

Out of these spiritual gifts arise the "fruits of the Spirit." In Christian symbolism the number nine is the mystery number. So St. Paul enumerates for us the nine-fold fruit of the

[13] *St. Matthew 12:31.*
[14] *Acts 8:17.*
[15] *See The Book of Common Prayer, p. 297.*

spirit—"the fruit of the Spirit is love, joy, peace, longsuffering, gentleness, goodness, faith, meekness, temperance."[16]

It is not as complicated as it may sound. The Holy Spirit is God in action—God sustaining the world which He has created and energizing human lives to whom He offers redemption through Jesus Christ. The easiest mistake we can commit is to think that we can make ourselves what we ought to be. Delicately timid about trusting God too far, we look upon Christ as a fine example of a wholesome life and resolve to emulate Him. Depending upon our own resources, we determine to improve ourselves according to the standard which He has set for us. But if there is one thing which the experience of life ought to teach us, it is that we cannot depend upon ourselves. We are always breaking down under pressure, our good intentions desert us, our firm resolutions prove to be as unstable as water. We simply can't do it on our own power. It may take a long time, and it may subject us to many hard knocks before we realize it, but sooner or later we are bound to face the honest fact that we are not sufficient of ourselves to do what we know we ought to do.

History is full of the men-on-horseback who have ridden rough-shod over their contemporary world, imposing their wills on submissive subjects and remoulding life to suit their own fancies. Some of them sky-rocketed to dazzling if temporary heights. Victor Hugo said of Napoleon that he became so arrogant that he "embarrassed God." Invariably they left a legacy of hardship, misery, loss and destruction for which their successors had to suffer. Over against them

[16] *Galatians 5:22-22.*

stands the long list of saints of God who became strong for Him in the recognition of their own weaknesses. For them ambition was transmuted into aspiration. They sought nothing for themselves but everything for God. They wanted to bring the world into subjection to God, not to themselves. Because of them our world today is better, happier, somewhat cleaner, a little more wholesome, and a step or two nearer to what God intends it to be. They did not fool themselves with egotistical notions of their own infallibility. They knew that without God their own best efforts were zero.

In His superior knowledge God understood this long ago, and He would not leave us helpless. The genius of the Christian religion lies not in the fact that Christ set us a noble example, but that His life is communicable to us by the operation of the Holy Spirit. We do not depend on ourselves— we depend on God. We do not attempt to reconstruct our own lives. We place ourselves in God's hands for redemption. He might have said, "I have taught them what to do and if they don't do it, it is their own responsibility." But He didn't. Rather, He said, "I love them. I want them to be right. I have given them what they need for holy living. In Jesus Christ I have shown them that it can be done. But I can't desert them now. I must stay with them. With infinite patience I must help them to arrive."

So He sends us the Holy Spirit.

XI

THE CHURCH

CHRISTIANITY is essentially biological. It may be decked out in forms and doctrines, but these are merely the clothing which covers the thing itself. Christianity has to do with life and therefore can be expressed only in biological terms.

This is true even back through the Old Testament preparation. The accounts of the Creation in Genesis are pictures rather than scientific treatises, but the important point about them is that they are stories of life personified in a pair of individuals. The truest features about the Creation stories are Adam and Eve—or John and Mary, if the ancient writer had been familiar with such names. Critically-minded people often object to the stories as puerile and unreasonable, and hence to be disregarded. It seems more unreasonable to subject such accounts to a kind of critical analysis for which they were never written and then throw them out of court because they are not scientifically accurate. They were not meant to be scientifically anything. They are life sketches. An inspiring picture of a sunset may be closer to the truth of human experience than the weather man's description of atmospheric conditions.

The Hebrews were God's "chosen people," not because God arbitrarily chose them, but because, out of their genius for religion, they, above all other people, chose God. The Old Testament is the record of God dealing biologically with the human race through the "chosen people." The Hebrews themselves were led, not by a form of teaching, but by God-inspired men—the judges, the kings, the prophets. The central nerve of their religious life was the Aaronic priesthood biologically transmitted by one person to another person. All this remained true until the Jews returned to Jerusalem from the Babylonian captivity in B.C. 538. Then everything was changed to their great religious loss. The personal leadership of living men was exchanged for the rigid enactments of the written Law. The result was a period of spiritual decadence when legalism prevailed and religion degenerated into a set of rules. In a word, as soon as the biological factor was obscured, spiritual vitality went into a decline.

Then "when the fulness of the time was come, God sent forth His Son."[1] The Incarnation is the reassertion of the biological principle. If God were interested only in the human intellect, He might have sent us a system of philosophy. As it is, He has sent us a Way of Life, expressed not in an argument but in His Incarnate Son. Birth, life, death, resurrection, ascension—these are the touchstones of the Christian religion.

In presenting His Gospel, Christ consistently adhered to this same principle. He set forth no system of regulations, no code of doctrine, no book of particulars. He declined to be

[1] *Galatians 4:4.*

embroiled in the legalistic debates of the Scribes. He told them the Kingdom of God was like leaven, like a seed, like a man. He taught them out of life as they knew it in order to lead them into the more abundant life which they did not know. And He centered it all about Himself personally. He did not ask: "How do you like this doctrine?" or "How does this theory appeal to you?" He asked: "What think ye of Christ?" He Himself is His own Gospel. The Christian religion does not consist in an intellectual assent to an idea, but in personal loyalty to a Person.

In view of all this, we might naturally expect that Christ would have made some provision for perpetuating His Gospel biologically. In this expectation we are not disappointed. He did not leave a system or a book. He left people. We call them Apostles, whom He trained, taught, and inspired to carry forward His mission. And He gave them just two things—a Commission and Sacraments. This constitutes the nucleus of the Church which St. Paul described as the Body of Christ—a spiritual organism prepared to receive and transmit the benefits of His redemptive life. It is one of the distinctive features of Christianity.

Now life comes only from life. It takes animal life to produce animal life. It takes human life to produce human life. Biologically speaking, it does not seem unreasonable that Christians should expect spiritual life to be derived normally in a similar manner—namely from the Body of Christ which we call the Church.

There are two ways of looking at the Church, from the outside in or from the inside out. Some think of it as a voluntary assembly of people who are already converted and settled in the Christian life. If you are good enough, you may be permitted to associate with other good people for a common purpose in which you have already acquired an interest. You join it, if you so desire, after you have become a Christian.

Others, however, think of it as a living organism, a corporate society, biological in character, into which you are admitted by spiritual birth. You do not first become a Christian in order to qualify. You grow into the Christian life in the company of your brethren as members of the Body. And you do not reach Christian maturity except as a part of that Body. From this point of view the Church is not a club for good people. It is a family in which we help one another to be better. You do not join it and resign from it at will, any more than you would from a family. It is a biological connection. By Baptism you are grafted into it and belong to it forever thereafter. "By one Spirit are we all baptized into one Body."[2]

The Church is organized but it is more than an organization. It is an organism. It is that which functions for Christ as a body functions for a human being. The Church is for the Glorified Christ what His human body was for the Incarnate Christ. It may be diseased by the sins of its members. It may be paralyzed in part, yet it is ideally His Body and must become actually so. St. Paul speaks of it as "a glorious Church, not having spot, or wrinkle, or any such thing; . . . holy and without blemish."[3] That is what Christ expects it to be. Weighed down by the inadequacies of its members,

[2] *I Corinthians 12:13.*
[3] *Ephesians 5:27.*

it is still far from its goal. But its destiny is assured because "Christ also loved the Church, and gave Himself for it."[4]

The Acts of the Apostles tells the story of the Church in its initial stage. Straight from Christ it came, and in its pristine vigor it was possessed of four special characteristics. The first disciples "continued stedfastly in the apostles' doctrine and fellowship, and in breaking of bread, and in prayers."[5] The "apostles' doctrine" is continued today in the historic Creeds. The "apostles' fellowship" is preserved in the Apostolic Succession which functions through the historic episcopate. We still have the "breaking of bread" in the Holy Eucharist. And the "prayers" never cease in the Church's public worship. An argumentative gentleman once put me in my place by breezily brushing all of this aside with the broad statement, "where Christ is, there is the Catholic Church." Whether he knew it or not, he was quoting St. Ignatius of Antioch, but he did not quote enough of him. At the beginning of the second century Ignatius wrote to the Smyrnean Christians as follows: "Where the bishop shall appear, there let the multitude also be; even as, wherever Jesus Christ is, there is the Catholic Church."[6]

In our Creeds we describe the Church as One, Holy, Catholic, and Apostolic. We have already said that we are admitted into it by Baptism. Therefore all baptized Christians are automatically members of His Body, the Church. That includes members in this world and those in the next world

---

[4] *Ephesians 5:25.*

[5] *Acts 2:42.*

[6] *Ignatius, Epistle to the Smyrneans, chap. VIII, Vol. 1, Alexander Roberts and James Donaldson, "The Ante-Nicene Fathers," Christian Literature Pub. Co., Buffalo, pp. 89-90.*

as well. The interruption of death cannot destroy the fellowship. Our Lord Himself said it—"upon this rock I will build my Church; and the gates of Hell (or Death) shall not prevail against it."[7]

There is therefore a fundamental spiritual unity of baptized Christians which extends into the future life. But that spiritual unity calls for a visible unity in this world where spiritual truth always requires external expression. That is the sacramental principle on which the whole universe is constructed. The divisions of modern Christendom are a blot upon the Church and must somehow be removed. The Church is ideally *One* not only in spirit but in visible manifestation. One of the best ways to achieve Reunion is to reiterate our belief in it.

The Church is *Holy* because it belongs to the Holy God and has received the Holy Spirit. At the beginning Christians were called "saints," people dedicated to God. It does not mean that the members of the Church have attained such a state of holiness that they can afford to look down upon their neighbors. Growth in holiness always increases personal humility. But it does mean that the Church has a holy purpose to fulfil, and leads its people in the way of sanctification. The Church may not yet have reached holiness but it is destined for that end. It is not a question of achievement but of character.

The term *Catholic* has unfortunately become involved in controversial issues. It was first used of the Church by St. Ignatius as quoted above, and its simplest meaning is "universal." Gradually it took on a technical meaning, and was

[7] *St. Matthew 16:18.*

used to distinguish the Catholic Church from various hereti-
cal sects which have sprung up at different times all along the
course of Church history. It implies wholeness—the Church
for the *whole* world, preserving the *whole* faith, imparting
the *whole* sacramental life, and possessed of the *whole* apostolic authority. "The term 'Catholic' is properly used of all
those Churches which maintain the faith of the Creeds and
the Ecumenical Councils, the practice of the Sacraments, and
the episcopate in historic succession from the Apostles."[8]
Plainly it is not a fitting title to be used for exclusive application to any particular denomination of Christians.

Finally the Church is *Apostolic* because it receives its commission from our Lord through the Apostles as a safeguard
for the apostolic teaching and tradition. It also carries the
apostolic responsibility of bearing full witness to Christ before the world. It dates from Christ and demonstrates its historic continuity from those leaders of Christ's own choosing.

But the question is sure to arise whether, granting all this,
we may not be just as good Christians without any direct
connection with the Church. In fact it is quite possible to
designate certain individuals of exemplary life who have
never had anything to do with the Church at all. Is it not
possible to be thoroughly loyal to Christ without concerning ourselves about the Church? Briefly the answer is—No.

There are people who live up to Christian standards and
pay no attention to the Church, but if it were not for the
Church they would have no Christian standards to live by. In
short, they are living on the Christianity of other people. It
is the Church which has preserved the Gospel, has proclaimed

[8] "*Doctrine in the Church of England*," The Macmillan Company, N. Y., p. 109.

Christ, and has inculcated the principles of Christian living. The Church is the normal avenue for the expression of Christian convictions. You cannot separate the two any more than you can separate feeling from your fingers or hearing from your ears.

One day a woman pugnaciously announced to me, "I've been converted and saved. I am a Christian and I feel no need whatever for the Church."

"That's interesting," I replied, "but I'm sorry you don't believe in the Bible."

"Why," she said, "that's the one thing I do believe in. That's my whole religion. As long as I have the Bible, I don't need the Church."

"Then," I continued, "if you believe so much in the Bible, it is too bad you don't read it."

"But I do read my Bible," she protested. "I read it all the time. That's why I am a Christian."

"You read your Bible," I said, "but you don't read all of it. Go home now and read the Acts of the Apostles which tells you all about the Church. And don't forget to read that part which tells you plainly that 'the Lord added to the Church daily such as should be saved.'"[9]

The primary function of the Church is to communicate the Incarnate Life of our Lord. It is not to entertain people, though it does greatly edify them. It is not to reform society, though it is responsible for an enormous amount of social improvement. In these days of much modern philanthropy too many people judge the Church by the extent of its practical charities. They complain that the Church keeps harping

[9] *Acts 2:47.*

on spiritual things while so many people are overwhelmed with physical needs. We are often told that the great charitable and philanthropic work of the world is done by secular agencies while the Church continues to theorize. That very criticism is the greatest compliment that could be paid to the Church. Today the parable of the Good Samaritan is the merest commonplace.

Mercy, sympathy, practical helpfulness—we never even question them. All you need do is to mention them and we say "of course." But it has not always been so. Once the parable of the Good Samaritan was a novelty. For twenty centuries the Church has been teaching it, and the Church has made it a commonplace. The very fact that non-Church agencies are feeding the hungry, clothing the naked, and binding up the wounds of the afflicted is in itself proof positive that the promulgation of the Christian Gospel has been an unparalleled success. The Church has succeeded in Christianizing the world just to that extent. All of these things are attributable to the Church, and without the Church supporting them, they would presently die off.

Over and over again we find the same sequence occurring. The Church has initiated something, taught the public its importance, and then turned it over to secular control to go on to something else. Education, for instance, has always been one of the Church's special interests. We are very proud of our American educational system, but it stems from Church schools established in Colonial times. The man who did more than any other for education in the early days of the American colonies was Bishop Berkeley who imported libraries from England. Gradually the secular educational system was developed and state and private universities established, but they began with the Church.

Hospitals were first built and operated by the Church, which still carries on a considerable part of this healing ministry. As the public has learned the importance of it, state, county, and municipal hospitals have been established on the foundation that the Church has laid.

The same may be said for homes, social settlements, orphanages, and a multitude of other charitable organizations. The huge modern programs of public relief, social security, and medical care of the aged have grown out of the age-old practice of alms-giving, which has always been a precept of the Church.

Today the Church is vitally concerned with issues of war and peace, of racial equality, and of social justice. It is interesting to note that as far back as 1892, the General Convention of the Episcopal Church addressed a communication to the responsible heads of the nations of the world commenting on the futility of war and urging international arbitration.[10] Through two World Wars and a succession of smaller ones the Church has never lost sight of the ideal of a peaceful world, though this ideal still seems far short of realization.

No one nation and no one Church can stand alone in this age of rapid communication and interdependence. Thus the nations have banded together in the United Nations, and the Churches have joined in national and World Councils of Churches to make their voices more effective.

[10] *General Convention Journal, 1892, pp. 89-90.*

The Episcopal Church, with other Churches of the Anglican Communion, has been an integral part of the World Council of Churches since its inauguration in 1937. In this country, it has cooperated with other members of the National Council of Churches in trying to apply Christian principles to the rapidly changing society of which we are a part.

Within the Anglican Communion itself, a new note of mutual responsibility and interdependence was sounded at the Anglican Congress of 1963, resulting in a broader concept of the mission of the Church, not only to all races and nations, but also to the increasingly complex urban society of our own and other countries. Moreover, the Episcopal Church is growing closer to the other Christian bodies, Catholic, Protestant, and Eastern Orthodox, in a common effort to reinvigorate the Church's life and to strive toward the unity for which our Lord Himself prayed.

Look at it any way you like, and you find that the Church is God's own blessing in a world that needs His blessing greatly. Take the Church out of the picture and the best features in modern civilization would dry up, starved out of existence for want of spiritual nourishment.

The Church is the most venerable institution in the world. It has outlasted kingdoms and empires. It has met and conquered every kind of adversity. It is strong, vigorous, and vital—and it has our Lord's promise, "Lo, I am with you always, even to the end of the world."[11]

[11] *St. Matthew* 28:20

XII

THE USE OF PRAYER

LET NO one imagine that it is a strained and unnatural thing for one to pray. It is far more unnatural for one not to pray. From the beginning of time men have turned in one way or another to pay their devotions to higher powers. Prayer is one of the most natural of human instincts. It has been so always and everywhere.

Well—what *is* prayer? It is not a padded club with which we make demands upon an unwilling God. Neither is it a kind of persuasion with which we cajole God into a kindly frame of mind. Prayer is not a species of magic by which we overturn the ordinary laws of nature. Prayer is not a pious whining intended to stimulate the divine sympathy.

A critical man once burst forth to me, "If I heard my boy on his knees in the next room begging me for something, I would give him a sound thrashing. I want him to come to me like a man." Of course, he was right. And he was wrong. Having cleared our minds of such misconceptions, we ask again, "What *is* prayer?"

There have been many definitions. Prayer is communion with God; it is exploring the mind of God; it is placing ourselves in God's hands; it is talking with God; it is spending time with God. Yes, these are all true, and we might add to them indefinitely. They are all descriptions of prayer. But for our purposes in this treatment of the subject, we are making a new definition of our own.

Prayer is the means by which God's power is released into human life. God is a God of law and order. He has created a world in which laws prevail which may not be violated with impunity. Some of these laws we know; some we guess at; some are still mysteries to us. But we know they are there, and we are convinced that we cannot live intelligently in this world unless those laws are constant and dependable. Apparent fluctuations do not tell us that natural law is unstable. They tell us that our understanding is incomplete. Thus science is constantly revising its conclusions as knowledge advances. The laws of the universe must be reliable. Even God cannot break them and remain true to Himself.

But just as there are natural laws, so are there also spiritual laws. To meet the limitations of human understanding we distinguish between the two but not always with perfect satisfaction. In God's sight there is probably no such distinction at all. His creation is a whole, a unified thing, in which natural and spiritual laws are interwoven, acting and reacting upon one another. An indication of this is to be found in the modern practice of medicine. Every physician knows that mental, moral, and spiritual upheavals affect the physical machinery of the body. It is often a simple matter to remedy a mechanical defect, but that does not necessarily make a person well.

Prayer is a spiritual law which we may call into play. Go into a great auditorium or a church building. Look up at the ceiling. You see a roof raised sixty, eighty, a hundred feet or more above the ground. The law of gravitation is inflexible, and it tells you that any object raised a hundred feet in the air will come down with a crash. Why, then, doesn't that roof fall? The answer is simple. Walls and arches and buttresses have been provided which hold it up. Has the law of gravitation been violated? Certainly not. There are other laws of strain and stress which every architect understands. These have been introduced to compensate the law of gravitation. In the absence of either, you would have a pile of bricks. By bringing the two together, you have a building. Nothing has been violated, but a different result has been achieved than either law by itself could produce.

Once I called on a mother whose little daughter was seriously ill. Suddenly she came out with this:

"Of course, I pray for my Mary. But I often wonder why. How can I expect God to change the course of nature and make my child well just because I ask Him to do it?"

"Did you send for the doctor when Mary was taken sick?" I inquired.

"Certainly," she replied, "but that's quite different."

"Not so very different," I answered. "You couldn't imagine yourself allowing the disease to run its natural course. You expected the doctor to call other forces into play which would check the disease and eventually overcome it. That is just what you are doing when you pray for her. You cannot separate Mary's spiritual life from her physical life. When destructive natural forces are at work, you introduce healthful spiritual forces to counteract them. They are bound to help. God has given you prayer as a means of tapping spiritual reserves. You would be a neglectful parent not to use it."

But there is a question. If we are honest with ourselves, we must admit that frequently our best judgment is defective. Without realizing it, we may be praying earnestly for something which in the long run will prove to be very bad for us. No honest-minded person can look back over years of life without remembering instances of wanting something badly, being disappointed at not receiving it, and now being deeply grateful that those desires were not fulfilled. We know how often we have been mistaken about what would have been good for us. How, then, can we pray with any assurance in the face of our own recognized fallibility? Maybe we are wrong when we think we are right. The answer is that God does know what is good for us even if we don't. So we pray "through our Lord Jesus Christ." Using the best judgment we possess, we pass our prayers through Him for cleansing, purifying, and correction, as it were, in transit. God's power is still released with all its beneficent effectiveness and our blunders are eradicated.

That suggests an answer to a further question which inevitably follows. Are prayers always answered? Yes, they are —though not always in just the way that we anticipate. Here I am struggling with a vexing problem. I lay it before God and ask Him to show me the way out. One evening I drop in to talk it over with my neighbor, John Smith. During the conversation Smith points out some aspects of the situation which I had overlooked and suggests the solution I am in need of. Do I then declare, "I asked God to help me and nothing happened—Smith did it?" Well, is there any good reason why God couldn't have worked through Smith? Must He answer you with fire out of heaven to prove that His spiritual laws are still operative? God is constantly working through people. The Incarnation, which is the heart of the Christian Faith, is sufficient evidence of that. Prayer does work. But it would be presumptuous for us to think we can control its operation to better effect than God Himself.

There was an attractive young woman who, for some unaccountable reason, became infatuated with a married man. Her friends knew the man was worthless and endeavored to reason with her to no avail. The more they talked to her, the more headstrong she grew. Finally she agreed to go away with the man to another country and passage was engaged on a boat. Her friends ceased their useless expostulations and began to pray for her. Of course they prayed that God would open her eyes to the folly of her behavior and lead her to give up the perilous venture. Then a strange thing happened. A few days before the boat was to sail the man coolly told her that he had changed his mind and everything was over. The girl was cruelly hurt but, in a flash, she realized the kind of man he was and the wretched position into which she had almost stepped.

Were those prayers answered? Of course, they were; and in a better way than the friends knew how to ask. If the girl had decided not to go, she would have had a perpetual question in her mind. As time went on, she would have had periods of discouragement when she might have wondered if possibly she would not have done better to have disregarded everything and to have taken the leap. The question itself would never have been settled. As it actually happened, there was no reason for later regrets. It hurt, but it settled the matter once for all. The prayers were not answered just as they were offered. They were answered in a better way because God knew a better solution.

We often become impatient over our prayers. We like quick results. Often it proves far better for us if the results are delayed. We do not stop our praying, but we learn to "wait upon God" and trust His greater wisdom. For many years St. Monica prayed earnestly that her son might be rescued from his dissolute life. Apparently there was no response. The young man continued in his evil ways but during those years his soul was tested, and eventually, when he did come out of it, the great Augustine brought a strength of character into his later life which successfully weathered many a stormy time. If in his case, quick results had been forthcoming, there would have been no *Confessions of St. Augustine* to help struggling Christians through all the centuries that have elapsed since his day. Who shall say that the mother's prayers were not effective?

Every honest prayer offered through the cleansing Presence of Jesus Christ is bound to be answered. It is a law of the spiritual realm and it always works. *Prayer is the means by which God's power is released into human life.* God's power is good and it always helps, however and whenever it is released.

Prayer is a spiritual law. It is just as normal to pray as it is to eat or to sleep. In either case you are using means which God has provided for a proper human life. The neglect of prayer cripples your ability to live. There are people who are satisfied if they have enough to eat, a place of shelter, and some clothes on their backs. The chief difference between them and the animals is that the animals grow their own clothes. Most humans desire something better than that. God meets the desire by equipping us with the faculty of prayer.

Prayer is a faculty and like every other faculty it needs to be developed. Certain people have natural gifts for music, but because of the gifts they are not freed from the necessity of study, practice, and training. Certain others have an aptitude for mathematics but they are not absolved from years of steady application before they arrive at proficiency. The old adage tells us that "genius is a capacity for hard work." A man says, "I have a yearning to be an artist. I will therefore sit down and paint a masterpiece." Capable artists smile at his presumption as they recall the sweat and labor they have expended to acquire the technique which is necessary for the expression of any artistic impulse.

Yet, strangely enough, many otherwise reasonable people seem to think of prayer as something to be taken up or set aside at one's convenience. There is nothing more pathetic than the self-sufficient person who has paid little or no attention to God, but who suddenly finds himself confronted with a desperate situation, and flings himself on his knees in a frantic appeal to the Throne of Grace. His spiritual faculties are stiff and apathetic from neglect. His soul is numb from disuse. He is a stranger in God's presence. He doesn't know how to talk to God. He cries, and moans, and cringes, and roars, and wonders why the comforting relaxation of trust in God's mercy is so difficult to attain. He is like an untrained craftsman trying to handle a delicate instrument. When we least feel the need of it is the time when we should develop our ability to pray. Then, when emergencies arise, we are prepared to face them with our spiritual faculties alive and alert.

There is no reason for us to be embarrassed about prayer and we will not be if we apply ourselves to it and exercise our prayer-faculty. People who read most easily are those who do a good deal of reading. Those who write with greatest facility are those who do much writing. So it is also with sewing, singing, walking, playing games. Everyone understands how easy it is to grow rusty in such pursuits if the practice of them is neglected. And if one has never even made a start, how can one expect to do anything with them?

It is not easy to learn to pray. There are periods of discouragement when timid souls feel like giving it up. But one is not to be governed by what one feels. A sensible person will approach it differently. He knows that feelings change with the weather, or with what he had for breakfast, but that the reality of his religious life has a much more stable foundation. He doesn't expect to feel an increase of education after every book he reads, nor does he expect to feel himself grow a trifle after every meal he devours. But he knows that reading and eating develop and sustain him whether he has any particular feeling about them or not. There are times when appetite slackens and no food is palatable, but we know that it continues to be necessary, and that presently the appetite will return.

The greatest of the saints all tell the same story. They, too, have experienced periods of "dryness" when their best spiritual efforts seemed futile and unavailing. Life is full of ups and downs. When the "downs" come, we don't stop living.

We go through them and discover greater heights beyond. It is not enough to pray. One must persevere in prayer. No one thrives on delicacies. Just as strength of character evolves out of adversities, so does one arrive at spiritual power through the testing process of blank moments. To the Christian the best known picture of prayer is Christ in Gethsemane. It must have been a trying time for Him that night. But to say that He "won through" is to put it mildly. If prayer were as easy as some people think it is, our souls would grow soft and our faith would be colorless.

There was a time when the single-cylinder motor car chugged down the street in uncertain lunges. It covered some ground but its action was slow, halting, noisy, and unreliable. Now the multiple-cylinder car rolls over the road in quick, sure motion—silent, powerful, and dependable. Increasing the number of cylinders has changed the life of the race.

It's a parable. Many, many people still struggle hesitantly, along the spiritual path finding nothing in prayer but a single purpose of asking things of God. Those who have really explored the inner recesses of spiritual life assure us that this is not only unnecessary but wrong. There are five distinct aspects of prayer, all of which need to be cultivated. For the sake of simplicity we set them down in alphabetical order:

> Adoration,
> Confession,
> Intercession,
> Petition,
> Thanksgiving.

All of these belong in a fully rounded prayer-life. Few of

us could follow through each one of them every time we go on our knees, but we should see to it that each aspect receives due attention over a period of time. On some occasions we will devote ourselves to thanksgiving, making no requests for anything. At other times we will concentrate on confession or intercession, asking nothing for ourselves. There is no reason why our prayers should always be alike. In fact, it is far better to make them varied.

A common danger to be avoided is that of falling into a spiritual routine, reciting over and over again the same familiar phrases. Such stereotyped habits make for artificiality. Our prayers need to be fresh, vigorous, interesting. We are talking with God, and any conversation lags if it constantly repeats itself. Therefore, we vary our prayers making sure that no single aspect is ever neglected. This calls for some thought and planning, but it saves us from the curse of unreality.

These five kinds of prayer are so many avenues into God's Presence. They need not all be used at once, but no one of them should be neglected. Our souls limp and stumble forward unevenly if we limit ourselves to a single aspect of prayer to the exclusion or the minimizing of the others. Of course they will run into one another, and we should not attempt to separate them into mechanical divisions.

While we are praying for ourselves, we will also pray for others. Seldom should we permit ourselves to approach God without offering some expression of gratitude. When we are confessing our faults we will also be giving praise to God for His understanding sympathy with our frailties. A reasonable balance should be secured and a spiritual equilibrium maintained. For prayer is not a hobby or a plaything. It is an art to be cultivated and a law of God to be observed.

Yes—prayer is a habit. Why shouldn't it be? Most of our daily living is based on habits. They are acquired by doing the same things over and over again repeatedly. When a child first begins to write, he strains and struggles with his pencil, expending much muscular energy to make a few legible lines. By reiterated practice he learns to form the letters without effort. Thereafter he does not think about how he writes. He does that automatically. He thinks about what he is writing. He has acquired the habit.

Thus prayer may be something of an effort to the beginner. He plans his time and his methods. Gradually it becomes a habit for him to pray. He does not worry himself about the words he uses or the technique he follows. Instead, he fixes his thoughts upon God.

Prayer is not to be considered as a luxury for occasional indulgence. It is both a duty and a privilege—a practical necessity for anyone who desires to live closer to God.

One suggestion might be added. Don't begin talking to God as soon as you fall on your knees. A few moments of complete quiet are the proper introduction to your entrance into the Presence of God. Let the spirit of devotion encircle you. You will pray better, and it is more polite to your Heavenly Father.

To sum it all up. We live in a world of law and order. One of the laws is the spiritual law of prayer. It is a faculty implanted within us which calls for training, practice, exercise. The spiritual realm has been deeply explored by men and women who have consecrated their lives to that purpose.

We make their experience our own. We acquire the technique by which we can best use our own souls. We begin simply but we do not stop there. We grow in grace. Difficulties and discouragements are to be expected. One reaches the heights only by surmounting obstacles. Gradually the enveloping atmosphere of prayer becomes the normal environment of the Christian who is on his way to God. Occasional kneelings give way to consistent habits. God is over all and in us all. We cannot live without Him. We welcome the opportunity to live with Him.

Prayer is the means by which God's power is released into human life. It is a law of God and God's laws are dependable.

XIII

CHRISTIAN SACRAMENTS

BACK IN Colonial days in the eighteenth century a wave of Calvinistic revivalism swept the settlements of the Atlantic seaboard. The name of Jonathan Edwards was stamped upon it, but the effects of it lived long after the period of his preaching. It was a lurid gospel couched in the fiery, sulphuric terms of literal hell and damnation. God was pictured as the inexorable Judge meting out rewards and punishments to His trembling creatures—chiefly punishments of a horrid and terrifying character. The shadow of it lay heavily on Christian preaching for several generations thereafter. Itinerant revivalists followed the retreating frontier to remind the adventurous pioneers that God was after them and eternal doom was just around the corner.

Such a distortion of Christ's Gospel could go just about so far, and then the inevitable reaction set in. Like all reactions, it sought the opposite extreme. People refused to contemplate God as a Judge at all. They looked to Him only as the loving Heavenly Father whose single desire was to shower blessings and benefits upon His children. Certainly, of the two, the latter is far more healthy, but either of them alone is out of balance. Most American Christians today expect

God to pet them, excuse them, and pamper them. They claim the privilege of imposing on His divine good-nature, demanding His fullest benediction in return for an occasional nod of recognition. To them religion has become a pleasing experience shorn of any obligations and drained of any sense of duty. They expect God to do everything for them whether they deserve it or not. Negligence on their part has nothing to do with the continuance of divine benefactions. God still loves them. What's the difference if they persist in slighting God?

For instance, there is the question of Holy Baptism. To be sure, Christians have always been baptized. Certainly Christ commanded it. But if they prefer to get along without it, why make a fuss about it? If they find it more convenient to be Christians in their own way rather than in Christ's way, what does it matter? There are plenty of good people who have never been baptized—why should they worry over it?

So Baptism frequently becomes not much more than an occasion for dressing up the baby and holding a family gathering. Bishop Gore said something about the perils of the popularizing of Christianity in the days of Constantine which might well be re-said for us today: "The real disaster happened when Christianity became the established religion and Baptism became really indiscriminate. 'Baptism doth represent unto us our profession'—it is the profession of discipleship; and it seems to me that no departure from the principles of Christ has been so serious as that which allowed membership of the Church to become a matter of course."[1]

[1] *Charles Gore, "The Reconstruction of Belief," Charles Scribner's Sons, N. Y., pp. 750–751.*

Let us make no mistake about it, the Christian religion is more than a pleasant state of mind. It is solidly anchored in the Person of our Lord Jesus Christ, and He stands for something more than an amiable disposition. If He had been content to talk about sacrifice, it would have been interesting. When He died on the cross, it became a fact. If He had stopped with a discussion of immortality, it would have been inspiring. When He rose from the dead, it became real. Could anyone expect Him to be less specific about the way of life to which He called His followers? He instructed them in prayer and then gave them a prayer to use. He told them they must be born again, and gave them Baptism as a means of regeneration. He taught them the need of spiritual nourishment and provided the Holy Communion for that purpose. How can Christian people give credence to His teaching and ignore His commands? God *does* love us, but just because He loves us He refuses to spoil us. The Christian life is a mutual experience in which God takes us into spiritual partnership. We qualify for His love by accepting and discharging the obligations of citizens in His Kingdom. Otherwise His love would be a cheap and meaningless gratuity.

Might it be that our Lord was using poetical language when He spoke of Baptism and the Lord's Supper? Did He really mean sacramental rites, or was it a symbolical appeal to our better natures? The answer is easily discovered. The Church wrote the New Testament record of our Lord's teaching. The Church would not have recorded one thing when it was actually doing another. What, then, was the

Church actually doing about Sacraments? It was baptizing people with water in the Sacred Name and was actually administering Holy Communion. Our Lord could have meant nothing else.

The Church catechism defines a Sacrament as "an outward and visible sign of an inward and spiritual grace given unto us; ordained by Christ Himself, as a means whereby we receive the same, and a pledge to assure us thereof." It is a good enough definition, since it expresses the principle underlying the whole created world—an outward form with an inward meaning. There is nothing strange about sacraments, because we live in a sacramental world. When the trees put forth their leaves in the springtime, it is an outward sign of the life within—a sacrament of nature.

Man himself is a sacrament. His bodily activities are outward expressions of the will and purpose by which he is animated. Consider such a thing as speech. What is it? One would be quite correct in saying that speech is merely the emitting of certain sounds produced by air pressure over vocal cords under the control of the lungs, lips, and tongue. Yet we know that speech is more than that. The sounds are outward expressions of ideas generated in the mind. Sounds and ideas together make speech and it is a sacrament.

This book consists of paper and ink which are the media for the conveyance of certain thoughts, and therefore sacramental. Food is a sacrament of nourishment. A handclasp is a sacrament of friendship. A school is a sacrament of education. A hospital is a sacrament of healing. And so on, without end. The universe itself is a sacrament of God's creative power. It is not a question of whether or not you wish to believe in sacraments. So long as you live in this world you can't get along without them.

Instinctively primitive people recognized the sacramental character of life in their religious practices. The ceremonial dance, the peace pipe, the animal sacrifices—they are all outward expressions of religious impulses. Speaking broadly, the created world is made up of material things and spiritual things. Without waxing philosophical it will suffice to say that "matter" means what you see, hear, feel, touch, smell —objects which you perceive through your senses. On the other hand, "spirit" would include that which is not responsive to the senses—love, thought, will, memory. God created all of them. So we say in the Nicene Creed, "I believe in one God the Father Almighty, Maker of heaven and earth, and of all things visible and *invisible*."

God's purposes are, of course, spiritual purposes. But He did not make material things and then abandon that part of His creation. He uses material things for spiritual ends. As a matter of fact, that truth is the very heart of the Christian faith. If God did not reveal Himself in the human life of Jesus Christ, then there is no Christianity. The Incarnation (the taking of our manhood by God) is the supreme Sacrament, and everything that flows from it partakes of its essential character.

The Church is a sacrament—the visible society of men and women who belong to Christ. That's why organic Church unity is a question of the utmost significance. Sectarianism cripples the working principle of the Incarnation. Christ is One, and the outward expression of allegiance to Him must be unified or it violates the sacramental principle without which life itself is meaningless.

So we might go on. The Bible is a sacrament. Prayer is a sacrament—the expression of spiritual communion in posture and words. So is worship, praise, self-denial, and Christian service in contributions of time, effort, or money.

In view of all this it would have been strange indeed if Christ had not designated certain means for sacramental use on the part of His disciples. To introduce the Christian faith into a sacramental world without specific sacramental ties would have been an anomaly. To have left a doctrine, an example, an ideal—and no more—would have been clearly out of character. Some means were necessary by which all these elements of His Gospel could be appropriated by His followers.

Christ did not come to start a discussion. He came to give life. The primary function of the Church is to impart that life. For this purpose He designated means which were simple enough to be universally available, and set them apart for special sacramental use—water for new spiritual birth, and bread with wine for spiritual nourishment. In specifying these particular elements He was not limiting the sacramental principle. He was pointing and applying it, just as in His Incarnation He made use of a particular human body without depriving men and women of their own physical inheritance. Therefore in a world of sacraments we have two which stand out above all others. Our Lord singled them out, placed His own mark upon them, and invested them with peculiar spiritual properties. He might have chosen something else which would have served equally well. The simple fact remains that He selected these two and backed them up with positive injunctions for their use. Whatever other rites may be recognized as Christian Sacraments, these two have always been received as the Major Sacraments—Holy Baptism and Holy Communion.

During the Middle Ages the Church went through a period of close theological analysis. In the earlier centuries many things entered into common Christian practice which were never clearly defined. The general attitude was much like that of Thomas à Kempis when he said, "I had rather feel compunction than know its definition." But then some question would arise and the Church would be forced to make definitions. This was true of the Sacraments. For a long time Christians lived in a large sacramental atmosphere, always laying supreme emphasis on the two Great Sacraments, but leaving open the question as to what other rites might warrant a similar title.

The Schoolmen (medieval philosophers who developed the system of scholastic theology) took up, among other things, a critical examination of the Sacraments. Different ones of them drew up different lists of what ought to be technically counted as Sacraments in the Church, and there was much discussion on the subject. In the twelfth century Peter Lombard wrote his *Book of Sentences*, in which he enumerated five Minor Sacraments, which in addition to the two Major Sacraments, made seven in all. Confirmation, Holy Matrimony, Holy Orders, Penance, and Unction were the five minors.

The distinction lay in the fact that Holy Baptism and Holy Communion came with specific commands of our

Lord behind them. The other five were not so precisely commanded, but they all had Scriptural authority to support them. Peter Lombard's writings were very widely read, and the *Sentences* became a textbook for centuries after his death. By unanimous consent his treatment of the Sacraments was accepted in eastern Christendom as well as in the west. So we commonly say that the two Great Sacraments are "generally necessary to salvation"—that is, they are meant for everybody and are directly enjoined upon us by our Lord. The other five obviously partake of the sacramental principle, but just as obviously they do not all apply necessarily to everyone—they derive from the New Testament Scriptures and fit into the apostolic teaching.

In this it must be remembered that we are not merely discussing theories—rather the actual experience of Christian people running over a period of twenty centuries. Even so, it may appear to some readers that we are making very large claims for a series of ordinances which are in themselves plain and unpretentious. Doesn't it all seem to be a little bit out of balance? We would be more likely to expect such great results from correspondingly significant efforts. We are told that in Holy Baptism we are united with Christ, made members of His Church, granted forgiveness of sins, equipped to receive further gifts of God's grace—all by means of a little water in the name of the Holy Trinity. Or we are told that in the Holy Eucharist we receive spiritual nourishment, the very life of Christ Himself with all its cleansing, purifying, revivifying grace—all for partaking of a morsel of consecrated Bread and a taste of consecrated Wine. Possibly it seems as though we do too little to get so much.

Well, let us see. Here is a great factory filled with imposing machinery which is standing idle and accomplishing nothing. At a given moment a workman throws over a switch. Immediately the wheels begin to hum, raw material starts on its way through intricate mechanical devices, finished articles begin to tumble out in profusion to be packed and shipped to the ends of the earth. A huge industry has come to life, supplying goods to the public and a means of livelihood to hundreds of employees. All because a workman moved a switch. Isn't it a disproportionately great result from a very small action?

Again—here is a chime of bells erected in the Holy Land to ring out sacred music in sacred surroundings. But the bells are silent. Over in the city of Philadelphia a man presses a button. Immediately the chimes peal forth in Palestine. A miracle has occurred. Isn't the result excessively great for the simple action of pressing a button?

But, you say, these things are different. Before the switch was thrown or the button pressed an enormous amount of labor had to be performed. The factory had to be constructed, the machinery had to be built, an organization had to be perfected, before the switch meant anything. In the case of the chimes, years of research, discovery, and invention in the field of radio-transmission had to be expended before the button was anything more than a button. To be sure, it is a simple thing to turn a switch or press a button, but it is a very great thing to erect a factory or to discover the secrets of radio-activity. The whole set-up must be considered before a comparison can be struck.

Very well—it must also be remembered that back of the

simple sacramental rites lies the life of our Lord—His birth, His ministry, His death, His resurrection, His ascension. All this is the set-up, if you like, which precedes the administration of the Sacraments. Without it they have no meaning. There is nothing small or trifling about Jesus Christ. If the results of the Sacraments are great, the preparation for them has been even greater. All of it must be considered before any comparison can be struck. The Sacraments themselves are the simple methods provided for making the connection. Purposely they are made simple because they must be available for all people everywhere.

XIV

HOLY BAPTISM

$\mathbf{A}$ MAN from another country comes to our country. He is an immigrant, a foreigner. He is not a citizen. He can live among us, secure work, make a living, send his children to school. He may be very successful, may possibly acquire a fortune. But he is not one of us. He is still a foreigner. One day he applies for his naturalization papers and takes the oath of allegiance. Now he is a citizen, with responsibilities to our country and a claim on the country. He is one of us.

Many people live in a Christian civilization much in the same way. They are surrounded with a Christian atmosphere. They have Christian standards to live by. They enjoy certain benefits which are fruits of Christian social ideals—hospitals, charitable institutions, educational systems, public libraries, freedom of speech.[1] But they are not citizens in the Kingdom of God. They have never been naturalized by Baptism. They are still spiritual foreigners living on the Christian faith of other people. Perhaps some day they seek Baptism. Then they become one of us. They accept their spiritual responsi-

[1] *These benefits, to be sure, may now be found in non-Christian lands, but many of them have been introduced under pressure of Christian influence, and where we find tyranny and excessive restriction of freedom in so-called Christian lands, it is because of a resurgence of non-Christian ideas.*

bilities and have a claim on the favor of God. They "are no more strangers and foreigners, but fellow citizens with the saints, and of the household of God."[2]

Like all analogies this one is only partial because it goes only part of the way. Nevertheless, up to a point it offers a parallel, though the significance of Christian Baptism goes far beyond that point.

The use of water for symbolical purposes was by no means new in the time of our Lord. As a cleansing agent it was, of course, universally recognized. It was quite natural that water should be taken over as a symbol of ceremonial purification in connection with religious rites. This is found to have been the case with many peoples, including the Jews. When St. John Baptist came preaching his message of repentance, he called his hearers to make an outward act of penitence. He announced the coming of the Messiah and instructed the people that they must leave their evil ways and turn to the path of righteousness if they would be worthy of the Messiah's Presence. In token of their change of purpose and the cleansing of their hearts they received baptism at his hands. But he himself told them plainly that there was a different kind of baptism to follow. "I indeed," he said, "have baptized you with water: but He shall baptize you with the Holy Ghost."[3] Our Lord also submitted to baptism at the hand of St. John Baptist as an act of fellowship with His people. To them it meant the burial of their past sinfulness and the beginning of a new experience. To Him it meant

[2] *Ephesians 2:19.*
[3] *St. Mark 1:8.*

"the fulfiling of all righteousness"—the identifying of Himself with the people He came to save.

All of this was preliminary to Christian Baptism. Jesus took something which was already highly regarded in the public mind and invested it with new properties for His purpose. The baptism of John is related to Christian Baptism much as St. John Baptist is related to Christ. It was preparatory and introductory. All that was represented by the baptism of John was absorbed into Christian Baptism and something else added. This is clearly indicated in the incident related in the 19th chapter of Acts, where St. Paul found a group of disciples in Ephesus who had heard of the Baptist and had received his baptism. St. Paul instructed them in the Christian faith, and then "they were baptized in the Name of the Lord Jesus," followed by the Laying-on-of-Hands or Confirmation.

One cannot very well read the New Testament without recognizing the primary necessity of Baptism for all Christian people. Said our Lord, "Except a man be born of water and of the Spirit, he cannot enter into the Kingdom of God."[4] His final command to the Apostles was perfectly clear—"Go ye therefore, and teach all nations, baptizing them in the Name of the Father, and of the Son, and of the Holy Ghost."[5]

The Christian community understood this to mean just one thing—Christians must be baptized, and they proceeded to do it. "Repent, and be baptized," said St. Peter on the day of Pentecost when those who had listened to his sermon asked what they were to do about it.[6] When St. Philip had

[4] *St. John 3:5.*
[5] *St. Matthew 28:19.*
[6] *Acts 2:38.*

finished explaining the Gospel to the Ethiopian eunuch, he did not merely leave him with some pleasant thoughts in his memory, but "they went down both into the water, both Philip and the eunuch; and he baptized him."[7] It was not enough for St. Paul to be converted; he also had to be baptized.[8] It was the same for Cornelius the centurion,[9] and for the jailor at Philippi.[10] The Epistles were letters of instruction written to congregations who already knew their Gospel, and the Epistles constantly refer to Baptism as something about which there could be no question.[11] It is safe to say that those first disciples would have been astounded at the idea of anyone claiming to be a Christian without first having been baptized.

REDEMPTION

Let us make another analogy. Suppose you should find, on a remote island, a race of men and women whose eyesight was gravely defective, so that they had to grope their way around, even in daylight. One of the elders of the tribe tells you that a legend has been handed down for generations that once upon a time their eyesight was excellent, but it had been ruined by deliberately eating some native herb which was pleasant to taste, but which they knew would damage their eyes. Nevertheless, they all ate it; they all became half blind, and this defect was passed on by heredity to the children of every generation.

[7] *Acts 8:38.*
[8] *Acts 9:18.*
[9] *Acts 10:48.*
[10] *Acts 16:33.*
[11] Cf. *Romans 6:3–4; I Corinthians 12:13; Galatians 3:27; Colossians 2:12; Titus 3:5; St. Peter 3:21.*

Now suppose you had with you a great doctor who could restore perfect eyesight to all those who would submit to his treatment. The hereditary taint would still be there; each new baby would need the treatment if it was to see properly; but all who came for treatment would go away healed and continue to see if they refrained from eating the poisonous herb.

The analogy falters, just as the story of the Garden of Eden falters in the book of Genesis. Both are parables. Nevertheless, whether you tell it in terms of damaged sight and a great physician or of an apple and a serpent, the moral is the same. God made man in His own image, capable of living a God-like life. Somewhere, somehow, man made a false choice and failed of God's high purpose for him. A moral and spiritual taint got into the blood. Our spiritual eyesight became clouded. In theology we call it the Fall of Man and the inheritance of Original Sin. There is nothing really formidable about such terms. Analyze as you will, everybody knows that we are naturally born into this world with certain inherited failings.

Now man owes to God the best he can give. When he fails, he is unable ever to make it up because he can never do more than the best which he already owes. Only God, the Source of perfection, can remedy the wrong of it. But since man is a free agent, the correction needs to come from his side. The Incarnation is the answer. God becomes man and instills the medicine of perfection into the current of human life. Men and women receive it by identifying themselves with Christ, and so possess an immunity against the ravages of Original Sin. They get a fresh start. The method of cure prescribed by our Lord is the Sacrament of Holy Baptism. It is a personal immunity to be acquired only at the Source. The effects are not magical, and can be crippled by non-coöperation, but the immunity is there and gradually asserts itself as men and women rise in the scale of Christian living. This is what theology means by Redemption. We might put it in popular language by saying that Baptism is a spiritual operation which restores our lost spiritual eyesight.

COVENANT

Baptism is a covenant which simply means a solemn agreement. We pledge certain things from our side and God promises certain benefits from His side. On our part we pledge *repentance, faith,* and *obedience*.

Repentance is not to be identified with remorse. Repentance involves an act of the will. Remorse may be only a state of feeling. To be sorry for something wrong is a commendable sentiment but one cannot live looking backward, even though one may look with regret. The Christian faces forward. He not only disowns a dubious past, but he is determined to achieve a better future.

Remorse, by itself, is a morbid recollection. Merged into repentance it becomes a bracing anticipation. The repentant Christian feels remorse, but he does not stop there. He addresses himself to preventing causes for future remorse.

Similarly, *faith* must not be identified with belief. Faith is an attitude of life. When St. Paul said that "a man is justified by faith" he did not mean verbal adherence to a doctrine, but personal confidence in a Person. Faith means trust in God, loyalty to Christ, reliance upon the Holy Spirit. Grounded in the facts of the life, death, resurrection of our Lord, faith is the governor of our spiritual action. Faith fashions our Christian intention.

Obedience is the outcome of faith. It represents a desire and purpose to practice what we profess. Christianity is more than a sentimental impulse. There are standards of Christian living which may not be disregarded. By a pledge of obedience we accept those standards as our own, recognizing that God knows better than we do how our lives ought to be lived.

BENEFITS

In Baptism we are formally admitted into the Church and become citizens in the Kingdom of God. It is an initiatory rite—the enabling Sacrament which qualifies us to receive God's spiritual gifts through His accredited channels. Baptism is the door into the spiritual realm where God's goodness operates. To expect to enjoy His Blessings without Baptism, where it may be had, is an imposition on His generosity. Christ would not have enjoined it if He had not meant it to serve a real purpose. It is a Sacrament that is not repeated, because it conveys an indelible "character." Once we become a "member of Christ, the child of God, and an inheritor of the Kingdom of Heaven," that character is stamped upon us and we can never be anything else. We have become members of God's family. We may be unworthy members, but we still belong.

As we, on our side of the covenant, pledge certain things, so God on His part promises three special benefits—*forgiveness, regeneration,* and *grace.* The New Testament is quite specific on these points and the importance of them can scarcely be minimized.

Over and over again *forgiveness* is coupled with Baptism: "Be baptized . . . for the remission of sins"; "Arise and be baptized, and wash away thy sins"; Christ cleanses the Church by the "washing of water"; the Corinthians have been "washed . . . sanctified . . . justified." But it is well to remember that this refers to the *forgiving* of sins, not the ignoring of them. The modern attitude toward sin is equivocal to say the least, and the neglect of Baptism is in close ratio to the disregard of sin. No doubt one reason for it has been the strange way in which the conception of sin has been extended to cover a wide field of personal dislikes.

The puritanical mind, which fails to distinguish between bad manners and bad morals, has catalogued a long list of trivialities as sin until healthy-minded people have been irritated to the point of discounting sin as a fanatical obsession. The literal mind which fails to distinguish between divine law and human ordinances has settled the whole matter out-of-hand by neatly classifying those who are in jail as sinners and those who are out of jail as obviously righteous. They forget that divine law represents permanent principles of conduct, while human ordinances may be only rules of temporary convenience for society. Many people who are rightfully enough in jail may have broken a city statute without at all violating the divine law. A person may be arrested for parking on the wrong side of the street, but wherein has he sinned against God? You may answer to the judge for stealing a man's coat, but you will answer to God for stealing a man's reputation. God is more interested in character than in overcoats. Some of the worst hurts from which the world suffers grow out of malicious gossip, poisonous insinuations, subtle half-truths, and arbitrary selfishness. No court may ever impose penalties for such violations of Christian decency, but they are clearly offensive to God.

The modern world needs a reassessment of sin if it is to secure a stronger hold on the Christian faith. It must distinguish sin from puritanical prejudices and the legal rules of a swiftly changing society. Sin means apostasy from God—the wilful choice of our own desires in opposition to God's purpose for us. That purpose is revealed in the person of our Lord Jesus Christ—His life, His ministry, His teachings, His Sacraments. These embody the divine law, and sin is the violation of that law. The application of it to the individual life is not so much a matter of codified rules and regulations as it is a matter of an instructed Christian conscience. We may have to particularize to meet a given situation, but we are dealing with principles rather than technical prohibitions.

If the final reason for human existence is to establish the Kingdom of God on earth ("Thy Kingdom come. Thy will be done,") then sin becomes serious, and the forgiveness of sin becomes a very important benefit. Baptism is the initial step in that direction, because it clears the decks of moral and spiritual rubbish. This is not to say that the baptized person will never again be guilty of sinning, but it does say that the character of sin has been replaced by the character of righteousness; and that the baptized person lives in the active current of God's forgiveness, where the correction of moral and spiritual deviations is always available.

Regeneration means new birth, and like any birth it is a gift.
Let us dissolve once for all a confusion between regeneration
and conversion. They are not the same. *Twice-Born Men* is
the title of a widely-read book which deals with conversions
achieved by the Salvation Army. The title is a misnomer—it
should be *Converted Men*. Conversion is a change of front
which we accomplish. Regeneration is a gift of God. The
two may meet in any life, but they arrive from opposite directions, and neither one can take the place of the other. Certainly there was never a more clear-cut case of conversion
than that of St. Paul, but he still found it necessary to be baptized. "The Church teaches always the priority of God. Regeneration in Holy Baptism is a birth into sonship. Conversion is the awakening to sonship. Regeneration is the act of
God. Conversion is the response of man. Regeneration is the
bestowal of life. Conversion is the conscious assimilation of
that life."[12] Just as we are born naturally into the world, so
we are spiritually born into the Kingdom of God. We do
not nominate ourselves for membership in God's family any
more than we choose our natural parents. Natural birth is
our point of entrance into human life. Spiritual birth (regeneration) is our point of entrance into eternal life. So our
Lord put it to Nicodemus—"Except a man be born again,
he cannot see the Kingdom of God." Nicodemus was puzzled, just as we may be, and asked for an explanation. Our
Lord replied—you feel the blowing of the wind but you cannot explain where it comes from or where it goes; if you are
baffled by such simple earthly things, how could you under-

[12] Paul B. Bull, *"The Sacramental Principle,"* Longmans, Green and Co., N. Y.,
p. 140.

stand such a heavenly thing as regeneration if I were to explain it to you?

The word "conversion" means turning—a turning away from evil and toward God. It may precede or follow regeneration. When you have turned your car up the highway, you are headed toward your destination; but you quickly discover that uneven spots in the road throw you out of line and you must make constant slight turns of the steering wheel to avoid disaster. So we are always in process of conversion. But we are born only once. Baptism, says our Lord, is the means of this regeneration. I cannot tell just how or why any more than I can tell the "how" or "why" of electricity, but I still turn on the light when I want to read.

Grace is the free gift of God, something which we have neither earned nor deserved. If God were to wait until we were worthy of His favor, no one knows better than we ourselves that our spiritual progress would never even get started. Says St. Paul, "By grace ye are saved through faith; and that not of yourselves: it is the gift of God."[13] It is an enabling spiritual power infused into human life by the Holy Spirit.

Take a piece of ordinary steel—hard, bright, smooth, strong. Lay it up against a magnet, and something happens to it. Apparently it is no different than it was before, but actually it is invested with a mysterious magnetic power which enables it to draw other metals to itself. So in Baptism a human soul is brought into contact with God and something happens to it. A new power is added which was not there before. We may call it *grace*; and it is renewed and

[13] *Ephesians 2:8.*

kept active by repeated contacts such as Confirmation and the Holy Communion.

One hesitates to call this "supernatural" because the word has been abused by association with things weird, spooky, and unnatural. We might call it "over-natural." At any rate, the point is that natural laws govern natural occurrences, and there are just as truly spiritual laws which govern spiritual occurrences over and above the natural. There is no conflict, though at times there may be a connection. Natural laws cover the action of magnetic steel. Spiritual laws cover the spiritual magnetics of Baptism. At the present stage of our understanding we cannot explain either of them, but we can experience both.

In the New Testament there is scarcely a reference to Baptism which is not definitely joined with the spiritual endowments of the Holy Ghost. Said St. John Baptist, "I indeed have baptized you with water: but He shall baptize you with the Holy Ghost."[14] "Be Baptized . . . and ye shall receive the gift of the Holy Ghost."[15] "By one Spirit are we all baptized into one body."[16] "Except a man be born of water and of the Spirit, he cannot enter into the Kingdom of God."[17]

Baptism is more than a sign; it is an instrument. It is not only an indication that something has been done, but it is the means by which it is accomplished. We are not baptized in order to show that we are Christians. We become Christians by union with Christ through His Sacrament of Holy Baptism.

[14] *St. Mark 1:8.*
[15] *Acts 2:38.*
[16] *I Corinthians 12:13.*
[17] *St. John 3:5.*

MATTER AND FORM

Every science has a language of its own. This is equally true of theology. When we speak of *matter* and *form* we are using technical terms which apply to the Sacraments. They have to do with the method of administration, and they are important because a Sacrament is "the outward and visible sign of an inward and spiritual grace," and its integrity depends upon both factors.

Matter is the material substance which is used in a Sacrament, and in the case of Baptism it is, of course, water. Conceivably, our Lord might have designated some other *matter*, but actually this is the one He did select and nothing could be more appropriate. Water is obviously the suitable symbol for spiritual cleansing. It is, on all counts, the most essential element for the preservation of human life. We can't live without it. Water is universally available wherever human beings exist, and its use requires a minimum of explanation. For a Sacrament which everyone is expected to receive the *matter* must not be difficult to obtain.

Spiritual things always have to do with quality rather than with quantity. Therefore the thing itself is important and not the amount of it. Complete immersion requires a considerable quantity of water, and we should scarcely expect our Lord to insist on that point. In the early days and in semi-tropical countries, immersion was the common but not the exclusive method. It may still be used if desired, but historically the Church has not required it. Immersion, affusion, or aspersion (that is, submergence under the water, the pouring on of water, or the sprinkling with water) are all in harmony with the intent of the Sacrament. So long as water flows upon the flesh of a person, the symbolism of the rite is complete. It is hardly likely, for instance, that immersion could have been used on the Day of Pentecost with the large number who were baptized on that occasion. It is almost impossible that it could have been used in the jail at Philippi. Descriptions of baptisms in early Christian writings and the pictorial representations of the Sacrament in the Catacombs and on other archaeological monuments show that affusion was commonly used in early times and it came to be the generally accepted method. Another substance may not properly be substituted, but the amount used is of no particular importance.

The *form* refers to the words of administration. This is settled for us, once for all, by our Lord's command, "Go ye therefore, and teach all nations, baptizing them in the Name of the Father, and of the Son, and of the Holy Ghost."[18]

Several places in the New Testament speak of being baptized "in the Name of the Lord Jesus" or "baptized into Christ." Whether or not this means that these words were actually used instead of the invocation of the Holy Trinity is a question on which scholars are not agreed. Many believe it means into the faith of Christ which is, of course, the faith of the Holy Trinity. It may be that there were variations in the form used in those very early days. Of this much, however, we can be quite sure—it was not long before the words given by our Lord were recognized as a definite *form*. And for a very good reason. While the Church was still young, distortions of the Gospel began to appear. Even before the

[18] *St. Matthew 28:19.*

New Testament writings were completed several phases of Gnosticism were corrupting Christian teaching. To preserve the purity of the Gospel the Church was obliged to define its position in a number of particulars. Baptism was too important to be left to the idiosyncrasies of opinionated people who might convert it into something which it was never intended to be. Therefore the Church found it necessary to state that Christian Baptism must be administered with water "in the Name of the Father, and of the Son, and of the Holy Ghost."

This might seem like throwing an undue emphasis upon certain words, but it is really a protection of the whole course of Christian life for the followers of Christ. They have a right to be sure they are being properly introduced into Christian discipleship, with no uncertainty as to the observance of our Lord's command. Modern experience of religious eccentricities (not to speak of religious rackets) proves the wisdom of this early decision. It is not a hide-bound Church, arbitrarily insisting on minor technicalities. It is an honest Church, determined to defend Christ's Gospel against manhandling on the part of irresponsible fanatics. Either Christ meant something by Holy Baptism, or He didn't. If He did, then we may not play lightly with what He meant.

THE MINISTER OF HOLY BAPTISM

It should always be borne in mind that Christ gave the Sacraments to the Church, and it is the Church which administers them. By remembering this simple fact much confusion may be avoided. The ability to convey spiritual blessings is not the monopoly of any individual person. In that way lies an open field of much superstitious practice. The Church does it acting through accredited agents.

At the beginning, Baptism was administered by the Apostles and later by the Bishops of the Church, because our Lord's command was to the Apostles originally. Even so, they were not acting as individuals but as spokesmen for the Church. The increase in the number of Christians and the expansion of the Church made it impossible for the administration of this Sacrament to be reserved exclusively to the Bishops. Authority to baptize was therefore delegated to the priests. Thus today the normal Minister of Holy Baptism is one who has been ordained priest, though in the absence of either priest or bishop Baptism may be done by a deacon.

In all cases the Minister is an agent of the Church. The personal worthiness of the Minister has nothing whatever to do with his capacity to baptize. If that were the case, baptisms would cease to occur. For no bishop, priest, or deacon would ever have the effrontery to declare himself personally worthy to act in the place of our Lord Himself. So long as he holds an office in the Church, it is the Church acting through him.

But emergencies sometimes arise when an accredited Minister of the Church may not be available. A sudden accident, a fatal illness, uncertainty as to the survival of a new-born infant—such emergencies may result in death before Baptism can be administered in the normal way. Long ago the Church recognized that emergencies have to be met. So we find that down through the ages it has been a common practice for anyone to administer Christian Baptism under extraordinary circumstances.

Take, for instance, the case of a new-born infant whose

strength seems insufficient to surmount the struggle of birth. The attending physician, the nurse, the midwife, or anyone present should feel no hesitation about administering Baptism to that wavering little life. Once an infant is born into this world, even for only a moment, it becomes part of the human family and a candidate for the fulness of eternal life. Baptism, being of primary importance, should not be denied to that life because of an unforeseen accident. Should the child survive, then it should be brought to the Church, not to be baptized again but to comply with the remainder of the baptismal service which the Church provides.

Every layman and laywoman who values his or her Christian profession, should know that in an emergency he or she is qualified to use water upon an unbaptized person with the declaration—"I baptize thee in the Name of the Father, and of the Son, and of the Holy Ghost." To raise the question as to whether a different *form* would answer just as well is simply beside the point. The Church confers Baptism acting through the individual. When the individual uses the *matter* and *form* authorized by the Church, he gives plain evidence that he intends to do what the Church does. Otherwise no one could be sure of anything.

CONDITIONAL BAPTISM

Modern sectarian divisions have caused a good deal of confusion among Christian people and have fostered a spirit of carelessness. Here is a sect which says that Baptism is a matter of indifference one way or the other. Another neglects the sacramental rite and is satisfied with a subjective experience which it calls "baptism of the Spirit," in spite of what our

Lord had to say about it. Still another goes in for sentimental effects and substitutes flowers for water. Many revivalists have failed to discriminate between conversion and Baptism, and reduce the Christian faith to a state of feeling. Baptism itself becomes neglected and many people grow to adult life without knowing whether or not they ever were baptized.

In the face of all these surface fluctuations, the historic Church is bound to take Christ seriously, and stands solidly for the necessity of spiritual regeneration. Yet Baptism is a Sacrament which imparts indelible "character" and should not be repeated. Once again the Church faces abnormal situations and must be prepared to meet emergencies. Therefore, in instances of uncertainty as to whether Baptism has been properly administered, or, indeed, ever administered at all, the Church provides a special *form* for "Conditional Baptism," as a safeguard for itself and for the person concerned. Should there be any defects, they are to be corrected, but the integrity of the Sacrament is to be preserved.

INFANT BAPTISM

In the early days discussions occurred concerning incidental questions regarding the baptizing of infants, but infant baptism was never an issue until the time of the Reformation. If spiritual regeneration is inherent in the Sacrament, there would seem to be little reason why infants should not be qualified to receive it. There is nothing in the Holy Scriptures to exclude them, and fifteen centuries of the steady practice of including them supplies a solid precedent. To break such a precedent demands some very sound reason.

Our Lord stated the necessity of being born again of water

and of the Spirit in order to enter the Kingdom of God. Obviously this must be understood to include all who are capable of entering His Kingdom. When the little children were brought to Him, He welcomed them, blessed them, and said, "Of such is the Kingdom of Heaven." Certainly He gave no indication that they were to be omitted.

St. Paul teaches that Baptism takes the place in the new Covenant which was occupied in the old Covenant by circumcision.[19] But circumcision was carefully performed among the Jews on the eighth day after an infant's birth. When St. Paul brought the Gospel to Philippi, a woman named Lydia and her family were all baptized together—"she was baptized, and her household."[20] It seems gratuitous to assume that there were no children in the household. Later in this chapter the same thing is recorded of the keeper of the prison and his family—"and was baptized, he and all his, straightway."[21] Again, St. Paul reminded the Corinthians that "I baptized also the household of Stephanas."[22] In none of these instances is there any suggestion that infants had been left out.

In view of the prevailing Jewish custom and the subsequent habits of the Church in administering Baptism to infants, the absence of any reference to them would seem to indicate that it was our Lord's intention to include them. Some clearly negative precedent is required to over-balance the positive temper of these records.

To be sure, it is sometimes contended that repentance,

[19] *Colossians 2:11-12.*
[20] *Acts 16:15.*
[21] *Acts 16:33.*
[22] *I Corinthians 1:16.*

faith, and obedience are necessary prerequisites for Baptism, and an infant is incapable of complying with any of them. The Church meets this by the appointment of adult sponsors for each child whose duty it is to see that the child receives the Christian training implied in this Sacrament. It must be remembered that spiritual regeneration is the beginning of something, not the end of it. There is no magical efficacy which closes the whole question of the Christian life at the moment one is baptized. Indeed, it is possible for the baptismal gift, either in a child or an adult, to be blocked by vicious habits until it is impossible for it to function. To guard against this there are supposed to be two male sponsors and one female for every male child, while for every female child there are two female sponsors and one male.

To "stand up" for a child is more than a social formality, just as Baptism itself is more than a pretty ceremony for a cute little baby. The spiritual seed is planted, and it is the duty of the sponsors to see that it is cultivated. If that is done there is every reason to anticipate a satisfactory outcome. To baptize a child and then leave him to the mercies of a semi-pagan world is a misuse of sacramental privileges.

If Baptism is the channel through which real spiritual gifts are conveyed, then those who are unbaptized are missing something. In the case of an adult, it is his own responsibility. He chooses to do without that which Christ offers to him. But what about the child whose Baptism is neglected by careless and indifferent parents and who dies in infancy before he can do anything about it himself? Is that little life automatically barred from all participation in the Kingdom of Heaven through no fault of its own?

In a word, what about this cruel doctrine of "infant damnation"? Fortunately one hears less of it today than formerly. This has never been any part of the teaching of the Church. It is one of those instances where human logic has intruded into the realm of divine generosity. Baptism is necessary to salvation; children are meant to be baptized; therefore unbaptized children are denied salvation and are condemned to eternal damnation. That is the rigid deduction of a cold-blooded Calvinism more intent on perfecting a closed system than in meeting the needs of human souls.

It is true that Christ has given us the Sacrament of Holy Baptism and calls upon us to use it. If we refuse, we are answerable to Him. But it is monstrous to suppose that He would visit us with penalties because we were denied the opportunity to follow His directions. God is not an arbitrary sultan. He is our Father. He expects us to observe the divine law, but He is not seeking occasions against us. Neglectful parents may answer to Him for depriving their children of the spiritual benefits He offers them, but the children are safe in His everlasting arms. Any other conclusion violates the whole spirit of the Gospel.

So, then, Baptism is the primary Sacrament of the Christian faith. It is the door into the Kingdom of God, the agency of a new birth, the beginning of a new life. It unites us with Christ, makes us members of His Church, imparts forgiveness of sins, and equips us to receive further gifts of God's grace.

"Baptism, whoever receives it, young or old, is the same Sacrament, with the same meaning and the same blessing. There is nothing magical about it. There is nothing more mysterious than there is in any other spiritual opportunity of our daily life. It is the benediction with which one is received into the membership of the Christian society on earth. It is the plain door which opens, at the touch of the humblest hand, into the Christian Church."[23]

[23] *George Hodges, "The Episcopal Church, Its Faith and Order," The Macmillan Company, N. Y., pp. 54–55.*

XV

HOLY COMMUNION

IT IS often said that we live in the age of electricity. We have become dependent upon it to an amazing degree. Electric power has been put to such a multitude of uses that one can scarcely think of modern life without it. Should it somehow be obliterated, modern society might well go into a total collapse. Yet nobody knows what it is or where it comes from. It is one of nature's greatest mysteries. The atmosphere in which we live is pervaded with free electricity. It is all around us. No one can escape from it. But its usefulness to us is dependent upon our ability to harness it with dynamos, run it through wires, and release its energy at a point of contact.

Well—there is also spiritual energy. God is everywhere. His whole creation is sustained by His ever-present divine power. No one can escape from God. "Whither shall I go from Thy Presence?" "In Him we live and move and have our being." But as human beings we require points of contact with God if we are to receive the benefits of His divine energy. That is the function of the Sacraments.

I sit in a darkening room eager for light. I am surrounded by electricity. My house is wired and equipped for its use.

But I am still in darkness. I press a button, make a connection, the energy flows through, and light flashes on. Similarly, I grope in spiritual shadows while God is all around me. I go to the altar, partake of the Holy Communion, make the connection, the spiritual energy flows through, and I find illumination. It is a mystery, to be sure. Both of them are mysteries.

Five names are widely in use for this second of the great Sacraments commanded by our Lord. It is called the *Holy Communion*, the *Lord's Supper*, the *Holy Eucharist*, the *Mass*, and the *Liturgy*. They all mean the same thing but each places a particular emphasis on one phase of the same Sacrament. It is like the facets in a precious stone, each reflecting its own angle of light but all deriving their brilliance from the same central point.

The *Holy Communion* points to the partaking of spiritual food. "The cup of blessing which we bless, is it not the communion of the blood of Christ? The bread which we break, is it not the communion of the body of Christ?"[1]

The *Lord's Supper* emphasizes the memorial feature of the Sacrament. Said our Lord, "Do this in remembrance of Me." It is a memorial act—not merely calling something up to memory, but identifying ourselves with the thing that was done.

The *Holy Eucharist* is the name used most commonly by the early Christians. The word "eucharist" means thanksgiving. While this Sacrament is a memorial of our Lord's death on the cross, it is more than that. The name "eucharist," in general use among the first Christians, adds the Resurrec-

[1] *Corinthians 10:16.*

tion to the Crucifixion. It is the Risen Christ whom we meet at the altar, and the whole sacramental service is an act of gratitude for Christ incarnate, crucified, risen, and ascended.

The *Mass* lays its stress upon the sacrificial aspect of the Sacrament. "The Son of Man came not to be ministered unto, but to minister, and to give His life a ransom for many."[2] The entire life of our Lord is an offering to the Heavenly Father which reached its climax on Calvary and was certified in the Resurrection. That offering was "once for all." It can never be repeated, but it can be reiterated. In the Sacrament we not only re-enact His sacrifice, but we personalize it by throwing our own lives in with His—"Here we offer and present unto Thee, O Lord, our selves, our souls and bodies, to be a reasonable, holy, and living sacrifice unto Thee." We receive something and we give something.

The *Liturgy* is the name particularly venerated by the Eastern Orthodox churches. It emphasizes the worship expressed in the Sacrament. Worship is the acknowledgment of God, the recognition of God, the appreciation of God. In no way can this be more completely done than by dramatic participation in our Lord's self-offering. We render praise as well as thanksgiving.

Whichever name may be used, the Sacrament itself is a memorial, a communion, a thanksgiving, an offering, and an act of worship. No one title can exhaust the significance of the thing itself. There is no use quarreling about different interpretations of the Sacrament. Most of them are likely to be right as far as they go, but they are also likely to be incomplete. Indeed, the differences which divide Christians into

[2] *St. Matthew 20:28.*

various denominational camps are usually due less to inaccuracies of understanding than to inadequacies. Many people are afraid of believing too much. Fractional Christianity is an evidence of human weakness and is apt to degenerate into negative prejudices. To declare that this Sacrament is a memorial does not deprive it of its sacrificial character or *vice-versa*. To name it as the summit of Christian worship does not deny that it is also communion. The Gospel may be studied in fragments, but it needs to be lived in its integrity.

BACKGROUND

The Lord's Supper must have been a matter of supreme importance to the first Christians because its institution is recounted four times in the New Testament.[3] Each of the first three Gospels tells the story. The fourth Gospel, which was written as a supplement to the other three, goes a step further with its remarkable passage about the Bread of Life.[4] Moreover it is to be noted that St. Paul's statement about it to the Corinthians is in the nature of a reminder of commonly accepted Christian teaching. He was not giving them anything new. Said he, "For I have received of the Lord that which also I delivered unto you," and then he proceeded to recount the story of the Last Supper and pointed out its exalted significance.

Four peculiar marks of the apostolic Church are given in the Acts of the Apostles—"they continued stedfastly in the apostles' doctrine and fellowship, and in *breaking of bread*, and

[3] *St. Matthew 26:26–28; St. Mark 14:22–24; St. Luke 22:9–20; I Corinthians 11: 23–25.*

[4] *St. John 6.*

in prayers."[5] Clearly the *breaking of bread*, grouped as it is with these other features, must have meant a sacred religious rite. This conclusion is verified by the incident of St. Paul's visit to Troas, where "upon the first day of the week, when the disciples came together to break bread, Paul preached unto them," and at the conclusion of his sermon he presided at the *breaking of bread*.[6] Evidently this was the custom at Troas just as it was at Corinth.

Therefore it is not at all surprising that in the earliest Christian writings outside the New Testament the Holy Eucharist stands out vividly as the very heart of the corporate life of the Church. In St. Paul's day it was often celebrated in connection with a common meal called the *Agape* or Love-feast. This proved to be an unhappy combination to which the Apostle strongly objected in his letter to the Corinthians, and it soon dropped out of sight. Early in the second century the Eucharist appears as a sacramental offering distinctive of Christian worship and regarded with peculiar reverence by the Christian faithful. Every Sunday they assembled to participate in it and in some quarters it was a daily occurrence. There never seems to have been any question about its primary importance among the followers of Christ.

During the first six centuries the Church fought many a battle to preserve the purity of the Gospel against the corruptions and distortions of the classical "heresies," but in all of those troubled times there were no controversies about the Eucharist. All accepted it as a sacred gift from our Lord. They made little effort to define it but they guarded it with

[5] *Acts* 2:42.
[6] *Acts* 20:11.

the greatest care. Converts in those early days were put through a long course of instruction before they were admitted to the family circle of the Church. They were called "catechumens." On Sunday (the Resurrection Day) they were allowed to share in part of the Christian worship, but were dismissed before the Eucharist itself began. Partaking of the Sacrament was reserved for those who were fully admitted to Christian fellowship—in other words, to communicants of the Church.

Not until well into the Middle Ages did discussion over the Eucharist reach any controversial form, and then it was not in the way of disputations over the Sacrament itself but over definitions in connection with it. The Schoolmen set out to define everything. They attempted to pack into words what had always been accepted without specific definition. The result was the doctrine of *transubstantiation* which was seriously called into question at the time of the Reformation when everything connected with the Christian faith was subjected to critical scrutiny. Other terms were advanced and other theories propounded in the effort to explain the unexplainable. The Anglican Church preferred to go back to first principles, take our Lord at His word, and commit itself to no elaborate analysis of holy things.

REAL PRESENCE

Sacraments are the vehicles for the conveying of divine grace. Think, for a moment, of a medicine prescribed for one's physical health. It consists of certain chemical elements which have been brought together. Those elements taken separately, are possessed of certain qualities, but when they are combined, a new medicinal virtue is produced. You may not be able to put your finger on that virtue but you learn from experience that it is there, underneath the chemical elements. You take the medicine and dispose of the elements, but the virtue remains with you and acts upon your body. It may not produce results until you take the medicine, but the virtue is there nevertheless whether you take it or not.

Something like this is meant by the Real Presence of Christ in the Holy Eucharist. The bread and the wine still remain bread and wine, but by combination with the spiritual act of Consecration they are invested with a peculiar spiritual virtue which is identified with the Body and Blood of Christ. "This," said our Lord, "is My Body . . . and this is My Blood." Christ is spiritually present under the forms of bread and wine. The virtue of His Presence produces its results when the Sacrament is received by the communicant, but the Presence is still there whether received or not.

There is a good deal of mystery in this, isn't there? Of course, there is. Why should there not be mystery when one is dealing with God? Over and over again people have attempted to strip Christianity of its over-natural elements and reduce it to a purely logical system of living. They have abolished most of the New Testament, discarded our Lord's nativity and resurrection, dispensed with the Sacraments—in short, they have amended His "Do this" to make it read, "Do nothing of the sort." What they have left is a dull, unattractive residuum of rationalism which has never been able to inspire anybody.

The truth is that God cannot be measured with the yardstick of the human mind. This must be so because human life consists of so much more than the human mind. Man is not merely an animated brain. He is also emotions, will, instincts, intuitions, and many other things. God cannot be kept out of any of them. Some of the most valuable factors in everyday living are entirely beyond the reach of straight logical analysis. Who ever dissected friendship? Yet we live by it every day. Who ever charted, diagrammed, or card-indexed love, and courtesy, and goodwill? They cannot be even accurately defined, yet we all know what they are and we live with them daily. They are mysteries just as Sacraments are mysteries—just as God is the greatest mystery of all. Because the Christian faith is meant for the whole of a man, Christ made it colorful and interesting. Drain the mystery out of it, and religion becomes flat and tasteless. Moreover, men and women refuse to submit to an existence gone stale. They will enliven it artificially with pomp and circumstance, military display, spectacular theatrical productions, or the elaborate pageantry of innumerable fraternal orders, and so make fictitious mystery. It is a natural human instinct, and any religion which overlooks it is not true to the kind of life which God has created. No one ever needs to apologize for the mystery that inheres in the Christian faith. It is there because Christ put it there. And He put it where it is because there is no other way by which God can be made real to the wistful souls of struggling humanity.

BENEFITS

"Christ died for our sins according to the Scriptures. . . . He was buried, and . . . He rose again the third day."[7] In the

[7] *I Corinthians 15:3, 4.*

chapter on Holy Baptism we said that our Lord came to communicate His divine life to men and women. How was that to be done? Scarcely by example or precept or historical reminiscence. Some personal contact had to be provided. Deductions from His own statements have always associated it with the Cross. But the Crucifixion cannot be torn out of its setting. Christ died, to be sure, but He also rose from the dead and ascended (returned) to the spiritual realm from which He had come. His death completed His sacrificial offering, His resurrection made it a living gift rather than a dead memory, and His ascension lifted it out of the world of time and space into the home of eternal experience. One thing more was necessary—namely, a means whereby this gift of His risen life might be applied to men and women, instilled into them, and made part of them. This is the reason for the Lord's Supper, which became part of the divine sequence.

When He instituted the Sacrament our Lord said, in effect, "I give Myself to you. Tomorrow I lay down My life. I do it through the agency of the Cross, but My death is only the termination of My human ministry. My risen life will still be available to you and to those who through you shall wish to receive Me. This is My Body. This is My Blood. It is My life I am giving to you under these sacramental symbols. Do this in remembrance of Me."

So He provides food for our souls. For our souls need spiritual nourishment just as our bodies need physical nourishment. You do not wait until you are physically famished before you go to a meal. You take your food at regular intervals in order to avoid becoming hungry. So your regular Communion keeps your spiritual life fit for its duties. You may not always be directly conscious of it but that does not matter. Who can say just what immediate benefit he has derived from any given meal? Yet you know that your daily food keeps you alive. Neither may you be able to say exactly what this particular Communion has done for you. But your soul requires its food. "Except ye eat the flesh of the Son of Man, and drink His blood, ye have no life in you."[8]

But there is more than a personal benefit to be considered. The Church is the Body of Christ, and the Sacraments are the arteries through which His grace is conveyed to all the members. The celebration of the Sacraments keeps the circulation flowing. Every time you make your Communion, you are not only doing something for yourself but you are strengthening the life of the Church. We are not so many separated units. We are a body, a society—each one dependent upon the others, and all dependent upon Christ.

One of the most difficult lessons for the average American is the lesson of corporate responsibility. He prefers to think that what he does is of no concern to anybody else. He likes to believe that his life is his own to do with as he may see fit. Under pressure he may learn that he is part of a closely-knit social structure in which every life exerts its influence upon other lives and each one contributes to the broad stream of common welfare. It is the same spiritually. The self-sufficient Christian not only cramps his own soul but retards the progress of God's Kingdom. The open enemies of Christ do not cause Him as great damage as those sometimes charming people who admire Him and neglect Him. The Holy Eucharist is a witness to the spiritual bond which unites us—we eat

[8] *St. John 6:53.*

of the same bread and drink of the same cup, enjoy common spiritual privileges and recognize common spiritual responsibilities. The earnest communicant knows that he does not live his Christian life to himself alone. So says the Invitation in the Communion office—"Ye who do truly and earnestly repent you of your sins, and *are in love and charity with your neighbors* . . . draw near with faith, and take this holy Sacrament to your comfort." It is a sign of Christian unity. That's why there is doubtful propriety in members of different churches communicating at the same altar when they have no intention of abandoning the divisions which separate them into various denominational groups.

MATTER AND FORM

As explained in an earlier chapter, *matter* and *form* in the Sacraments are important as assurances that the sacramental intention is sound. It is the Church which administers the Sacraments through its Ministers, and when the *matter* and *form* authorized by the Church are used, it is evidence that the Minister is doing what the Church intends to be done. The Sacraments do not depend upon the Minister, but upon the Church which commissions him, and the people have a right to be sure of what they are receiving.

Both *matter* and *form* for the Holy Eucharist were given by our Lord Himself. The *matter* is bread and wine similar to that which He used at the Last Supper. The bread may be either leavened or unleavened, though it is most probable that the kind used the night before the Crucifixion was unleavened. The wine is the fermented juice of the grape mixed with a little water. There is no reason whatever for thinking that our Lord used any description of unfermented grape juice.

The liturgies used among the Christians may be traced back to very early times. They differed according to local usage, but they always had one point in common. The central feature of every liturgy was the re-enactment of the Last Supper, with a careful recital of our Lord's words of institution—"Take, eat, this is My Body, which is given for you. . . . Drink ye all of this; for this is My Blood of the New Testament, which is shed for you, and for many, for the remission of sins." This is the heart of it—the *form* of the consecration. Around this other parts of the sacramental service are built. They may vary considerably, but without this central *form* there could not be a Eucharist, whatever else there might be.

MINISTER

At the Last Supper our Lord Himself administered the Sacrament to the Apostles and commanded them to perpetuate what He had begun. With the passing of the Apostles the bishops succeeded to their leadership in the Church and it was they who celebrated the Eucharist for the people. The bishop consecrated the elements at his own altar and the Bishop's Eucharist was sent from that altar to Christians who lived any distance away. Obviously, as congregations increased in number this became more and more difficult to do. The right to consecrate was gradually delegated to the local priests, and this became the prevailing custom throughout the Church. Down to the time of the Reformation nobody but a bishop or a priest was authorized to perform this function, and in line with Christian history it has been the consistent practice of the Episcopal Church down to the present day.

ADMINISTRATION

Always the consecrated Bread has been administered individually to each communicant, but there has been some difference in the use of the chalice. From early times it became the custom in the Eastern Church to dip the consecrated Bread in the Wine and administer both together by means of a spoon. In the Western Church, however, each communicant received directly from the common chalice until well down into the Middle Ages. It was out of a sense of reverence, apprehension over a possible accident in handling the chalice, that the laity became reluctant to receive it. No regulation withdrawing the chalice from the laity was promulgated until the custom had become well established by popular usage. After the twelfth century it was common practice to communicate the people "in one kind," that is, by administering only the consecrated Bread. In many quarters a return to the common chalice came at the time of the Reformation.

Every now and then some agitation is aroused in objection to the common chalice today. The modern motive, however, is quite different from that which prevailed in the Middle Ages. Instead of being impelled by a feeling of reverence, it is inspired by a sense of fear. Some people are frightened by the possibility of germs. The danger is so remote that it might reasonably be dismissed, but the feeling is nevertheless present with many people. Some churches have endeavored to meet it by resorting to the use of individual communion cups. The involved mechanics of this method are not helpful to the sacred character of the Sacrament. In some places administration by "intinction" is preferred—whereby the wafer is moistened in the Wine and so given to the communicant.

This much may be said. There is no reason for any such considerations to keep a communicant away from the Altar. Any person, if he so desires, may receive the Bread without partaking of the chalice, and in doing so makes a full communion. Christ cannot be divided. He is fully present in either of the consecrated Elements, and the benefits of the Sacrament are obtainable whether received in "both kinds," in "one kind," or by the method of intinction.

FASTING COMMUNION

Christian records going back into the earliest centuries tell the story that Christian people were accustomed to make their communions at the beginning of the day. It has been a mark of reverence that the Sacrament should be received before any other food is taken for the day. Obviously the Sacrament itself is more important than the time of receiving it, and circumstances may qualify many a wholesome custom, but the discipline of fasting has a spiritual value. The bishops of the Church have described fasting communion as "reverent in its intention, with the guarantee of long usage, and with the commendation of very saintly men."[9]

[9] *General Convention Journal, 1895, p. 386.*

RESERVATION

When the Bishop's Eucharist was celebrated in the early days and the consecrated Elements were sent out to those who lived at a distance, it was necessary, of course, that the Sacrament should be "reserved"—that is, part of the consecrated Elements were kept after the service itself was over. There were also other reasons for this. It was considered so important for the faithful to receive their Communion that provision was thus made for those who might be sick—the Reserved Sacrament was carried to them. Particularly was this true in the case of imminent death. No Christian wanted to die without his last Communion—the *Viaticum*. Also, during those periods when persecution frequently raged against the Church, and many Christians were held in prison awaiting martyrdom, the Sacrament was always ready to be taken to them. Indeed, the primitive custom went even beyond that. Sometimes people carried the Sacrament back to their own homes in order that they might communicate themselves on days when there might be no Eucharist which they could attend. This last custom raised so many problems that it was eventually discontinued.

Reservation for the sick and for the dying was embedded in the normal tradition of the Church. It was done everywhere down to the time of the Reformation. In the Church of England it has never been discontinued. The first English Prayer Book of 1549 definitely called for it, and that provision has never been invalidated either in the Church of England or in the American Episcopal Church.

During the Commonwealth period, in the middle of the

seventeenth century, many careless habits gained currency even to the extent of carrying away from the Church any surplus of consecrated Elements and using them for ordinary and profane purposes. When the Restoration took place and the Prayer Book was again revised in 1662, this sacrilegious custom was corrected by the addition of a rubric which says —"And if any of the consecrated Bread and Wine remain after the Communion, it shall not be carried out of the Church; but the Minister and other Communicants shall immediately after the Blessing, reverently eat and drink the same." It is quite clear that the purpose of the rubric was to rectify this sorry condition, and that it had no bearing on the reservation of the Sacrament for the following reason. Thorndike, one of the revisers who was responsible for the rubric, writing eight years later, observes: "As concerning the Eucharist . . . the Church is to endeavour the celebrating of it so frequently that it may be reserved to the next communion. For in the meantime it ought to be so ready for them that pass into the other world, that they [the priests] need not stay for the consecrating of it on purpose for every one."[10] People still fall sick and they still die unexpectedly. The Sacrament ought to be ready for them.

And the Church continues to meet emergencies by a further provision contained in a rubric in the office for the Communion of the Sick. Sometimes a sickness is of such a character that the patient is physically incapable of receiving the Sacrament in the usual way. Under such circumstances

---

[10] *Clarke and Harris, "Liturgy and Worship," S. P. C. K., London. Chapter on Communion of the Sick, by Charles Harris, p. 592.*

he is assured that in a spirit of penitence and faith and with a sacramental intention he may make a *spiritual Communion* by which he may truly partake of the benefits of the Sacrament. This is an emergency provision, and does not relieve the communicant of the duty of making his Communion normally, or relieve the priest of the duty of making it available.

Always the Eucharist has been the central act of Christian worship and so it must always be. It is the instrument designated by our Lord Himself through which His redemptive gifts may be appropriated by us today. To know that two thousand years ago a perfect life was lived, a pure and holy Offering made, and a peerless Example erected—all this is no more than a matter of antiquarian interest. How can it reach us in the life of the twentieth century? How can it become vital, active, and impelling in the daily life of the modern world? Christ anticipated such a need and provided for it.

The offering of His life is an eternal fact—something which never ceases. More than an event in past history, it is an ever-present reality. It is going on now. As He gave Himself to the Apostles in the Last Supper, so the giving never fails while we perpetuate the Eucharistic memorial. He continues to come in spiritual reality as He once came in physical form. Our offerings may be poor and feeble, but they become worthy by identification with His.

So when we make our Communion we come with a *special intention*—that is, we bring a special need, petition, or intercession and give it to Him. Incompetent as we may be in ourselves to make any claims on God, we find dependable access to the Heavenly Father by identification with Him who has made the Perfect Offering.

XVI

CONFIRMATION

THE OTHER five Sacraments or sacramental rites stand in a different category from those of Holy Baptism and the Holy Eucharist. They do not come with a direct command of our Lord attached to them, but they all have Scriptural backing and the support of a long Church tradition. Hence the distinction between the Major Sacraments and those we call the Minor Sacraments.

Confirmation fits in so closely with our Lord's teaching and was so clearly the practice of the Apostolic Church that it has been widely understood to be one of "the things pertaining to the Kingdom of God" which He discussed with the Apostles just before His ascension.[1] Years ago the Rev. Dr. Little put it this way: "If, at the Battle of Waterloo, Wellington had been known to summon twelve generals to headquarters to receive instructions from him; and forthwith the twelve generals, in all parts of the battlefield, had begun and carried out a definite plan of *concerted* action, who would doubt that *that* was what the great leader had commanded?"[2] This very well fits the case for Confirmation.

[1] *Acts 1:3.*
[2] A. W. Little, "*Reasons for Being a* **Churchman**," Morehouse-Barlow Co., N.Y., *p. 25.*

Soon after the Church began its work St. Philip the Deacon went to preach the Gospel in Samaria. He made converts and baptized them. But that was not enough. The Laying-on-of-Hands followed the Baptism, but Philip as a deacon was not qualified to do this. So he sent to Jerusalem for St. Peter and St. John, who were Apostles, and they "laid their hands on them, and they received the Holy Ghost."[3]

Later St. Paul was preaching in Ephesus. He also made converts, who had previously known only the teaching of St. John Baptist. St. Paul baptized them, but that was not enough. "When he had laid his hands upon them, the Holy Ghost came on them."[4]

These two instances indicate clearly the common practice of the Apostolic Church. That this was the common practice is strongly supported by the Epistle to the Hebrews where the writer reminds his readers of certain fundamental points which were so well known that it was unnecessary to repeat them. Six of these fundamentals were enumerated—"repentance from dead works, and of faith toward God, of the doctrine of baptisms, and of the Laying-on-of-hands, and of resurrection of the dead, and of eternal judgment."[5] The Laying-on-of-Hands is coupled with Baptism, faith, repentance, etc., as one of the unquestioned steps in the Christian life.

Shortly after the close of the apostolic age this Rite is found to be a regular feature in the Church's work. Tertullian, who was born about 150 A.D., writing of Baptism, adds: "Next to this the hand is laid upon us, calling upon and

[3] *Acts 8:17.*
[4] *Acts 19:6.*
[5] *Hebrews 6:1–2.*

invoking the Holy Ghost through the Blessing."[6] St. Cyprian, who was born about A.D. 200, says: "They who have been baptized in the Church are brought to the Bishops of the Church, and by our prayer and by the Laying-on-of-hands they obtain the Holy Ghost and are consummated with the Seal of the Lord."[7] Other writers bear the same testimony.

Until the fourth century Confirmation was called the Seal or the Anointing. The use of these terms strongly suggests other Scriptural references where an objective Rite is indicated as "anointing" and "sealing."[8] St. Augustine of Hippo is the first one to use the title "Confirmation," which came to be the generally accepted name in the West. In the East it has continued to be known as the Seal or the Anointing down to the present day.

From all of this certain conclusions are inevitable. Confirmation or the Laying-on-of-Hands was closely related to Christian Baptism. It was administered at first by the Apostles and then by the bishops of the Church. It was always considered to be a means by which spiritual gifts were conveyed from God to His people through the ministry of the Church, and no Christian life was complete without it.

Confirmation is the completion of Baptism. By Baptism one is admitted into the Kingdom of God; in Confirmation one receives spiritual strengthening to live a Christian life within the Kingdom. This is the central theme of the Confirmation office in the Book of Common Prayer, as expressed in the Prayer of Invocation, which has been in use

[6] *Tertullian, "On Baptism," Chapter 8.*
[7] *Cyprian, "Epistles," LXXII, 9.*
[8] *II Corinthians 1:21–22; Ephesians 1:13.*

all over Christendom for at least fifteen hundred years. In this prayer the seven-fold gift of the Holy Spirit is called down upon the candidates. It is a kind of lesser ordination to the "priesthood of the laity." It is not merely something which we do but something which is done to us. We do not confirm ourselves. We *are* confirmed.

The *matter* of Confirmation is the laying of the hands of the Bishop upon each candidate individually. The *form* is a prayer for the Holy Spirit. In the Roman Catholic Church and in the Eastern Orthodox Churches the Laying-on-of-Hands has been modified into anointing with chrism, serving the same purpose and signifying the same thing.

Down to the time of the Reformation Confirmation was always a function of the bishops. It is true that in the Eastern Orthodox Churches the priests have confirmed, but they have done so by using chrism consecrated for them by the patriarch who is a bishop. (*Chrism* is a mixture of olive oil and balsam consecrated for special purposes.) In the past four hundred years some Churches which do not have the Historic Episcopate have continued to administer Confirmation, but at the hands of the local pastor.

The recipient of Confirmation is any unconfirmed person who has been baptized with water in the Name of the Holy Trinity. In the primitive Church it followed directly upon Baptism both for adults and for infants. This is still the practice in the Eastern Church where babies are baptized and confirmed at the same time. In western Christendom where Confirmation was administered only by the bishops the practical problem became difficult. Bishops could not always be available when baptisms occurred. Therefore the custom arose of postponing Confirmation until the Bishop could make his visitation to this or that parish. Nevertheless, a formal separation between the two ordinances was not authorized until the sixteenth century. Since that time Confirmation has been postponed for children until they reach "years of discretion" and have received instruction in the basic principles of Christian living. Plainly there are advantages in this method, but it has led many people to think that Confirmation is nothing more than a public profession of faith on the part of the candidates. This is quite contrary to the whole body of Church teaching. Whatever profession may be made by a candidate is strictly secondary to the spiritual gift of God's strengthening power, which is the real purpose of the Laying-on-of-Hands.

There are three pertinent directions in the Book of Common Prayer which should be noted:

1. The sponsors at the baptism of an infant promise to see that the child shall be "brought to the Bishop to be confirmed by him" when the proper time arrives. This keeps Confirmation as the normal sequel to Baptism.

2. At the end of the Office of Holy Baptism a rubric says, "It is expedient that every Adult, thus baptized, should be confirmed by the Bishop, so soon after his Baptism as conveniently may be; that so he may be admitted to the Holy Communion." This means that both for children and adults Confirmation is expected before one receives Holy Communion.

3. Another rubric at the end of the Confirmation office states, "And there shall none be admitted to the Holy Communion, until such time as he be confirmed, or be ready and

desirous to be confirmed." This clarifies and defines the other rubric mentioned above. The first part of this rubric was written into the first English Prayer Book of 1549 and was the regular rule of the Church—that people should be confirmed before making their Communion. In the middle of the seventeenth century, during the English Commonwealth, Confirmation was prohibited for a dozen years, and many children grew up with no opportunity to receive it. When the Protectorate ended in 1660 it was not deemed right to refuse Communion to those who had been unable to be confirmed and make them wait until the reduced number of bishops could catch up with the accumulated duties of visitations to parishes. Therefore the last phrase was added to the rubric to meet the needs of those people. But it was not intended to change the rule that they ought to be confirmed.

So Confirmation comes to us as an apostolic Rite administered by the bishops of the Church, grounded in the Holy Scriptures and the steady practice of the Church, a sacramental means of receiving spiritual strengthening, and the normal method of approach to the Altar. If one proposes to be a disciple of Christ, it seems reasonable to follow the accredited order—Holy Baptism, Confirmation, and the Holy Communion.

XVII

CHRISTIAN MARRIAGE

Bishop McDOWELL has called attention to a valuable distinction between a marriage, a wedding, and the Solemnization of a marriage.[1] A marriage consists of the mutual consent on the part of a man and a woman to live together as husband and wife. A wedding is the ceremony by which the consent is certified and made public. The Solemnization is the blessing by which the Church sanctifies the union. Much confusion may be avoided by keeping this distinction in mind.

A marriage is contracted by a man and a woman—they marry each other. The state does not marry them, neither does the Church. The state regulates the conditions of marriage for the best interests of society. The Church adds its sacramental blessing through which the man and the woman receive divine grace to help them in keeping their vows. It is a universal human institution dating as far back as we know anything about human life. Following the example of our Lord the Church has ratified and blessed it.

The essence of marriage lies in free consent given before witnesses. Long before the development of our modern sys-

[1] "*The Living Church*," July 31, 1937.

tem of public records, this was accomplished by a wedding ceremony which proclaimed to the public that a marriage was being contracted. Only about two centuries ago the custom of issuing licenses was established by law as a matter of legal record and for the protecting of property rights. The public ceremonies gathered about themselves a large variety of wedding customs and traditions, many of which have been preserved in attenuated forms down to the present day. The price that was once paid for a bride is now represented by the gift of a wedding ring. The reception of the woman into the man's family is symbolized by the joining of hands. To carry a bride over the threshold of her new home is a relic of the days when women were captured and carried away for marriage.

In olden days the "espousals" (that is the "engagement") and the "nuptials" constituted two distinct ceremonies, often with an interval of several months between them. But the espousal was just as binding as the final marriage itself. This is one of the elements in the Scriptural account of our Lord's birth, where it is told how St. Joseph was espoused to the Blessed Virgin Mary.[2] Both among the Jews and the Romans marriage was supposed to be a permanent union lasting for the duration of life, but in actual practice divorce had become so common and easy that no marriage was secure.

Our Lord gave evidence of His approval of marriage as an institution by His attendance at the wedding in Cana of Galilee.[3] He further stated the Christian standard in His

[2] *St. Matthew 1:18.*
[3] *St. John 2.*

teaching as recorded in three of the Gospels.[4] Briefly it is as follows: the marriage of a man and a woman is part of God's purpose for mankind, it unites the two into "one flesh," and is an indissoluble union. "Those whom God hath joined together let no man put asunder." He pointedly condemned the divorce habits which prevailed in His day, allowing for a possible exception (as recorded in St. Matthew) in the case of unfaithfulness. This exception is a matter of debate among biblical scholars.

St. Paul had several things to say on the subject in applying the teaching of Christ to conditions existing in the pagan world as he met them during his missionary travels. His most important statement was to the Corinthians,[5] in which he emphasizes the life-long character of marriage, and disowns the pagan practices of divorce. In writing to the Ephesians St. Paul goes a step further, comparing marriage to the mystical union between Christ and His Church, which is, of course, the ultimate Christian ideal.[6]

Such was the situation when the Church entered upon its career to carry out our Lord's mission. Marriage itself and the prevailing wedding customs were taken over by the Christians, and a distinctive touch was added as the newly married couple made their Communion together and received the eucharistic blessing. In this way their marriage was dedicated to God and became more than a natural institution. It was converted into a sacramental experience through which God's blessing descended upon a family and

[4] *St. Matthew 5:31-32; St. Mark 10:2-12; St. Luke 16:18.*

[5] *I Corinthians 7:10-18; Romans 7:1-3.*

[6] *Ephesians 5:22-33.*

through which two lives offered their united loyalty to Christ.

Down through the centuries the Church has struggled to uphold the Christian standard in a world which was slowly becoming conscious of Christ, but which was still impregnated with many remnants of unchristian paganism. Today the Church finds itself faced with a double duty—it must uphold the ideal, and at the same time must minister the Gospel of Christ to many people who have never known what a Christian ideal is. The easiest way would be for the Church to adopt a set of rules and demand that everybody should conform. The difficulty is to find any such rules which will fairly meet the intricate variety of circumstances which entangle bewildered individuals in a net of domestic problems. The first business of the Church is to minister to people rather than to execute rigid rules. The relationship of the sexes is an inflammable matter at best, and human emotions are not easy to regulate.

From those who have been brought up in the Church certain things may be expected. But many people who have had no such training will ignorantly violate the laws of the Church and later honestly seek entrance into the Church. This is greatly aggravated by mixed marriages where divergent convictions call for adjustment. Moreover, the state has qualified the clergy to officiate at marriages as officers of the state as well as priests of the Church. And the secular state sets up its laws of marriage and divorce largely on grounds of expediency, with little or no consideration for the claims of Christian morality.

The Church upholds the historic standard of Christian

marriage which cannot be lowered. Then it attempts to deal with people as generously as possible without sacrificing the standard. Marriage is a life-long union, not to be dissolved when a different union may seem desirable. Most marriages could be made to work if the two persons concerned were determined to keep them permanent. No priest of the Church is permitted to solemnize the second marriage of a person whose original mate is still living, unless the previous marriage has been declared null by the Bishop.

A communicant who violates this rule is automatically excommunicated. However, should one who has contracted a marriage contrary to this standard desire to take his place in the Church and be admitted to the Sacraments, he may apply to the Bishop of the diocese in whose jurisdiction he resides and the Bishop, being fully informed of the facts, may give a dispensation, each case standing on its own merits.

It is important to remember that this does not mean a person is condemned for life to a hopeless and degrading union. Such unions do occur and there are times when divorce is entirely justifiable. Neither does such a separation make any difference in a person's relationship to the Church. That question arises only in the event of remarriage after divorce. Often it is a practical necessity for a husband and wife to separate and live apart, safeguards being secured through divorce proceedings. Seldom is it necessary for either one of them to remarry. Too many bachelors and spinsters do very well with their lives to prove any real necessity for divorced persons to contract other unions.

The Church has the deepest sympathy for persons who

become involved in the toils of domestic tragedy, but that is not the crux of the matter. Once it is accepted that marriage is a temporary contract, easily made and easily dissolved, it becomes little more than an experimental experience. The divorce habit and the divorce psychology take hold. Small domestic differences are readily magnified into disruptive issues and the basis of family life becomes a quicksand.

Divorce follows divorce, men and women leave a succession of husbands and wives behind them, children are bandied about and deprived of the parental affection which is their natural right, love degenerates into emotional impulse, and the fiber of character which should be strong enough to stand a strain becomes soft and wayward and ineffective. This is the "divorce evil" which the Church opposes—not so much the occasional case, where honest effort has broken down, as the flippant disregard of any sound standards of married life because some people want to do whatever they want to do.

There are, of course, marriages which are not true marriages at all, and should never have been contracted. The Church recognizes that these may properly be declared null and void, relieving the parties concerned of any responsibility. A marriage which has never been consummated is a fiction. Certain conditions existing before marriage constitute "impediments" which invalidate the whole intention of the free consent required—for instance, mistaken identity, insanity, impotence, bigamy, etc. In such cases the Church provides means whereby an annulment may be procured and the marriage itself cancelled. In every instance the judgment must be rendered by the Bishop with competent legal advice.

The "ministers" of marriage are the man and the woman who are being united. The *matter* and *form* consist of the mutual consent and the declaration which proclaims it. The officiating priest adds the Church's blessing by which the benefit of God's help is introduced to make the marriage true and permanent. Strictly speaking, the persons who receive the blessing should be baptized Christians, since Baptism is the basic Sacrament which qualifies the recipients for other sacramental grace. By ancient tradition marriages are discouraged during the period of Lent because of the penitential character of that season in the Church Year. The old custom of joining the Solemnization with a nuptial Eucharist is fortunately increasing in frequency.

Obviously these provisions are intended for professing Christians. Actually many persons who have little or no concern with the Christian religion come to the clergy to be married because the clergy are commissioned by the state to officiate on such occasions. The situation is anomalous and sometimes embarrassing. It is worth raising the question as to whether the Church might not do well to decline the secular commissioning of its clergy, leave the marriages to be contracted before civil magistrates, and provide for Christian Solemnization (preferably with the nuptial Eucharist) after the civil ceremony for those who propose to establish really Christian homes.

XVIII

THE CHURCH'S MINISTRY

"THIS IS where Christianity is fundamentally different from other religions. Confucius left his Classics. Buddha left a system of instruction. Mohammed left the Koran. But Jesus Christ left disciples. . . . Life comes only from life, and it takes Christians to make Christians."[1]

Therein lies the essence of the much-disputed question of Apostolic Succession. The Church rests upon the principle of the Incarnation—God expressing Himself in the life of our Blessed Lord. He might have done it some other way, but we are bound by the historical facts of what actually did occur. Christianity is an historical religion taking its origin from Christ as an historical Person. True to this principle of His own Incarnation, our Lord provided for the continuation of His work through other persons. It is important to remember that Christ never wrote a book. He never promulgated a system of philosophy or a code of ethics. He taught a small group of people whom we call the Apostles. Having selected them out of a larger number of followers, He kept them close to Himself over a period of three years, training, instructing, preparing them, and finally commissioning them.

[1] *The author's "Common-sense Religion," The Macmillan Company, N. Y., p. 130.*

He made them the accredited leaders of the Church which was to carry on what He had begun. He invested them with the authority of "binding" and "loosing"—that is, they were to determine what was permitted and what was forbidden when questions arose within the Church.[2] At the end of His earthly ministry He sent them forth as His representatives—"Then said Jesus to them again, Peace be unto you: as My Father hath sent Me, even so send I you. And when He had said this, He breathed on them, and said unto them, Receive ye the Holy Ghost: whose soever sins ye remit, they are remitted unto them; and whose soever sins ye retain, they are retained."[3]

The Apostles proceeded to carry out their commission on the authority personally received by them from our Lord. For many years the Gospel was preached, the Sacraments administered, and the Church planted through this personal witness of the Apostles, with no written records and no organized machinery. It was God working with and through human lives by personal contact. As the Church expanded, as the number of Christians increased, and the Apostles advanced in years, their witness was reduced to writing in what we now call the New Testament Scriptures, and the growing burden of their work was delegated to other carefully selected individuals ordained for that purpose. Always it must be remembered that the Scriptures are the record of what the Apostles were already teaching. The Church does not receive its authority from the Bible. It is the other way around.

[2] *St. Matthew 18:18.*
[3] *St. John 20:21–23.*

One cannot read the New Testament without being impressed with the unique position accorded to the Apostles in the early Church. One of the first things the Christian community felt it necessary to do was to fill the vacancy in the number of the Apostles left by the death of Judas Iscariot.[4] After St. Paul's conversion, he had to be presented to the Apostles before being accepted into the Christian family.[5] Questions about the reception of Gentiles were brought before the Apostolic Council, and the decision was pronounced by St. James, one of the Apostles.[6] Hear St. Paul rebuking the wayward Corinthians—"Now some are puffed up, as though I would not come to you. But I will come to you shortly. . . . What will ye? Shall I come unto you with a rod, or in love, and in the spirit of meekness?"[7] Repeatedly such messages reveal the Apostles as the recognized leaders and directors of the infant Church.

Not long after the Church began to function it was found necessary to divide the ministerial responsibilities. The first important step was taken in the setting apart of seven deacons as assistants to the Apostles—"whom they set before the Apostles: and when they had prayed, they laid their hands on them."[8] So they were ordained. Later elders were chosen and similarly ordained. (The Greek word for elder is "presbyter", which was later contracted to "priest.") They looked after the affairs of the Church in their several localities after the fashion of what we would now call local parish priests.[9]

[4] *Acts 1:16–26.*
[5] *Acts 9:27.*
[6] *Acts 15.*
[7] *I Corinthians 4:18, 19, 21.*
[8] *Acts 6:6.*
[9] *Acts 14:23, 20:17; I Timothy 5:17; I Peter 5:1.*

So the three-fold ministry was evolved out of the apostolate. There were others who performed certain functions in the Church—evangelists, prophets, teachers, etc., and, later, deaconesses—but not as orders in the Christian ministry.

Inevitably the time came when the ranks of the Apostles began to be depleted by death, and others had to be found to continue their duties of direction and leadership in the Church. Such men as Timothy and Titus were chosen who were respectively the Bishop of Ephesus and the Bishop of Crete. They were known as bishops, the title "Apostle" being reserved especially for the original Twelve as a mark of peculiar honor. They were ordained for this purpose, and one of their prerogatives was to ordain elders (priests) and so pass on the commission which they had received.[10]

This method of operation was standard for the early Church. To be sure, in a fast growing movement there were bound to be irregularities here and there for a time, but it is quite certain that soon after the opening of the second century this standard prevailed throughout the Church—that is, bishops, as successors of the Apostles, ordained priests and deacons, thus completing the three-fold ministry. These were the "Sacred Orders" recognized by the Christian world for the next fifteen hundred years, and were always conferred by the bishops who were the recipients of the apostolic commission. One can convey only that which one possesses. The Apostles received their commission directly from our Lord and have perpetuated it through the bishops in successive generations by personal ordination.

The Apostolic Succession is not a mechanical device

[10] *II Timothy 1:6; Titus 1:5.*

designed to retain a monopoly on spiritual ministrations. Obviously there must be some seat of authority when many people are united in a common cause. The ultimate Authority in the Church is Jesus Christ. Immediate authority is logically that which is derived from Him. He sent forth His Apostles as His representatives. They transmitted their responsibilities to their successors—and so on down. Thus the apostolic witness has been preserved on the principle of the Incarnation. From person to person it has been passed on, beginning with the Apostles who themselves began with Christ. However much God may have blessed other ministries, self-constituted and detached from the apostolic line, they are simply not the same as the apostolic ministry.

This is not to say that ministers of the Apostolic Succession have some magical powers which others do not possess. Christ is really the Minister of all Christian Sacraments, and He acts through His mystical Body which is the Church. In the case of Holy Orders it is the Church which conveys them, following again the principle of the Incarnation which works through persons. Bishops do not act on their own initiative. They are the accredited agents of the Church. Their authority is conditioned by the Church, which is its field of operation. Holy Orders are not conferred according to the whim and fancy of any individual prelate. They are conferred by the bishops *in the Church*. Such an apostolic ministry is a guarantee of the authenticity of the Church which Christ loved and for which He gave Himself. It is a preservative of the integrity of the Gospel which was entrusted to the Apostles. It is a magnetic core of Christian unity and a compass of spiritual direction from that which began with Christ to that which must end with Him.

The Episcopal Church has carefully preserved all this in its official Ordinal. In the Prayer Book, the Preface to the Ordinal states: "It is evident unto all men, diligently reading Holy Scripture and ancient Authors, that from the Apostles' time there have been these Orders of Ministers in Christ's Church—Bishops, Priests, and Deacons . . . And therefore, to the intent that these Orders may be continued, and reverently used and esteemed in this Church, no man shall be accounted or taken to be a lawful Bishop, Priest, or Deacon, in this Church, or suffered to execute any of the said Functions, except he be called, tried, examined, and admitted thereunto, according to the Form hereafter following, or hath had Episcopal Consecration or Ordination."

Always the Minister of Ordination is the Bishop. Following the Scriptural precedents the *matter* consists in the laying on of the Bishop's hands. The *form* is prayer to the Holy Spirit for the particular office to which the candidate is being ordained. The benefits are the transmission of the Apostolic Commission and grace to fulfil the functions of the office. The sacramental marks are evident—"an outward and visible sign of an inward and spiritual grace given unto us." Holy Orders are "indefectible"—that is, like Baptism, they set a permanent "character" upon the person ordained and he may not properly be ordained a second time. As a matter of discipline, which may be modified or changed from time to time, certain precedent requirements are called for by the canons of the Church involving study, examination, and general preparation for the ministry.

A Deacon must be a baptized and confirmed communicant of the Church, and must have passed through the preliminary stages as a Postulant and Candidate for Holy Orders. He must be at least twenty-one years of age. Having been recommended by the Standing Committee of his diocese, he is presented to the Bishop for ordination. He is invested with a copy of the New Testament as the chief symbol of his service. His stole is worn diagonally over one shoulder as a sign of his partial ministry. The Deacon is directly responsible to his Bishop, by whom he is appointed to certain duties and licensed to preach the Gospel. He may not be rector of a parish. He may assist at the Holy Communion, but he may not celebrate. In the absence of a priest he is qualified to baptize. He may conduct other services except for pronouncing the absolution or the benediction. He serves as a Deacon for a year, which for special reasons may be shortened to a minimum of six months, before he qualifies for advancement to the priesthood.

To be ordained Priest the candidate must have been episcopally ordained to the diaconate and must be at least twenty-four years of age. Having met the other requirements, he is presented to the Bishop. Other priests who are present at the ordination join with the Bishop in the Laying-on-of-Hands as a sign of the fellowship of the priesthood. He is invested with the Holy Bible, his stole is placed over both shoulders, and, according to an ancient custom, a chalice and paten may be placed in his hands as symbols of his commission to celebrate the Holy Eucharist; also, he may be clothed in eucharistic vestments. One may not be ordained to the priesthood without a "title"—*i.e.,* a specific field of service to which he is ordained must be provided for him. As a Priest he is qualified to perform all spiritual and ecclesiastical functions except Confirmation and Ordination. He is formally attached to some particular diocese, and is under the general supervision of his Bishop.

To be consecrated, a Bishop-elect must be possessed of priest's Orders and must be at least thirty years of age. He must have been canonically elected, and consent to his consecration must have been given by a majority of all the bishops in the Church and by a majority of all the Standing Committees in the several dioceses, or by a concurrent majority of the House of Bishops and the House of Deputies at General Convention. The Presiding Bishop is the consecrator, or another bishop appointed by him. At least three bishops must participate in the consecration of a new bishop as a witness to the fact that the whole Church is acting in the conferring of this highest order. The new bishop is invested with the Holy Bible, and in accordance with ancient custom may also be invested with ring and crozier as symbols of his episcopal authority.

A "Diocesan" is a bishop who is formally in charge of a diocesan jurisdiction. A Coadjutor Bishop is an assistant to the Diocesan who takes over a specific part of the jurisdiction and succeeds as head of the diocese upon the death or resignation of the Diocesan. A Suffragan Bishop is an assistant to the Diocesan without definite jurisdiction and without the right of succession. The Bishop is the chief pastor over his diocese, administering the discipline of the Church. He is the executive head of the diocesan organization. He administers Confirmation and confers Holy Orders. He presides at diocesan Councils and Conventions, and he sits with his brethren in the House of Bishops. A Missionary Bishop is elected by the House of Bishops, with concurrence by the House of Deputies. All bishops are elected for life, subject to retirement at such age as authorized by the General Convention.

The Presiding Bishop is elected by the General Convention, with bishops, other clergy, and laymen all having a share in his choice. He relinquishes his former diocesan responsibilities, and devotes his full time to the pastoral and executive responsibilities of the Chief Bishop of the Church.

The General Convention consists of all the bishops of the Church, comprising the House of Bishops, and a House of Deputies, consisting of equal numbers of priests (or presbyters) and laymen, elected by the dioceses. It is the supreme legislative body of the Church, and has responsibility for enacting or amending the Constitution and Canons by which the Church is governed. It also is the only body that can alter the Book of Common Prayer, authorize proposed changes for trial use throughout the Church, or adopt a new Prayer Book. In the intervals between General Conventions, many of its responsibilities are carried out by an Executive Council, over which the Presiding Bishop presides.

God created an orderly universe. So, the Church needs to be anchored to some central fact which is definite, permanent, understandable, and which speaks with authority in His name. The apostolic ministry serves this purpose.

XIX

CONFESSION AND ABSOLUTION

"IF WE say that we have no sin, we deceive ourselves, and the truth is not in us. If we confess our sins, He is faithful and just to forgive us our sins, and to cleanse us from all unrighteousness."[1]

In these words St. John was writing to baptized Christians. In their Baptism they had been cleansed of "original sin" but that was not a guarantee of perfection. St. John knew, as we ought to know, that many unchristian influences pervade the world in which we live, and that under the pressure of them we are frequently driven or enticed out of the way that Christ sets before us. We may ignore or discount our sins but we are only deceiving ourselves. In our honest moments we know that we do many things which could never stand our Lord's inspection. Now the Christian religion is meant for use—not merely for discussion. It is intended for life as it is actually lived in a complicated world. Our Lord reckoned with facts, even the unpleasant ones, and kept open the way for dealing with post-baptismal sins in order that we should not be discouraged. He would not minimize the grievousness of sin, but He would provide all the means required to

[1] *I John 1:8-9.*

overcome it and march on to God in spite of it. He gave the Apostles a graphic illustration the night before His crucifixion when He proceeded to wash their feet. St. Peter protested at the indignity of it, but our Lord said, "If I wash thee not, thou hast no part with Me." Whereupon St. Peter replied that in that case he would be glad to be washed all over. But our Lord reminded him, "he that is washed needeth not save to wash his feet."[2] That is, the cleansing of Baptism had prepared him for the Kingdom of God, but he still needed to remove the recurrent impurities gathered on the road of human life.

So the Ministry of Forgiveness is a vital part of the Gospel and lies close to the heart of the Church. After His resurrection our Lord said to the group which comprised the nucleus of the Church: "Thus it behooved Christ to suffer, and to rise from the dead the third day: and that repentance and remission of sins should be preached in His Name among all nations."[3]

The divine forgiveness is offered to men and women through the Gospel. We do not earn it. Always it rests upon the Passion and Resurrection of our Lord. By repentance and faith we qualify to receive it. But, true to the sacramental pattern of the whole Christian religion, it must be brought out of the realm of theory into the world of practice. Therefore it is committed to the Church to be taught, preached, and mediated through the Ministry of the Church by the Church's accredited representatives.

Once our Lord was healing a sick man. The first thing He

[2] *St. John 13:3–12.*
[3] *St. Luke 24:46–47.*

said was, "Son, thy sins be forgiven thee." Immediately His critics declared this was blasphemy, that only God could forgive sins. Whereupon He replied, "That ye may know that the Son of Man hath power on earth to forgive sins, (He saith to the sick of the palsy,) I say unto thee, Arise, and take up thy bed, and go thy way into thine house."[4] Later He sent forth His Apostles to continue His work—"As My Father hath sent Me, even so send I you. . . . Receive ye the Holy Ghost: whose soever sins ye remit, they are remitted unto them; and whose soever sins ye retain, they are retained."[5] Put those two together. Christ declares His power to forgive sins, and then He commissions His Apostles to do likewise in His Name. Certainly, only God can forgive sins. Christ, being God Incarnate, exercises that divine prerogative. When a priest says, "I absolve thee," he is speaking for Christ just as when he says, "I baptize thee." No priest can forgive anybody's sins. He points and personalizes the forgiveness of God which becomes available through the Passion and Resurrection of Christ.

It is the sacramental principle all over again—the goodness of God coming to us through human channels because we are human beings. Sins are concrete things and require concrete handling. Therefore the Church which is His visible representative on earth is the agency through which His forgiveness normally operates. "We do not receive forgiveness of sins in order to enter the Catholic Church; we enter the Catholic Church in order that we may have our sins forgiven."[6] There is no suggestion of interfering with free

[4] *St. Mark 2:3–12.*
[5] *St. John 20:21–23.*
[6] *Report of a Conference at Fulham, December, 1901, p. 14.*

access to God. It is a case of using instruments provided for the exercise of spiritual privileges. One can't think without a brain, or speak without a tongue, or see without an eye, because one is a human being and made that way. Spiritually, we are conditioned by human requirements, and God meets us accordingly.

It should always be remembered that the Christian is a member of the Body of Christ and he lives a corporate life. His sin is not only an offense against God but a blemish on the Body which affects his fellow-Christians. Therefore he stands in need, not only of the forgiveness of God, but also of reconciliation with his brethren. The early Christians recognized this quite clearly. A notorious, persistent, and unrepentant sinner was excluded from the company of the Church and denied admission to the Holy Communion—he was excommunicated. To regain his Christian standing he had to be restored to his place in the Church. For this the Church required evidence of repentance and amendment of life. So a penitential system began to develop.

At first the offender was expected to confess his wrongdoing publicly in the congregation, accept whatever penance might be given him, and be publicly restored and readmitted to Communion. These open confessions raised obvious practical problems, and gradually they came to be withheld in favor of private confession to the priest acting in the name of the Church. During the Middle Ages private auricular confession became the fixed custom. In the later medieval period the hardening rigidity of ecclesiastical discipline did strange things to the whole penitential system. Sins were weighed and classified. The theory of the Treasury of

Merits and the granting of indulgences led to a traffic in forgiveness. Confession was made compulsory and a tariff was established which poured a blight on spiritual sincerity. This proved to be the immediate issue on which the continental Reformation hinged. The reaction was rather violent. Many of the revolting bodies abolished confession and penance.

In this, as in many other matters, the Anglican Church endeavored to correct abuses by reform rather than by destruction. The mediating office of the Church was preserved, cleared of the mechanical calculations of indulgences. In the services of the Prayer Book a general confession was inserted and a general absolution was provided. Worshippers were expected to examine themselves, particularly before receiving the Holy Communion, and clear their consciences before approaching the Altar. In the absolution in Morning Prayer it is stated that God "hath given power, and commandment, to His Ministers, to declare and pronounce to His people, being penitent, the Absolution and Remission of their sins," and in the Communion office the priest, performing that function, announces, "Almighty God . . . have mercy upon you; pardon and deliver you from all your sins; confirm and strengthen you in all goodness; and bring you to everlasting life." It is getting back to the spirit of the early Church when reconciliation with the congregation is coupled with forgiveness from God.

At the same time the English Prayer Book also made provision for private confession and absolution—but as a voluntary privilege rather than a compulsory duty. The second Exhortation to Holy Communion urges the need of self-examination and adds, "If there be any of you, who by this means cannot quiet his own conscience herein, but requireth further comfort or counsel, let him come to me, or to some other Minister of God's Word, and open his grief; that he may receive such godly counsel and advice, as may tend to the quieting of his conscience, and the removing of all scruple and doubtfulness." While in the office for the Visitation of the Sick a rubric provides—"Then shall the sick person be moved to make a special confession of his sins, if he feel his conscience troubled with any matter; after which confession, on evidence of his repentance, the Minister shall assure him of God's mercy and forgiveness."

It is significant that leading psychologists have recently been discovering the therapeutic value of private confession. The Church knew it long ago but the Church goes a step further. It is not only good psychology for one to get something off one's mind which is festering and causing "nerves," but it is good spirituality to receive the assurance of absolution as potent medicine for a spiritual hurt. It is the outward expression of a spiritual gift, and therefore partakes of the sacramental character. The benefit is spiritual cleansing and reconciliation with God and His Church. The *form* is the declaration of absolution. The *matter* is contrition, confession, and satisfaction on the part of the penitent.

Contrition means the recognition of the wrong done to God together with a desire and intention to avoid repetition of it. Confession means an honest statement of what the wrong is. Not only must sin be confessed but sins. If we are to grapple with our faults it is necessary to face them and realize what they are. This may be done without squeamishness, because the "seal of confession" is binding upon every priest; under no circumstances does he reveal what he may have heard except with the consent of the penitent. Satisfaction simply means that something shall be done as an evidence of contrition. It is not a question of satisfying God but of building up a wall of resistance. If we have inflicted an injury upon another person, we should make some sort of restitution. If we have shamed ourselves, we should undertake some spiritual exercise as an antidote to a possible recurrence of the fault. With contrition, confession, and satisfaction accomplished, one becomes a candidate for absolution.

God's forgiveness is broad and generous, but God is not to be imposed upon. We do not get forgiveness merely for the asking. In order to be forgiven we must be forgivable. Christ provides the ground for it. We establish our claim by repentance, faith, and our willingness to forgive others: "If ye forgive not men their trespasses neither will your Father forgive your trespasses." [7] We prove our sincerity by contrition, confession, and satisfaction. Then we are qualified for the assurance of absolution. The picture needs to be kept complete.

Of course, there are two dangers. In a general confession it is possible that we should be vague, indefinite, unreal. On the other hand, in repeated private confession it is equally possible that we should be formal, settled in a routine, and sometimes trivial. We shall avoid either of these pitfalls insofar as we keep an active recollection of what Christ has done for us and how much we owe to Him. In this the Holy Spirit can and does help us.

[7] *St. Matthew 6:15.*

XX

THE MINISTRY OF HEALING

"IF I can only keep my children healthy, I shall be perfectly satisfied." Some such statement is often thrown out by parents. Before one approves or quarrels with such a remark, it is necessary to know just what the speaker means by it. If, as is unfortunately too often the case, the parent is concerned purely with the physical mechanics of bodily health, he is missing the point in two ways. In the first place, he is ignoring the moral and spiritual factors which determine the right or wrong use of a healthy body. And in the second place, he overlooks the fact that the moral and spiritual condition of any person has a great deal to do with the proper functioning of his physical machinery.

Modern psychology is catching up with the Christian practice of many centuries. It is now recognized on all hands that a human being consists of something more than muscle, bone, and sinew, and that a person's health depends upon mental attitude and spiritual condition as well as upon lungs and glands. If a person is to be really well, he must be *all* well, and if he falls sick, all of him needs to be treated. Therein lies the reason for the Church's Ministry of Healing, which was part of the commission given by our Lord to the Church and exercised by the Church from the very beginning.

Not only did our Lord Himself heal the sick, but He instructed His disciples to continue doing so. "And when He had called . . . His twelve disciples. He gave them power against unclean spirits, to cast them out, and to heal all manner of sickness and all manner of disease."[1] He sent the Seventy into various cities and among other things told them to "heal the sick that are therein, and say unto them, The Kingdom of God is come nigh unto you."[2] This the Apostles proceeded to do, and spiritual healing, consisting of prayer together with the Laying-on-of-Hands or anointing with oil (or both), soon became an established feature in the general ministry of the Church. One of the practical directions in that most practical epistle of St. James is very specific—"Is any sick among you? Let him call for the elders of the Church; and let them pray over him, anointing him with oil in the Name of the Lord: and the prayer of faith shall save the sick, and the Lord shall raise him up."[3]

In primitive times it was customary for the sick to be brought to Church in beds or litters, and at a fixed place in the Liturgy the Bishop blessed them and prayed for them. Where they could not be brought from their homes, the clergy visited them for prayer and unction. Says one of the early writers, "As regards the sick, their healing depends on their coming frequently to Church, and enjoying [public] prayer, except in the case of one dangerously ill. Let such a one be visited daily by the clerical body, that they may give him fuller assurance [of recovery] "[4] This became such a

[1] *St. Matthew 10:1.*

[2] *St. Luke 10:9.*

[3] *St. James 5:14.*

[4] *Clarke and Harris,* "*Liturgy and Worship,*" *S. P. C. K., London, p. 476, footnote 1.*

regular part of Christian practice that Christian churches came to be known as "temples of healing." The early office books contain forms of prayer for the Bishop in consecrating the oil to be used for healing purposes.

Just as it was most appropriate for water to be used as the symbolic element for the cleansing effect of Holy Baptism, and as bread with wine was most appropriate for the sacrament of Spiritual Nourishment, so it is most natural that oil should be the sacramental instrument of spiritual healing. Oil has a mollifying effect, especially in bodily wounds, and has long been used as one of the ingredients in many medicinal compounds. In our Lord's parable the Good Samaritan gave first-aid to the wounded traveler by pouring in wine and oil.[5] As an outward symbol of spiritual renewal it is a fitting substance for the *matter* of this sacramental rite, and one which was used by the Apostles under our Lord's direction when He sent them out on a missionary tour—"and they cast out many devils and anointed with oil many that were sick, and healed them."[6]

The *form* consists of prayer to the Holy Spirit for strength to overcome the attacks of illness. The benefit is the refreshing and reinvigorating of spiritual powers which in their turn have their effect on one's physical condition. The recipient is any baptized person who may be sick. The minister is ordinarily a priest, though in the absence of a priest it may be a layman—but in either case the oil has been consecrated for this purpose by a bishop or priest. The usual custom is for the Bishop to consecrate sufficient oil for use in his diocese

[5] *St. Luke 10:34.*
[6] *St. Mark 6:13.*

during the period of a year from Maundy Thursday, which is the traditional day when such consecrations are made. In the administration of Unction the sign of the cross is made with the consecrated oil upon the forehead of the patient, together with appropriate prayers, and preferably after the reception of the Holy Communion.

Does this always cure a sickness? Sometimes. Always it helps. Faith makes a great deal of difference—not the amount of faith but the quality of it—for faith is the medium through which the benefits of any Sacrament are assimilated. Yet a word of caution needs to be said about the popular conception of "faith cures." The Church has never disparaged the curative efforts of medical science. To the contrary, the Church has always encouraged and fostered them. Priest and physician work together toward the same end. Their ministrations are complementary, never opposed. It is an unwarranted assumption to declare that health and sickness are purely physical states, and it is equally unwarranted to assume that they are entirely mental or spiritual.

A human being is a unit. For purposes of analysis and discussion we divide him into body, mind, and spirit, but actually no one of the three can be separated from the other two. If such a separation could be made we would have on our hands a corpse, or a disembodied spirit, or something else—but not a human being. A person is a unit. If something goes wrong with him, he must be treated as such. The thing that goes wrong may be a physical obstruction or a mental or spiritual obstruction. In either case the whole person is affected. Just as a bruise, a tumor, or an infection may cause a physical impediment, so worry, remorse, or sin may be responsible for a mental or spiritual impediment. Any one of these will cripple the health of a person and requires treatment. A person is never really well until he is well in all three directions. Therefore, when a person is sick, he ought to be prayed for just as he ought to go to bed and take his temperature. For *prayer is the means by which God's power is released into human life,* and that power always does good.

In the early centuries of Christian history the administration of Unction was always associated with the healing ministry of the Church. During the Middle Ages a different emphasis appeared connecting this rite with the preparation for death. Naturally people became reluctant to call for it in any ordinary illness. By the twelfth century it was commonly known as Extreme Unction, and was resorted to only when death seemed to be imminent. This has continued to be the practice of the Roman Catholic Church down to the present time, where it is often called the "Last Rites."

Here again at the time of the Reformation the Anglican Church stepped over a medieval distortion and re-established the practice of the Primitive Church. In the first English Prayer Book of 1549 a form for the administration of Unction was provided in the office for the Visitation of the Sick. The prayer which accompanied the anointing in this office contained the following: "and vouchsafe for His great mercy (if it be His blessed will) to restore unto thee thy bodily health and strength, to serve Him; and send thee release of all thy pains, troubles, and diseases both in body and mind." The intention is obvious—not only to fortify the soul at the point of death, but to counteract the effects of the spiritual debility which is an accessory to, if not the cause of, any sickness which may overtake us.

During the past two or three centuries of excessive material progress, popular attention has leaned predominantly in the direction of physical remedies for physical ills, and this sacramental ministration has been widely neglected. Recently a considerable change has set in. In some quarters it has run to extremes in "faith cures." Gradually, however, the sane and reasonable position of the Church is winning its way, and people are taking more seriously what the Church has to offer them. In our American Prayer Book the office for the Visitation of the Sick contains a section for Unction or the Laying-on-of-Hands, thereby conforming to the principles and practice of the Apostles as well as the example of our Blessed Lord. It is expressly provided for the patient "that all thy pain and sickness of body being put to flight, the blessing of health may be restored unto thee."[7] Any parish priest, out of his own pastoral experience, can bear witness to the beneficent results which increase as Church people grow in the appreciation of what their Church can do for them.

A word to the clergy. Spiritual healing is part of the normal ministry of every priest. It is not restricted to those who may be possessed of unusual powers, because the Ministry of Healing is part of the commission given by our Lord to the Church. It is not the priest who heals—Christ heals through the power of the Holy Spirit and the priest is His representative. The priest administers Unction and the Laying-on-of-Hands just as he administers any Sacrament because he is an

[7] *The Book of Common Prayer, p. 320.*

agent for Christ. When a call comes, he accepts it naturally as part of his Ministry. If circumstances permit, he directs the patient to make a particular confession, or he may use the General Confession, after which he pronounces absolution. He recites a verse or two from the Scriptures, like the text from St. James, and offers appropriate prayers. Holy Communion may be given to the patient. Then he makes the sign of the cross upon the patient's forehead as he says, "As with this visible oil thy body is outwardly anointed, so may our Heavenly Father grant of His infinite mercy that thy soul inwardly may be anointed with the Holy Ghost, who is the Source of all strength and power." Then he lays his hands upon the patient's head pronouncing a benediction. Extempore prayer may properly be used quite freely. Not often is it possible to do all of this. Selection must be made to fit the circumstances.

A word to the laity. Do not hesitate to call upon your priest for this ministry any more than to call in your physician. You should do both. Lend your support to the Ministry of Healing by your prayers, for the corporate faith of the Church provides the atmosphere in which it operates most effectively. Parish prayer circles are an enormous help. They are composed of groups of people who pray for the sick in the parish and meet at appointed times in the Church to unite their intercessions. We cannot do better than to quote from one of the best books on this subject which has yet come into print: "In regard to the laity, one finds that Prayer Circles, formed for the purpose of praying for the sick, are springing up in many parishes, and are very faithfully attended. The pioneer work done during the last twenty-five years has convinced large numbers of the laity that Spiritual Healing can be found within the borders of their Church, and their requests to receive this great blessing from Christ, through His Church, are now so numerous that it is becoming clear that this work can no longer be left to such a limited number of priests as it is at present."[8]

[8] R. A. Richard Spread, *"Stretching Forth Thine Hand to Heal,"* Skeffington, London.

XXI

ETERNAL LIFE

EVERY one of us will die—some day. To some people this is a terrifying thought—so terrifying that they refuse to make room for it in their minds. They say they would rather think of pleasant things. So they bring up their children with a shrinking aversion to the very idea of death, and teach them to live in a state of self-delusion. Then one day death strikes near at hand. Totally unprepared for it, these unwilling mourners are overwhelmed, stricken, broken in spirit by something which they might very well have anticipated. If there were any possibility of escaping death, there might be some sense in ignoring it. But of all the things which may or may not happen to us, death is absolutely certain. When we know something is sure to occur, ordinary judgment tells us to face it frankly and be ready for it. When we are dealing with the facts of life, there is no use evading the one fact which is clearly inescapable.

The common attitude toward death assumes that it is invariably a calamity. Look at it the other way—suppose there were no such thing as death? In one of his essays Stephen Leacock pictures a world in which disease and old age had been conquered and natural death abolished. Accidents were the only perils to life, and they became the single cause of popular anxiety. Anything which might produce an accident was carefully removed. Motor vehicles were forbidden —railroads, automobiles, street cars, airplanes—elevators were discarded; machinery was reduced to a minimum; sharp instruments were not allowed. Civilization slowed down to a creep and drowsed along in the one universal concern of keeping alive. With no one dying the question of over-population soon became acute. Births had to be abolished, and it presently became a childless world. People lived interminable years heavy with the accumulated wisdom of endless old age. Youthful enthusiasms were unknown because there were no youths. The spirit of adventure was lost. There were no fresh faces, no spring-time courting, no gaiety, no zest in life—only quantities of aged wisdom. Who would want to live in such a world—where there was no death?

Is it really such a fearful thing? Why should people be afraid of it? Is it because it is accompanied with so much suffering? As a matter of fact it isn't. Most deaths are far more peaceful than the illnesses and accidents from which we recover. Is it because it means separation? There are many separations in life which are far more tragic than those which accompany death. Is it because it disrupts our plans and interferes with what we are working for? The answer is that we should always take death into our calculations, and lay out our plans accordingly.

No—the real reason is that we have admitted death into our minds as the direct antithesis of life. We cherish life, therefore we shun death. But if life continues through and after death, we cannot think of them in opposite, contradictory terms. The only basis for the fear of death is the absence of any faith in immortal life. Death is a point of transfer —it is not the end of the line.

Some sort of belief in immortality has prevailed among all kinds of people everywhere. Since the dawn of human history there has been a strange universality about the conviction that death cannot be the end of all things. To be sure there have been individuals who have denied it and some sporadic systems of philosophy which have ignored it, but they are mere trickles in the broad stream of human assurance. There is something instinctive about it and men have gathered up reasons to support their instinct. They find their own intellectual and spiritual capacity so much greater than anything they can achieve in this life that they know there must be more life to come. Their moral attainments on earth fall so far short of their moral desires that it would be irrational to suppose they could stop when earthly life ceases. And then there is the claim of justice. In this world too many people wax fat and prosperous on the fruits of iniquity, while decent folk endure storms and tribulations. There must be something more beyond this perplexing world or justice itself becomes a cruel phantom.

That this is more than a matter of wishful thinking is borne out by our knowledge of ourselves. I know that I am more than a collection of chemical elements which dissolves at the touch of death because I learn that I can rise above so many physical handicaps. I may lose an arm or a leg, but I am just as much "I" as I ever was. As a matter of fact I wear out several physical bodies in the course of a lifetime, but though

I may shuffle off bodies, I still retain my own identity. The physical particles of my brain dissolve and are replaced by new cells, but my memory still carries on. The music is not the violin, though the musician may use the instrument to express the melody. I may be conditioned by my body but I am not identified with it. Knock off the chains of a prisoner and the man himself goes on unchained. If I can live through several bodies and if my identity remains constant even with a partial body, then I myself am more than my body or any part of it. My body may be mortal but I am not.

When we speak of the "immortal soul" it is something hard to define because nobody has ever been able to isolate and analyze it. It means the life-essence, including reason, memory, will, personal identity, self-consciousness—what is signified when we say "I." To make a human being this soul is encased in a human body, but the more we know about life in general, the more we realize that the soul has an existence of its own superior to its bodily container. Sometimes an accident occurs to the brain effectually blocking the ordinary mental processes. But a circuit may be gradually built up around the injured member and the mind begins to function again as clearly as before the injury. Certainly it indicates that the soul of the person remained active and intact though the instrument through which it expressed itself was temporarily disabled. Or there is that strange phenomenon which we call telepathy. It is now quite well established that communication does occur between persons without recourse to the usual physical agencies. If the soul can rise above physical limitations even in the human stage of life, certainly there is good reason to believe that it does not perish with the dissolution of the physical body.

This is all well and good as far as it goes but it is not nearly enough for the Christian. To him the immortality of the soul may be a reasonable expectation but he cannot be satisfied with anything less than eternal life, which is something far greater. To be sure that life continues after death might not in itself be a very desirable assurance. Many a hard-pressed person would look forward with dismay to the endless continuance of a life which meant only worry, and care, and a burden to him. If he could not anticipate a better kind of life, he might well prefer to be done with it. Mere endlessness might be a horror rather than a blessing.

That is where Christ comes in with His gift of eternal life which means quality as well as duration. Eternal life means life from above which carries with it the experience of vital fellowship with God. Christ possesses it in full measure, and He imparts it to those who accept Him and enter His Kingdom. "As the Father hath life in Himself; so hath He given to the Son to have life in Himself."[1] And "God so loved the world that He gave His only begotten Son, that whosoever believeth in Him should not perish, but have eternal life."[2] —or as the Authorized Version has it, "everlasting" life, but the two words are the same. It is something which begins now and continues into eternity. "We know that we have passed from death unto life."[3] Here the distinction is not between existence and non-existence but between spiritual destitution and living fellowship with God. This is what St.

[1] *St. John 5:26.*
[2] *St. John 3:16.*
[3] *I John 3:14.*

Paul meant when he said "the wages of sin is death; but the gift of God is eternal life through Jesus Christ our Lord."[4] Our Lord Himself summed it up in His final intercessory prayer—"This is life eternal, that they may know Thee the only true God, and Jesus Christ, whom Thou hast sent."[5] Eternal life is a participation in the divine nature. It is the gift of God to the Christian disciple by the Holy Spirit and must be nourished after it has been received. "Ye must be born again,"[6] said our Lord, and "whoso eateth my Flesh, and drinketh my Blood, hath eternal life."[7]

The study of evolution shows successive stages in the advancement of the created world with certain clear-cut and unaccountable breaks between the stages. It checks in quite consistently with renewed applications of God's creative power. At the beginning was the inanimate, inorganic world —the rocks and the hills and the minerals—with nothing present of what we call "life." This was followed by vegetation and organic life. There is no connection between the two. The one does not come out of the other. Some new force entered in—another touch of God's creative power raising creation to a new level. Later appeared animal life, something new and different from vegetable life. Once again another force broke in—another evidence of God's creative power rising to another level of creation. Came the time when human life appeared. It was something intrinsically different from animal life and without any essential connection in spite of physical similarities. Something had happened

[4] *Romans 6:23.*
[5] *St. John 17:3.*
[6] *St. John 3:7.*
[7] *St. John 6:54.*

for which no theory of evolution can account. A new force came in—God's creative power again in action and another level of creation attained. But that was not the end of it. In the fulness of time that same divine creative energy was once more manifested in the gift of eternal life. A still higher level was reached. A new kind of life was imparted. It is a life which could not be evoked out of human conditions by natural means but is a gift from above.

This is what the Christian means by eternal life. To be sure it is immortal but much more than immortal. It is possessed of divine qualities, beginning here and rising to limitless heights hereafter. It is not merely a prolongation of existence, but the purification and intensification of life through direct and intimate connection with the Source of all living.

"What shall it profit a man, if he shall gain the whole world, and lose his own soul?"[8] It is a question of simple foresight. Any person of sound judgment will relinquish a temporary benefit if it involves a future loss, or, conversely, he will accept an immediate sacrifice if it promises a greater benefit in the future. What would you say of a young man who spent his year's income on high living in the month of January, knowing that he would starve the rest of the year? To say the least, you would call him foolish. Even the squirrels do better than that, as they lay up a winter's supply of food in advance. Yet there are plenty of attractive and otherwise intelligent people who immerse themselves in the affairs of this world without ever a thought for the life-to-come.

We are often warned against the dangers of too much "other-worldliness." We have often been told that in the

[8] *St. Mark 8:36.*

old days the Church concerned itself with too much teaching about the beauties of heaven and too little about the human needs of this world. There may be some merit in the criticism, but it scarcely warrants us in flying off to the other extreme where we drop even below the instincts of a squirrel.

We need to remember that life is a continuous process, beginning here and continuing hereafter, with an experience between which we call death. There is a distinct connection between the two. We can dispense with the childish mathematical idea that so many bad deeds in this world will cost us just so much in the world-to-come. But we cannot escape the plain logic that a bad life here handicaps us for a good life there. St. Paul pictures it in terms of the seed which is planted and disappears as a seed but reappears as grain.[9] Poor seed is bound to produce poor grain. Likewise an evil life on earth is bound to make an unfortunate carry-over into the future life. That is the plainest common sense.

Our problem is to cultivate that aspect of human life which has eternal worth. It is a matter of proportionate values. Which is of greater significance—earthly things that perish or spiritual things that do not perish? Life may have many uncertainties but one point is sure—namely, that there are no pockets in shrouds, and you will leave behind you your possessions when you die.

Our Lord tells us that this world is properly a preparation for a better world to come and that we must learn how to fit the one into the other. If He were here today, He would undoubtedly warn us against the success artists who go about

[9] *I Corinthians 15:35-44.*

preaching a shallow psychology of self-assertion. "Blow your own trumpet," they proudly declaim, "magnify your importance, inflate your ego, claim everything, act as though you owned the world, and soon someone will come and give it to you."

Well, suppose someone did come and give you the world, what will you do with it when you die?

Said our Lord, "A man's life consisteth not in the abundance of the things which he possesseth,"[10] but rather "seek ye first the Kingdom of God."[11] Sixty generations of Christians attest the truth of His solution.

[10] *St. Luke 12:15.*
[11] *St. Matthew 6:33.*

XXII

PARADISE

ONE DAY I received a pathetic letter from a woman who was engaged in a struggle between her conscience and her natural instincts. Someone had died whom she loved dearly and for whom she had always been accustomed to pray. She had been taught that the souls of the departed go straight to heaven where their final destiny is settled at once, and that it is wrong to pray for them. Yet it seemed like a violation of her best instincts to stop praying for that person. She was in a quandary as to what she ought to do.

Certainly we ought to pray for one another. Is there any good reason for us to cease because death intervenes? There is nothing in the Bible that says so, and for fifteen centuries Christians never thought of such a thing. Four hundred years ago the question arose out of a harsh teaching of Purgatory which was developed during the Middle Ages. Along with it came a theory of a Treasury of Merits and Indulgences which set up a mechanical system offering every inducement to widespread abuse. As a money-making scheme it had its points, but the spiritual effects were disastrous. This was the occasion of Martin Luther's original outburst, and the response which ensued tore western Christendom apart. In the

Eastern Orthodox Church no such issue was raised because they never shared these purgatorial ideas. Under this system the commercializing of prayers and intercessions for the dead provoked such a violent reaction that many Christians lost all sense of distinction between the spiritual reality and the artificial system which had been added. As a result they abandoned all thought of an Intermediate State after death, assumed that all souls went directly to heaven, and called an abrupt halt to prayers for one another as soon as death occurred. It is hard to overcome the prejudices which are born in a period of bitter strife, and we shall do better if we retrace our steps to the earlier days before these fiery differences appeared.

In the time of our Lord's ministry the Jews had several terms which they used for the abode of departed souls— Sheol, Hades, Abraham's Bosom, Paradise. The most common of these was Hades which in the Authorized Version of the Bible is translated "hell." But as we have already seen, language grows, and in the course of time words take on new shades of meaning. At the beginning of the seventeenth century the word "hell" had no such ominous significance as it has since acquired. It meant the place of waiting souls, not a place of eternal punishment. The Revised Version of the Scriptures notes the distinction far more accurately. When in the Apostles Creed we say that our Lord after His crucifixion "descended into hell," the phrase is made clear by a rubric in the Prayer Book which says it means "He went into the place of departed spirits." It means neither "hell" nor "heaven," but the Intermediate State which we usually call Paradise.

To the thief on the cross our Lord gave the promise, "To-day shalt thou be with Me in paradise."[1] But after His resurrection He said to Mary Magdalene, "I am not yet ascended to my Father."[2] Evidently there was something between this world and the final blessedness of heaven.

So the Church understood, and so the Church taught in the early period of Christian history. There are three stages of life—first, the probationary stage in this world; second, the waiting stage in Paradise; third, the final completion in heaven. In the parable of Dives and Lazarus the latter was carried after his death into Abraham's Bosom, the former was in Hades (not hell, in the modern sense).[3] Allowing for all the imagery in the parable, it does indicate a difference of condition for the two men but not necessarily a final judgment. The various features of this parable are thoroughly Jewish so that the whole story fits in with the Jewish conception of a waiting period before the "great day of the Lord." Our Lord did not return to the Father immediately after His crucifixion, but St. Peter says He preached the Gospel "also to them that are dead."[4] If our ultimate destiny is really determined at the moment of death, what reason would there be for preaching the Gospel to the dead? The only sensible interpretation, and the one which has always prevailed, is that those who died before our Lord came into this world were not to be deprived of the benefits of the Gospel, and that they were in some waiting state capable of receiving such benefits and profiting by them.

[1] *St. Luke 23:43.*
[2] *St. John 20:17.*
[3] *St. Luke 16:19–31.*
[4] *I Peter 4:6.*

All through the writings of the early Church Fathers it appears again and again—an Intermediate State for waiting souls. For fifteen centuries that was the common teaching of the Church which has been obscured in modern times by the reaction from serious abuses as noted above. To be sure speculations have been numerous as to details and implications of the doctrine. Difficulties always arise when we attempt to particularize about the future life in Paradise. Most likely we, with our limited human understanding, would not be able to grasp it even if reliable information were forthcoming. We may, however, draw a few general conclusions both negative and positive.

Materialistic considerations are quite inappropriate. It is a spiritual state, not a place in any sense of time or space. Of course, this is beyond our power to visualize. Paradise as a location is purely a figure of speech. There is no reason to anticipate anything like physical suffering. When we say that the dead are "at rest," or are "fallen asleep," we are again using figures of speech. It is not an inactive, comatose condition but one in which the cares and turmoil of this world are relieved. Whether there can be communication with those who are on the other side is a complicated question. On the face of it, there is no reason why there might not be. It is quite possible that under certain circumstances a breaking-through might occur, and it is not impossible that some people in this world might be peculiarly sensitive to spiritual impulses from the other world. But any such manifestations will depend upon the laws of the other life and will originate there. Spiritistic efforts to command the attention of departed souls is a presumptuous trifling with the laws of God. Fraud and chicanery have been discovered too often to justify much confidence in such attempts. Even if they could be proved, they have no necessary religious value, any more than a telephone conversation is necessarily religious. It might deal with religious subjects, in which case it would have some sort of religious significance. But there is nothing religious about table-tipping, board-knocking, or directions for finding lost jewelry.

In positive terms a few points may be made about the future life in Paradise.

1. Personal identity will be retained in a conscious life. "It is I myself" said our Lord after His resurrection.[5] When He promised the thief on the cross that they would be together in Paradise, it would have been a cruel jest if He meant nothing more than oblivion. This "I" which transcends physical deficiencies here on earth could scarcely be obliterated by passing through death. Whatever survives, "I" will survive, and it will be the same kind of "I" that developed in earthly life. If I have been selfish, vicious, dishonest and unChristian in this world, how can I expect that death will suddenly reverse the trend of character which I have deliberately constructed? As Paterson-Smyth puts it, "acts make habits and habits make character and character makes destiny." When I enter Paradise I shall be the same kind of person I have been here. It is to be expected, then, that since personal identity continues in a conscious life, we shall recognize one another in the future life.

2. There will be further growth and progress in Paradise. Certainly there needs to be. Not one of us would consider

[5] *St. Luke 24:39.*

himself really fit for heaven at the end of his earthly life. If character persists, we are all conscious of imperfections in our own characters which will need straightening out, and of moral and spiritual blemishes which will require eradication. Advancement "from glory to glory" does not cease at the end of our earthly life. Just how much of another chance this may mean for those who have ignored their Christian opportunities in this world we may not know. The fact remains that life here is truly a probationary period in which we set a course for the future. A person who consistently turns his back on God, throttles his better impulses, chooses evil rather than good, and refuses all of Christ's offers—such a person is guilty of the "sin against the Holy Ghost" which cannot very well be forgiven "neither in this world, neither in the world to come"[6] because in the nature of the case he is not susceptible of forgiveness. Such instances, we may trust, are rare. Most wrongs are the result of weakness, faulty judgment, or the pressure of difficult circumstances. These may well be subject to correction in the clearer and cleaner atmosphere of Paradise.

3. In Paradise there will be active service to be rendered to God. It is impossible to think that we would be expected to serve God in this world and then slip into a state of eternal sloth on the other side of death. A freer and less restricted life should mean greater and keener service. Our Lord commands us to love our fellowmen, and to be forever diligent in our missionary efforts to carry His Gospel to them. It would not be Paradise with love excluded, and with it the incentive to help one another. Souls will not find a comfortable

[6] *St. Matthew 12:32*

haven where they may enjoy their selfish ease, indifferent to the needs of backward strugglers. There would be nothing Christian about that. As in other matters Christ set an example in this also when He preached His own Gospel to departed souls. At the end of His earthly ministry He instructed His disciples to take up what He had begun and spread His Kingdom to the ends of the world. We may be sure He will expect some similar missionary enterprise in the future life. Too many humorists have drawn caricatures of winged people decorated with halos, sitting on damp clouds, picking out dreamy melodies on harps. They are, of course, misusing the symbolic pictures found in the Apocalypse. They might better give attention to another picture in the same book of those who have passed through tribulation to the throne of God where "they serve Him day and night."[7]

4. In Paradise we shall be with Christ. Just what all that may mean we cannot tell. "Now we see through a glass, darkly; but then face to face: now I know in part; but then shall I know even as also I am known."[8] Our faith in Christ and our partial knowledge of Him in this present life are the most ennobling elements of human experience. How much more so when the veil is lifted, and the mists are dissolved, and our vague gropings become ascertained reality!

Now and then we meet a fine personality whose presence is a benediction. Wherever he goes something good emanates from him. As he enters a group discords cease and a spirit of harmony, confidence, and goodwill prevails. We say we would always like to be in his company. Multiply

[7] *Revelation 7:15.*
[8] *I Corinthians 13:12.*

that indefinitely, and you get a slight foretaste of what it will mean to "be with Christ." Sometimes in an exalted moment of prayer or in an intense sacramental experience you are lifted out of yourself, time ceases, and you are absorbed in an instant of spiritual concentration. It gives you a suggestion of what eternity means in contrast with time, and what the eternal presence of Christ may mean when human distractions have been left behind. On the Mount of Transfiguration St. Peter said, "Master, it is good for us to be here."[9] That was a fleeting glimpse into the life-to-come. It will be better for us to be there.

Human curiosity might like to delve more deeply into the condition of the life that awaits us, but it is probably just as well that we have no particulars about it. It is too easy for people to grow morbid or hysterically sentimental. We are simply not equipped to comprehend the spiritual realm, and it is not surprising that our Lord discussed it only in parables and metaphorical statements. Nevertheless, in view of the assurances which we do possess, we can frankly face the question at the beginning of this chapter about prayers for the dead. It was an accepted custom among the Jews. If our Lord had disapproved of it, certainly there would have been some indication of His disapproval. On the contrary He seems to have taken it for granted, and His early followers found it entirely consonant with their Christian profession. For instance there is St. Paul's letter to St. Timothy in which he refers to one Onesiphorus who had been kind to him. Twice he sends greetings not to Onesiphorus himself but to his family. Evidently the man was dead, yet St. Paul prays for

[9] *St. Mark 9:5.*

him—"the Lord grant unto him that he may find mercy of the Lord in that day."[10] If there had been anything unchristian about the practice, St. Paul would have been quick to condemn it. Inscriptions on the catacombs show how thin the separation was felt to be between Christians in this world and their departed brethren for whom they continued to pray. The early Christian Fathers commended it in their writings, and it became an established custom throughout the Church.

The Communion of Saints is a cardinal doctrine of the Christian faith. The Gospel tells us plainly that the separation of death is superficial and temporary. The Kingdom of God is a spiritual realm. It penetrates human life but extends far beyond it. His spiritual laws can by no means be confined to that portion of His Kingdom which appears in the world of human affairs. We pray for one another in this earthly life. What logical reason can there be for stopping it when death removes certain of our number from human sight? Why should we stop praying for them or why should they stop praying for us? Does our love for our dear ones cease because they die? If Christ deserved reverence and adoration as God incarnate during His earthly ministry, does He deserve anything less because He was crucified? To pray for our dear ones while they are in the flesh and to stop it abruptly when they enter Paradise is a serious wrench upon our human sensibilities which is hard to reconcile with Christ's emphasis on eternal life. We may know little of their condition or their needs, but every Christian instinct tells us that our prayers

[10] *II Timothy 1:18.*

for them are acceptable to God who is their Creator as well as ours.

Thus in the Communion Office in the Prayer Book—"we also bless Thy holy Name for all Thy servants departed this life in Thy faith and fear; beseeching Thee to grant them continued growth in Thy love and service." And in the Burial office—"Remember Thy servant, O Lord, according to the favour which Thou bearest unto Thy people, and grant that, increasing in knowledge and love of Thee, he may go from strength to strength, in the life of perfect service, in Thy heavenly kingdom."

XXIII

JUDGMENT, HELL, AND HEAVEN

THE THESSALONIANS had earned a mild rebuke—at least some of them had. They focused their attention so closely upon the second coming of Christ that they twisted their spiritual vision out of its proper perspective. They figured that if Christ were likely to return any day, it did not much matter whether they applied themselves to their daily vocations. So they grew neglectful and indolent—waiting for the Lord. St. Paul wrote a letter to set them straight. Yes, he told them, some day Christ would come, but the time of His coming was no concern of theirs. They must attend to their affairs and be ready for Him whenever He might come. They were not to indulge in futile speculations for "the day of the Lord so cometh as a thief in the night."[1] They would do better to leave that to God, and "study to be quiet, and to do your own business."[2]

Certainly it was good advice which might well be followed by prophetically-minded persons of our own day who insist on playing tricks with the Holy Scriptures and setting dates for the Second Advent. Recurrent announcements of

[1] *I Thessalonians 5:2.*
[2] *I Thessalonians 4:11.*

the end of the world which fail to materialize have led many people to laugh off the whole idea of a second coming of our Lord. The predictions may be ridiculous, but the coming of Christ is definitely part of the Christian Gospel. Obviously there will be an end of the world sometime. When it does occur, Christ will take charge in a fitting climax to the drama of creation. He said so repeatedly to His apostles. When at His trial the high priest placed Him under solemn oath, He declared, "Hereafter shall ye see the Son of man sitting on the right hand of power, and coming in the clouds of heaven."[3] At the time of the Ascension the Apostles were told, "This same Jesus which is taken up from you into heaven, shall so come in like manner as ye have seen Him go into heaven."[4] Said St. Paul to the Corinthians—"Then cometh the end, when He shall have delivered up the Kingdom to God, even the Father."[5] And to the Thessalonians—"the Lord Himself shall descend from heaven with a shout, with the voice of the archangel, and with the trump of God."[6] Of course the language is pictorial but the event itself is clearly forecast. Meantime we are living in the millennium, the Christian dispensation which is now going on. The millennium does not mean a literal thousand years. These figures are symbolical. The number "one thousand" means a very great many years—nobody knows how many. Christ reigns on earth now, and His kingdom is gradually winning the ascendency in a world of mixed values.

Someday it will end in a great divine transformation when

[3] *St. Matthew 26:63–64.*
[4] *Acts 1:11.*
[5] *I Corinthians 15:24.*
[6] *I Thessalonians 4:16.*

two notable events will occur—the general resurrection and the general judgment, both of which have been grossly misconstrued by popular cartooning of the last things. We say in the Creed that we believe "in the resurrection of the dead," and many people promptly jump to the conclusion that Christians look for a magical reassembling of disintegrated bones to be reconditioned into bodies of flesh and blood—all of which strikes them as absurd. Our Lord did say—"thou shalt be recompensed at the resurrection of the just,"[7] and again "the hour is coming, in the which all that are in the graves shall hear His voice, and shall come forth; they that have done good, unto the resurrection of life; and they that have done evil, unto the resurrection of damnation."[8] St. Paul spends some time explaining this in the passage we often read for the burial service. It is like a grain planted in the ground which must die, go to pieces, disappear before the new growth can arise out of the dead seed—"God giveth it a body as it hath pleased Him, and to every seed his own body."[9] In the resurrection life a complete personality will need an instrument through which to express itself and that instrument shall be for that life what corresponds to a flesh-and-blood body in this world. There may be a connection between the two, but they will be quite different as St. Paul himself points out in this same passage—"flesh and blood cannot inherit the kingdom of God."[10] It will be a spiritual body, glorified and incorruptible, in contrast with

[7] *St. Luke 14:14.*
[8] *St. John 5:28–29.*
[9] *I Corinthians 15:38.*
[10] *I Corinthians 15:50.*

the natural body. Of course we cannot explain the process. Nobody can tell just what matter is anyhow or what it is possible to do with it. The doctrine of the resurrection does place a touch of sanctity on the human body as in some sense the germ of the resurrection body. It is not a matter of indifference to the Christian how he treats his human body for it is "the temple of the Holy Ghost."[11]

There has been a great deal of by-play concerning the Judgment Day but no one can read the Christian Bible without facing it. As rational beings equipped with a sense of moral values, we are responsible for our actions, our habits, and the characters which grow out of them. It would be unreasonable for us to think of God providing us with certain standards of life and then paying no attention to the way in which we used them. God has built a universe designed to operate according to moral and spiritual laws. He must be true to Himself. We expect Him to keep His promises of mercy and loving-kindness. How can we expect Him to ignore the claims of simple justice? Our confidence in the divine order would vanish very quickly if we were to believe we could get away with violations of God's laws as we please without ever being called to account. It is not a matter of vindictive punishment but of inevitable penalty. So our Lord declares—"the Son of Man shall come in the glory of His Father with His angels; and then He shall reward every man according to his works."[12] St. Paul said that God "hath appointed a day, in the which He will judge the world in righteousness by that Man whom He hath ordained."[13] St.

[11] *I Corinthians 6:19.*
[12] *St. Matthew 16:27.*
[13] *Acts 17:31.*

Peter testified that "it is He which was ordained of God to be the Judge of quick and dead."[14]

This judgment goes on day by day in our earthly lives. We are constantly writing our own record of rights and wrongs. At death comes a summing up in what we call the *particular judgment* based on the quality of character we may have achieved in our earthly progress. The correcting, purifying, strengthening process goes on for waiting souls in Paradise. Finally comes the *general judgment* which our Lord presents in the well-known picture of separating the sheep from the goats while He says to those on the right hand "Come, ye blessed of my Father," and to those on the left hand "Depart . . . ye cursed."[15]

Always we must remember that these pictures are symbols —the Great Assize, the sheep and the goats, the opening of the records and so on. We run to all manner of extravagances when we attempt to apply them literally to God in His judicial capacity. What it means is that there will be a final reckoning and a final disposition of men's lives in whatever way and by whatever method God deems to be best. There will be no rule-of-thumb decisions such as we are obliged to follow in our inadequate human judgments. In our manmade legal systems we deal with overt acts and consequently commit endless blunders. In the wisdom of God motives, purposes, and intentions receive due consideration. The things that we have done are not the whole of it. Very bad people can often do good things and *vice versa*. That's why

[14] *Acts 10:42.*
[15] *St. Matthew 25:31–46.*

we say that we are not saved by works but by faith—faith being the determining purpose behind our deeds. Any rascal can go through the motions of an honest Christian without any Christian intention to give reality to what he does. On the other hand, people who mean the best may be pressed by force of circumstances into equivocal situations which can hardly be explained. We are incapable of judging them accurately because there is so much that we do not know. But God does know and will know. That's what our Lord must have meant when He said to the chief priests—"the publicans and the harlots go into the Kingdom of God before you."[16]

Christ will be our Judge, and His justice will be tempered with the mercy which comes from sympathetic understanding. He too lived a human life and faced its problems—"for we have not an high priest which cannot be touched with the feeling of our infirmities; but was in all points tempted like as we are."[17]

Beyond that we cannot say much. There will be a Judgment. It will be real justice mitigated by the atoning mercy of our Saviour's redemption. There will be no appeal—to whom could one appeal above God? Heaven and hell will be opened. Christ said so.

HELL

Around the city of Jerusalem on three sides runs a deep valley. The southern portion of it is known as the Valley of Hinnom. The Hebrew word for valley is "Ge," and combined with the name "Hinnom" it gives "Ge-hinnom,"

---

[16] *St. Matthew 21:31.*
[17] *Hebrews 4:15.*

which was transposed into Greek and so into English in the form, Gehenna.

Seven centuries before Christ an evil king named Manasseh reigned in Jerusalem who for a time corrupted the religion of Israel even to the point of introducing human sacrifice. These horrible rites were held in the Valley of Hinnom. When the good king Josiah came to the throne he abolished all such practices and formally defiled the place where they had been carried on. The Valley of Hinnom became unholy ground full of evil memories. It was turned into a dumping place for the refuse of the city where a fire burned day and night consuming the useless things which were cast out for destruction. This is the history of the name Gehenna which has been translated "hell" in the English Bible.

It is easy to see what His hearers must have understood when our Lord spoke about certain ones being "cast into hell, (Gehenna) into the fire that never shall be quenched; where their worm dieth not, and the fire is not quenched."[18] Certainly He was not indicating a place of physical agony— of flames and brimstone and little devils armed with pitchforks. Some of these fanciful accessories have been drawn from the Apocalypse which is all symbolical, and the rest have come from sources outside the Scriptures which have nothing whatever to do with Christian teaching. Our Lord was issuing a solemn warning that stubborn resistance to the will of God made people spiritually worthless, fit for such a rubbish-pile as might be seen any day at the foot of the cliff in Gehenna.

The words "hell" and "damn" have hardened into mean-

[18] *St. Mark 9:45-46.*

ings which they never had when the English Bible was translated, and which have never been intended in Christian
teaching. Damnation means simply an adverse judgment.
Hell means the receptacle for lost souls—those that have
made themselves worthless. In one way or another both
words have acquired a flavor of profanity though there is
really no particular reason for it in either case. The extrava-
gant sulphurous trimmings have largely extracted the reality
out of hell, and people make jokes about it without giving
it much serious consideration. This is unfortunate, for the
real Christian teaching about hell is a definitely serious
matter.

The moral malignity of sin is nothing to be laughed away.
Persisted in, it disqualifies one for the company of God.
There is a strain of severity in the Christian Gospel as well as
of love and mercy. Indeed the love and mercy would be
softly unreal without the stiffening presence of judgment and
penalty. Said our Lord to the hypocritical scribes and Phari-
sees, "Ye serpents, ye generation of vipers, how can ye escape
the damnation of hell?"[19]—how can ye escape the judgment
of the worthless? Those are grave words. There is a hell for
those who are finally impenitent. They will be excluded
from the company of their more honest brethren and will
be denied a place in the household of God. They will suffer
loss of spiritual privileges and will be consigned to a state of
unhappy deprivation. How could it be otherwise? If we
flout the God of all life, can we expect it will make no difference in the end? That would be the abrogation of all justice
and would make a mockery of the very essence of moral

[19] *St. Matthew 23:33.*

responsibility. There is such a thing as spiritual retribution. Not because God wants to get even with us but because He must be true to Himself. Just what it will comprise, we do not know. The Scriptures are reticent about describing it, and our Lord discussed it in parables. But there it is, a solemn and serious fact.

Will it really go on forever and ever through all eternity? There are the words of Christ "these shall go away into ever-lasting punishment: but the righteous into life eternal."[20] The two words "everlasting" and "eternal" mean the same thing, and as we have already pointed out, they have to do with quality rather than duration. It is difficult for us to think that God's purposes will not be completely successful in the long run or that there can be two conflicting states, one of righteousness and one of unrighteousness, existing forever in clear opposition to each other. St. Paul says that "God may be all in all,"[21] and somehow that must come to pass. So far as the Holy Scriptures are concerned, it remains an unanswered question. The best we can do is to leave it so, knowing that God has a way of working out even seeming contradictions, and He has not seen fit to tell us how. Of this much Christ assures us plainly—that unrepented rebellion against God faces a final penalty commensurate with the gravity of the offense. It may not be diluted with the off-hand remark that, "I get my hell in this world with the troubles I have to bear." Perhaps it finds its beginning here, but Christ is talking about something far more important in the future life of eternity.

[20] *St. Matthew 25:46.*
[21] *I Corinthians 15:28.*

HEAVEN

Golden streets, pearly gates, shining towers, with St. Peter standing guard at the entrance somewhere far off in the bright blue sky—it is a familiar but not exactly stimulating picture for one who is accustomed to a vigorous, robust life in this world. We always run aground when we try to turn poetry into prose. Because heaven is far beyond our limited imagination, prophets and poets have been obliged to depict their visions in terms of what we count most brilliant, and beautiful, and intrinsically valuable in our everyday living. Neither everyday life nor its sundry accompaniments can be transferred to heaven. Our allegorical anticipations are not and cannot be descriptions. "Eye hath not seen, nor ear heard, neither have entered into the heart of man, the things which God hath prepared for them that love Him."[22]

In our contemplation of eternal realities we simply *must* clear our minds of the possessive idea. Grubbing along as we do in this earthly sphere to snatch a living out of modern society, we sink ourselves into a struggle for goods and chattels until nothing else seems to count. Experience does its best to correct us but we still persist in the same old blunders. Having expended our energies in the acquisition of wealth, position or power, we discover that they are incapable of producing the happiness which is the object of our pursuit. Yet we still keep on. And when we think of heaven we wrap up our minds in notions of things to be had and special privileges to be enjoyed. But heaven means to be something

[22] *I Corinthians 2:9*

rather than to get something. It is concerned with character, not possessions.

The pious soul may be happy with the thought of heaven as a perpetual existence filled with incandescent bliss. To most of us that does not mean much. Whatever the best may mean to any of us, heaven will be that multiplied indefinitely. God's will shall be done perfectly, not as an extraordinary achievement but as a normal fact. Theologians call it the *Beatific Vision,* which is a technical way of saying that what we glimpse as a faint reflection in our best moments will be our natural portion there. Selfishness, and jealousy, and envy, and all such human annoyances will have been sponged out together with the causes of them. Happiness for one will not be obtained by the contrast of less happiness for another. There will be an abundance for all. Yet this will not mean a monotonous, dead level of existence. Our Lord hinted, "in my Father's house are many mansions."[23] We cannot analyze this but we can see where something of the kind would be right and good.

There will be no sorrow in heaven. How could there be? Sorrows come from accidents and maladjustments which turn our hopes into disappointments. Where our hopes coincide with the will of God and His will is assured, neither maladjustments nor disappointments are possible. For the same reason there will be no sin in heaven, and its blighting consequences will not cloud memories or raise regrets. There will be work to be done, not as a burden and care with anxiety as to the results, but as constructive service of the Heavenly Father always fruitful and always satisfying.

[23] *St. John 14:2.*

People sometimes say—my heaven is here and now rather than there and then. There is no reason for any such contrast. It may be both because it is concerned with character which begins to be built in this life and continues to unfold in the hereafter. The "I" which God created in the first place is the same "I" which is finally redeemed, exalted, and perfected.

Does all this seem super-sweet, too good to be interesting, an over-refinement of excellence? What about the value of struggle against adverse circumstances? What about the stimulating benefits of uncertainty, the fortitude bred by the manly facing of failure and defeat? Such things give color and glamour to life as we know it. Are they all to be smothered in an eternity of debilitating security? No, they will all be there, but stripped of the grief, and the hurt, and the tragedy. Just how this will be, we may not know. But we may be sure that nothing good will be lost out of all God's creation. The human means by which these virtues are realized may be discarded with the conclusion of the human age, but the essence of the virtues remains for such expression as fits the heavenly life. Certainly there will be strength and fortitude, color and vigor, patience and perseverance, enthusiasms and aspirations. Far from being suppressed, they will be heightened, sharpened, and glorified. In this world they are mixed with evils, and it is hard for us to conceive of them without that context. In heaven the evils will be abolished—not the stirring interests.

God's purpose must come to pass just because it is God's purpose. It will be the absolute of all that is good, right, true, and beautiful. The when, the where, the how of it—that's what we call Heaven.

XXIV

THE SPIRITUAL WORLD

FAR DOWN beneath the surface of the sea a kind of life goes on which is totally different from that with which we are familiar on the upper surface of the globe. It is inhabited by creatures who have never seen the light of the sun nor felt the touch of the air. Their conditions of life are at such complete variance with those in which we live that they could not, in their wildest flights of imagination, conceive of air, and light, and dry land, and all the rest of it. Occasionally some inhabitant from the upper world may momentarily touch their realm of existence on a deep-sea diving expedition. Such a visitor might startle the denizens of the deep but would leave them in all their former blank ignorance as to what life on the higher level could mean.

Is there anything necessarily illogical in supposing that there may be still another level of existence above that in which we live and equally unknown to us? It might be a spiritual world peopled with persons of a very different nature, living in conditions which are quite beyond our comprehension, and which we could not understand if it were described to us because we have so little basis of comparison. Occasionally an inhabitant from this other world might touch our life here, but he would only startle us and leave us in the same state of ignorance.

It is something of this sort which we mean when we talk about angels. They are not disembodied spirits. We do not become angels when we die—an impression which is all too frequently planted in the minds of children. They are another order of creation, quite distinct from us in the human sphere. They are spiritual beings, possessed of different properties from ours, and serving a different purpose in the economy of God's universe. Is there any reason for thinking that creation ceased with man, that there are not other grades of created beings of which we are capable of knowing little or nothing?

Certainly anyone who takes the Bible seriously cannot escape the angels. They are frequently in evidence—visitants from God with some mission to perform in our human world. The word "angel" means messenger, one who is sent. Just as God uses human agents for certain aspects of His work, so He uses angelic agents for other purposes. There is nothing strange or eerie about it. We are part of God's creation, but not all of it, and not necessarily the summit of it. Every now and then there is a spell of popular discussion as to whether or not some of the other planets in the heavens might be inhabited. But we always go on the assumption that if they are inhabited, they must be occupied by human beings like ourselves. The question is, why should we be the only kind of beings to be considered? Conditions in other planets might not be at all suitable for our kind of life, but they might be eminently suitable for a different kind. And there may be other worlds in God's universe not dependent on any planet or other place but of a spiritual character unknown to us.

The angels are God's agents from a spiritual world which surrounds us. Through them God's will may be expressed to men, perhaps far more frequently than we realize. Now and then an angelic presence may be noticeable. It is not unlikely that we are influenced by them more often in quiet and unnoticeable ways. "Are they not all ministering spirits, sent forth to minister for them who shall be heirs of salvation?"[1] An angel came to encourage Joshua as he was about to lead the people of Israel into Canaan.[2] When Elijah was hiding for his life an angel came to help him.[3] The annunciation of our Saviour's birth was made to the Blessed Virgin Mary through an angel.[4] The "man of Macedonia" who urged St. Paul to carry the Gospel over into Europe was an angelic messenger.[5]

Such instances keep recurring over and over again. Sometimes the angels are in companies or "hosts" as those who sang praises to God on the night of the Nativity.[6] Indeed this is the reason for the title frequently assigned to God in the Old Testament, "the Lord of Hosts," meaning that He has multitudes of them at His command.[7] When St. Peter drew a sword to defend our Lord against the soldiers led by Judas Iscariot, Jesus told him to put it away because if He needed

---

[1] *Hebrews 1:14.*
[2] *Joshua 5:13–15.*
[3] *I Kings 19:5.*
[4] *St. Luke 1:26 ff.*
[5] *Acts 16:9.*
[6] *St. Luke 2:13.*
[7] *Psalms 24:10; Jeremiah 9:7; Amos 4:13.*

help He could call for "more than twelve legions of angels" to protect Him.[8]

Naturally there is a good deal of mystery about it which has been productive of much pious speculation. In the story of the Garden of Eden we read that Cherubims were placed, after the Man and the Woman were driven out, "to keep the way of the tree of life."[9] When Isaiah was called to his prophetic ministry by the "seraphims," one of them touched his lips with a live coal from the altar.[10]

Some are called archangels, and a few are given personal names like Gabriel or Michael.[11] St. Paul says that Christ is raised "far above all principality, and power, and might, and dominion,"[12] and that by Him all things were created in heaven and earth "visible and invisible, whether they be thrones, or dominions, or principalities, or powers."[13] Out of all this three hierarchies of angels have been deduced: first, Seraphim, Cherubim, and Thrones; second, Dominions, Virtues, and Powers; Third, Principalities, Archangels, and Angels. All of which is fanciful and poetic.

When we attempt to describe angels we are in difficulties and are driven to symbolic imagery. The usual sentimental picture is that of a female figure clothed in flowing white garments and equipped with large fleecy wings. As a matter of fact the angels are more probably sexless beings. White garments are symbols of purity. Wings are symbols of celerity in the service of God. We simply do not know what

[8] *St. Matthew 26:53.*
[9] *Genesis 3:24.*
[10] *Isaiah 6:6–7.*
[11] *St. Jude v. 9; St. Luke 2:26; Revelation 12:7.*
[12] *Ephesians 1:21.*
[13] *Colossians 1:16.*

angels look like or if they have any "looks" as we know them.

A significant statement was made by our Lord in speaking of little children—"I say unto you, That in heaven their angels do always behold the face of my Father which is in heaven."[14] It has been surmised from this that to every child is assigned a Guardian Angel who watches over him during his earthly life and safely conducts him into the future life. Whether so much can be warranted may be a question, but it does fit into the general scheme of things that through some sort of guardian angels God exercises His providential care over His people.

One cannot consider the question of angels on any Scriptural authority without giving consideration to the more somber reference to spiritual powers of evil. Here we are confronted with a confused mass of hysterical superstitions in which it is virtually impossible to find one's way about. It is not a pleasing story to trace the course of the fears and terrors which have gripped men's souls in their struggles with the darker side of life. The supposed traffic with evil spirits, the unreasoning fright over devils and hobgoblins, the gruesome witch-hunts which have stained the annals of man's inhumanity to man—all of these create disturbed and debasing episodes which we would much prefer to forget. The result is one of those typically popular reactions which lead people to throw everything overboard and deny the very existence of any powers of evil. The Devil is laughed away as the product of a fevered imagination, and evil spirits are consigned to the fictitious realm of childish ignorance.

[14] *St. Matthew 18:10.*

Frankly we cannot tell much about the world of darkness, but we dare not shut our eyes to it because we have a greater liking for all that is sweetness and light. There is a world of spirits in which the contest between right and wrong is relentlessly waged. "There was war in heaven: Michael and his angels fought against the dragon; and the dragon fought and his angels, and prevailed not."[15] Whatever this symbolical language may mean, it fits in with our Lord's reference to "the Devil and his angels"[16] and St. Peter's remark about "the angels that sinned."[17] Among the angelic hosts there were some who rebelled against God and were thrown into the category of "fallen angels." How, when, or under what circumstances, we may not know, but that they constituted an opposition to God's will and a menace to human welfare we cannot very well deny. Just as good angels would surround men and women with helpful influences, so would bad angels entice them into evil ways and afflict them for evil purposes. In the end, of course, God is victorious and the rebellion ceases, but in the meantime we are engaged in a spiritual contest between powers of good and powers of evil which tries our souls and tests our courage.

Not so long ago there was a tendency to minimize the accounts of our Lord's casting out of "unclean spirits" as an evidence of primitive demonology which had been quite discredited by modern knowledge. Those "possessed of evil spirits," so we were told, were merely mental cases subject to a greater or less degree of insanity. Perhaps they were.

[15] *Revelation 12:7–8.*
[16] *St. Matthew 25:41.*
[17] *II Peter 2:4.*

However, while such a diagnosis may explain the condition, it does not account for it. Recently a deeper understanding of mental irregularities has made us far less dogmatic about them. Strange things continue to happen. There are spiritual forces which baffle us but with which we must somehow reckon. Certainly our Lord wrestled with "unclean spirits," and we do not materially change the situation by substituting other terms which eventually mean much the same thing.

And when it comes to the Devil, we will do well to walk with some circumspection. His pictorial representation as a dark, naked figure with a cloven hoof, a long tail, and a pair of wicked horns is not all child's play. Of course it is not a picture of him, but it is a symbolic contrast with the other representation of the angel of light. As the white robe of the angel stands for purity, so does the dark, naked body indicate impurity. The hoof and the tail represent a carnal, bestial character, and the horns are symbols of strength and power. The name "Devil" is a Greek word for "accuser" or "adversary," and is the counterpart of the Hebrew "Satan" which has the same meaning. Our Lord speaks of him as "the prince of the devils,"[18] or as "the prince of this world"[19] (where "world" means the sphere of discord with God). St. Paul calls him "the prince of the power of the air, the spirit that now worketh in the children of disobedience."[20] Whatever we may name him, he is the instigator of evil, even so presuming as to tempt Christ Himself at the beginning of His ministry.[21] Our Lord recognized him as a serious contender, and we

[18] *St. Matthew 12:24.*
[19] *St. John 12:31.*
[20] *Ephesians 2:2.*
[21] *St. Matthew 4:1–11.*

cannot expunge him from the drama of human life without doing violence to the whole of the Christian Gospel.

There is not much more we can say. There is a spiritual world which penetrates our human world bombarding us with influences both good and bad. The choice rests upon us to make alliance with one or the other. Using the means which God gives us, we develop an increasing sensitiveness to the powers of light and a stronger resistance to those of darkness. As we acquire an affinity for the right, God's messengers find more ready entrance into our lives. We learn the significance of St. Paul's advice—"put on the whole armour of God, that ye may be able to stand against the wiles of the Devil. For we wrestle not against flesh and blood, but against principalities, against powers, against the rulers of the darkness of this world, against spiritual wickedness in high places."[22] In the Eucharistic offering, "with Angels and Archangels, and with all the company of heaven, we laud and magnify Thy glorious Name." We know our own needs, and in unison with the faithful we raise the Advent petition, "give us grace that we may cast away the works of darkness," and with it the further plea which the Church has wisely set for All Angels Day:

"O Everlasting God, who hast ordained and constituted the services of Angels and men in a wonderful order; Mercifully grant that, as Thy holy Angels always do Thee service in heaven, so, by Thy appointment, they may succour and defend us on earth; through Jesus Christ our Lord."[23]

[22] *Ephesians* 6:11–12.
[23] *The Book of Common Prayer, p. 251.*

XXV

CHRISTIAN WORSHIP

CHRISTIAN worship rests upon two principles. The first is that God is the center of all creation. It is one of those fundamental facts that needs reiteration. In modern times there has been a certain tendency to shift the central emphasis from God to man. The enormous strides made in the natural sciences and the swift developments in the field of industrial organization probably account for it. In the past century we have learned a great deal about man and the world in which he lives. We have also been successful in mechanical inventions which seem to supply mankind with everything he needs for the steady enrichment of his daily life. The study of human relationships has become an absorbing passion for people of a sociological turn of mind. Psychology and its natural offspring, psychiatry, have turned attention inward in the search for the secret of human behavior. Humanism has been the inevitable result—the attempt to solve human problems in a purely human atmosphere and by strictly human means. Theology has been discounted, God has been passed by, and worship has fallen into neglect. Popular religion has largely gone humanitarian and has contented itself with doing good to one's neighbor. In short, for many people man has become the center of the universe.

However, the cycle seems to be turning. More and more it becomes clear that man's efforts to raise himself by his own boot-straps is both unworkable and irrational. Mechanical improvements do not create happiness. The knowledge of right social relationships is not enough without some additional impulse to set them in motion. The further we explore our mental attitudes, the more we see that there is something deeper to be accounted for.

Through all the turmoil of modern progress Christianity has kept repeating that above man there is God; that man comes from God and returns to God; that there is no rhyme, reason, logic or common sense in a creation without a Creator; and that the real center of all things is God. "Thou shalt love the Lord thy God—and thy neighbor as thyself."[1] The sequence must be kept straight. The love of God comes first and supplies a reason for loving one's neighbor. Such a reason is necessary because frequently neighbors are not exactly lovable. Being creatures of God we are dependent on Him. Since He is the Source of all life, our very existence is conditional upon His will. Take away God and the universe explodes, carrying human life to annihilation.

God is the center of it all. Everything revolves around Him. Therefore to Him we pay our reverential respects, we acknowledge His sovereignty, we offer Him our prayers and praises—in short, we worship Him. Our fumbling answers to the problems of life are contingent on His wisdom —therefore we go to Him for guidance. Our physical needs are met by the physical laws which He has established—

[1] *St. Matthew 22:37–40.*

therefore we make Him suitable returns of gratitude. Once we recognize God to be central, we cannot reasonably avoid worshipping Him.

All that has been said thus far might be sufficiently covered by the regular practice of personal, private prayer on the part of those who recognize their human relationship to God. That brings us to the second principle—namely, that Christian worship is a corporate act. Important as personal prayer may be, it can never take the place of public worship. Our Lord's redemptive work is not only for individual Christians but for the Christian Society, the Church, the Family of God, the Body of Christ. We are dependent on one another even as we are all dependent on God. Through the Church God mediates His spiritual blessings, and from the Church worship is to be returned to Him. We are joined together by spiritual bonds which extend beyond death. The community of the faithful includes us in this world and also those in Paradise. Worship is an offering to God rendered by the whole family, both here and there.

The practical advantages of corporate worship are perfectly obvious. Ordinary experience teaches us the value of concerted action. The strength of a hundred men is more than one hundred times the strength of one. United effort adds a plus something to the combined efforts of any given number of individuals. It may be difficult to put your finger on it but you know it is there. A person of feeble voice might be reluctant to sing praises to God by himself, but place him in a choir and he will sing with confidence. The *esprit de corps* of a regiment, a lodge, or a labor union gives a lift to the individual members. So the spirit of worship in a congregation of people is a spiritual incentive to the individual worshipper. Of course, it goes far beyond this in the Church because the Church is more than a voluntary organization—it is a living spiritual organism.

Now any common movement, involving a considerable number of persons, must be planned and ordered if it is to escape confusion. Imagine a congregation of people each one expressing his worshipful self according to the private impulse of the moment! Imagine the singing of hymns where each singer selected his own words, tune, and tempo! God is a God of law and order. Any worship worthy of him must be dignified and regulated. Issues have been raised at times between so-called "free" worship and "liturgical" worship. As a matter of fact there can be no such thing as "free" worship where each person does spontaneously whatever he happens to think of. The old objection to a liturgy is fast disappearing. It is not so much a question of liturgy as it is a question of which one and what kind.

Worship is an art. Devotional expression requires training and cultivation just as much as musical or literary expression. Certain persons are gifted along devotional lines and have applied themselves to a careful study of the art of worship. The accumulated experience so acquired has been conserved in the historical liturgies of the Church. Certain methods have been tried, tested, and found to be most conducive to a suitable expression of common or united worship. There are liturgical principles which can be violated only at the cost of spiritual edification. In them "we see the good manners of created beings before their Maker."

The worship of God calls for a time, a place, and a method.

It is all very well to say that one can worship out in the open country or on the golf course. Everyone knows that it isn't done and, if it were, it would be violating the principle of corporate action. Worship is not a matter of passing compliments to God but of fulfiling a duty which is owing to Him. No recurrent duty can ever be performed without definite arrangements as to ways and means. So the Church has constructed the Christian Year with its seasons, feast days and fast days, and the regular observance of the Lord's Day. In the Christian Year engagements are made with God to be kept at specified times. Every Sunday is a special day of worship because it is the Resurrection day. Every Friday is a day of abstinence when we deny ourselves in memory of our Lord's crucifixion on that day. Each season throughout the year calls us to the recollection of some particular feature in the life and teaching of our Lord—His birth, death, resurrection, ascension, His Church, His Gospel, the expansion of His Kingdom, His gift of eternal life, final judgment, and our responsibility for Christian living. The full cycle of Christian teaching is kept before us as we make the annual pilgrimage of the Church seasons in company with Christ. Thus the *time* element is provided to keep our worship definite.

The *place* is, of course, our local parish church. It does not just happen that our churches are built and equipped as they are. A language of symbols has been developed which speaks just as accurately as any language of words. Churches are built for the glory of God. That is why we beautify and embellish them. Not that we need the embellishments for practical use, but because they are means of expressing our devotion to God, and they help create that atmosphere in which devotion is deepened in our actual worship. Always the most important point is the altar, symbol of God's presence. Nothing is allowed to obscure the altar, nothing stands before it, nothing impedes access to it. The center aisle runs straight through the church from the entrance to the altar, symbolizing the pathway of life which leads straight to God. By the door of the Church is placed the font where we are baptized. It represents the beginning of Christian life just as the altar represents its goal. The center aisle is the narrow way that leads from Baptism up to God.

The Bible is the guide book on our Christian way. It is not the end of the Christian life but a help in our progress. Therefore it is not placed before the altar, but at the side of the way upon the lectern.

Preaching is for instruction and encouragement on the way. We do not live to hear sermons—we live for God. Therefore the pulpit is not placed before the altar, but at the side as another help on our way.

Likewise music and singing are meant to inspire us on our way. We do not worship the organ—we worship God. Therefore the altar is kept clear while the organ and choir are divided on either side as further helps on the way.

The Church is built on three levels—the nave, the choir, and the sanctuary. The nave symbolizes life in this world, the choir means Paradise, and the sanctuary is the fulness of God's Presence in Heaven. From life in this world the way advances to God, and progress is always upward.

In the center of the altar stands the cross, chief symbol of everything Christian. It represents Christ. Flanking it are candles to remind us that Christ is the Light of the World. Flowers are placed beside the cross to symbolize the resurrection. These ornaments keep telling us that we worship Christ who through His death and resurrection has become the light of the world.

Throughout the building there may be many symbols in carving, painting, or stained glass of the God we worship. Maybe it is the triangle for the Holy Trinity, the hand emerging from the cloud which means God the Creator, the sacred letters IHS which stand for Jesus Christ, or the descending dove which represents the Holy Spirit. They are not merely decorations. They have a meaning. In what other place could worship be so profitably offered as in a church building where the reverential habits of the ages have been gathered together to meet our sense of the fitness of things?

The *method* is supplied by the liturgy—a form of worship which has been evolved out of centuries of Christian devotion and which is built upon recognized principles and accompanied by actions of definite significance. Worship is meant to be an active experience for the worshippers. They are not meant to be spectators but sharers in a common offering to God. Certain parts of a liturgical service belong to the congregation. They are supposed to join in and make it their own both by what they say and by what they do. Briefly their actions are governed by the following formula—we kneel for prayer, we stand for praise, we sit for instruction.

Worship is intended to be dramatic without being theatrical. Theatrical worship is showing off and easily becomes artificial. But dramatic worship is the performing of certain outward acts as expressions of a real meaning lying behind them. Worship is a changing, developing thing, reflecting the needs and concepts of the people in different times and places; but its basic principles remain the same. Liturgy is literally "the people's work," the way in which the people of God respond to the love of God.

The liturgical movement in recent years has affected the worship of the people in every part of the Christian Church. Protestants are placing more emphasis on the Lord's Supper, or the Holy Eucharist. Roman Catholics are offering the Mass in the language of the people. Episcopalians are emphasizing anew the importance of the laity in congregational participation. In many churches the altar has been brought closer to the congregation, and the priest celebrates facing the people. A new form for the Holy Eucharist, incorporating both old and new features, is being tried out, possibly for eventual incorporation in a revised Book of Common Prayer. New insights have been gained in the relationship of Holy Baptism and Confirmation. Provision has been made for commemoration of post-Reformation saints and heroes of the Faith. And members of different Christian Churches are beginning to have a new appreciation for the treasures of their varying traditions, and to worship together whenever possible. We are living in an age as exciting (and confusing) as that of the sixteenth century Reformation, but without the sharp intolerances that caused the strife and separations of that era in the Church's history.

The central act of worship is the Holy Eucharist, which is essentially a drama of salvation. The first act is the preparation for Christ in the ministry of the Word—readings from the Scriptures, prayers, praise, and the preaching of the Word of God. Then comes the presentation of Christ and the re-enactment of the Last Supper, with the consecration of the Bread and Wine and the administration of the sacrament of Holy Communion to His people. Finally, we express our thanksgiving, and go out into the world to do His work in our several callings. We are participants in the dramatic action, joining ourselves with Christ in the eternal offering which He has made in our behalf.

The worship of the Church keeps the lines of communication constantly open between God and man. God is always reaching out to us. He can find us only as we respond to His invitation. In our worship we make the responses, complete the connection, and God's power flows through.

Worship is the most important part of a Christian's life. Upon it depends our ability to receive God's grace and to put into practice the precepts of Christian living. To neglect it is plain discourtesy to God. To allow it to degenerate into a perfunctory formalism is a dishonor to God. It is a serious business—truly, "the people's work."

One needs to perfect oneself in the art of worship, never forgetting our Lord's injunction—"they that worship Him must worship Him in spirit and in truth."[2]

[2] *St. John 4:24.*

XXVI

THE PROBLEM OF EVIL

HERE IS a man who has always lived an honest, thrifty, decent life. One day, through no fault of his own, he is struck by an automobile and carried off to a hospital. An unscrupulous lawyer trickles in, gains his confidence, promises damages, and then by one ingenious trick after another defrauds the injured man out of all his savings and leaves him hurt and destitute. Certainly it is all wrong, and we can see no reason or sense in it. Once again we fret over the problem of evil.

But here is another man who has lived a neutral kind of life, never having done anything particularly commendable. One day a passing motorist good-naturedly picks him up and drives him home. A friendship grows out of the casual contact and the motorist does many kindnesses for the man, helps him solve his problems and gives him a start on a prosperous career. Why do we not become agitated over such a situation? Why are we not worried over a "problem of good"?

For some reason we assume that things ought to be right and we are not surprised when they are. We expect the good and we are troubled when it fails us. But why should we?

If the world is merely a mechanical device, churning out purposeless events, there is no more reason for expecting good things than bad things. There is no problem of evil because there are no standards of right and wrong. The machine grinds on, and we are thrown into the hopper for such impersonal treatment as a blind and heartless chance may arbitrarily dictate. We can theorize on such a cheerless possibility but we simply cannot live that way. Something in us rebels.

Instinctively we postulate a Will for Good as the guiding influence in life. We would all go mad if we did not believe that the world was meant to be right, and that goodness was the normal condition of human existence. Evil is abnormal and out of place. That's why we are perplexed over it while we take good for granted. As Christians, of course, we go a step further. We look to a Heavenly Father who made the world and said it was good. He is a God of holiness and righteousness who wants His holy and righteous principles to prevail among men. Evil is out of character with God, and it puzzles us to find it present in His good world. Are we wrong about God or are we inaccurate in our estimate of evil? Maybe some of the things we consider to be evil are not really so at all.

There are four classes of occurrences which we commonly designate as evil. Let's look them over.

1. There are the harmful deeds committed by men and women, perverted actions which cloud the characters of those who perform them and often inflict injury on others at the same time. The answer is simply—sin. God does not will these deeds and does not want them. They are products

of human selfishness and the denial of God's will. Sin is an evil thing and needs correction. God Himself has realized this so clearly that He has provided a way of redemption through the incarnation of our Lord Jesus Christ.

But there is still another troublesome point about it. Men may sin and incur divine disfavor for their misconduct. But the consequences of it often affect innocent persons who must suffer for the wrongs of others. Frequently the heaviest penalty of sin falls upon those who are not guilty. Why should that be so? It is so because we are all bound together in a common life. No man lives to himself alone. What I do has an inevitable effect on those who live about me. But this is true of good as well as of evil. I can make it easier or harder for others to live properly. I contribute to the well-being or the ill-being of my community as the case may be. It is not all one way. If someone commits a sin, I may suffer for it undeservedly. But if someone does a good deed I may benefit undeservedly. As a member of the human race I share its hurts and its blessings. I cannot be exempt from either one. It is because Man has sinned that I, as a man, must face the consequences of it. But it is also true that because Christ became Man, I, as a man, become a partaker of His divine grace. Personally I have not deserved either one. Therefore the evil of sin lies in human resistance to God and because I am human, I am part of it. Also because I am human, I shall find ultimate release in the Sacred Humanity of my Saviour.

2. Natural catastrophes—earthquakes, fires, floods, volcanic eruptions, tornadoes—occurrences which we call "acts of God" or simply "accidents." They comprise an exceedingly complicated state of affairs, and it is impossible to sift

them out with any degree of accuracy. For instance, it seems fairly well established that some of our most disastrous floods are largely due to our abuse of our natural resources—wholesale deforestation, the draining away of our swamps and marshes, unwise blocking of streams and rivers, the destructive cultivation of fertile lands, and so on. Also there are some places which are known to be danger spots—active volcanic districts, some of the mountain slopes, windswept regions, or low-lying areas always in danger of submergence. If we take chances and build towns and villages in what are known to be perilous locations, there is no real cause for surprise in the event of natural catastrophes. We can scarcely expect God to protect and deliver us from our own questionable recklessness.

Of course, that is not all of it. There are natural laws of which we know something, probably little of what there is to be known. Many disasters arise out of ignorance of what we ought to expect, and we suffer. Such calamities may seem to us very evil. Perhaps there is a good in them of which we are not conscious at the time. God has established natural laws and it may be more important in the long run for these laws to be upheld than for a relatively small number of people to be saved from a catastrophe. Probably we cannot see far enough but occasionally we can get a glimpse. A city is destroyed by an earthquake with much loss of life and property. A new city is erected on the ruins, far better than the old, cleansed of festering corners and disreputable haunts, a much finer place for a new community. In the end the catastrophe may have had its beneficial aspects—to be sure, at the cost of loss and suffering. It may be hard for us to reconcile the two. There is too much which we do not understand. The point is, some of the things we call evil may not be as evil as we think. A temporary loss is often the way to a greater final gain. In any case we trust the goodness of God to turn the scale in the right direction, recognizing that circumstances are complex beyond our powers of analysis, and that we must withhold final judgments on what we may be justified in calling "good" or "evil."

3. More than two thousand years ago an unknown writer composed the Book of Job in an effort at least to present the problem as to why good people are visited with a succession of troubles. Job was "perfect and upright, and one that feared God, and eschewed evil."[1] Adversities descended upon him until he was all but overwhelmed. "Job's comforters" came to reason with him over his sorry state but no one of them seemed able to provide a satisfactory answer. Finally the Lord Himself spoke to remind the questioners that they know very little of God's purposes, that with all the other things they cannot explain they must trust God in these mysterious visitations also. This poetic drama is as good an answer as anybody has yet advanced.

According to our little measurements of right and wrong, fortune should smile on the good and the righteous, while trouble and difficulty should be the lot of the wicked. Often the situation is quite reversed and we call it a problem of evil. Why should such things happen? One answer is that sometimes these apparent evils are not evil at all. Adversity may prove to be a rousing experience to test the mettle of our courage. Many people can date the best period of their lives

[1] *Job* 1:1.

from some violent disturbance which, at the time, seemed to them inexplicably unjust and unnecessary.

However, there are instances of totally undeserved hardships which never seem to do anybody any good. Why should they be permitted? Again we must remember that our lives are intertwined with other lives, and we cannot be insulated from the good and the bad which flows around us. I say the good and the bad because we are the undeserving recipients of both. If as innocent bystanders we suffer hurts from the evil doings of others for which we are in no way accountable, it is also true that we are frequently beneficiaries of blessings for which we have done nothing. Think of all the inventions and discoveries which have brought within our reach comforts and conveniences of life which we could never otherwise have enjoyed—yet what have we done to deserve them? Through painstaking research someone has produced anesthetics which have reduced the sufferings of the world immeasurably, and we reap a benefit to which we have made no contribution at all. All this does not wipe out the problem, but it hints at the direction in which an answer might be sought.

4. Finally comes the problem of pain—the most common and the most acute aspect of the whole question of evil. The sum total of physical agony under which the world staggers is appalling. Certainly a good God cannot wish this on us, and why should He allow it to be? Once again the question is not a clear-cut issue between good health and ill health. A large amount of disease and pain is attributable to our own bad living, to our violations of the laws of health, or to our straight-out sins. Sometimes the infliction of pain is remedial

and produces a greater joy in the long run. And not infrequently physical suffering induces refinements of character which could never result from any amount of ease and luxury however attractive they may be. The verses left by a patient in a Denver hospital greatly mitigate the problem of pain, if not the pain itself.

> "The cry of man's anguish went up unto God:
>   'Lord, take away pain!
> The shadow that darkens the world Thou hast made;
>   The close-coiling chain
> That strangles the heart; the burden that weighs
>   On the wings that would soar—
> Lord, take away pain from the world Thou hast made,
>   That it love Thee the more.'

> "Then answered the Lord to the cry of His world:
>   'Shall I take away pain,
> And with it the power of the soul to endure,
>   Made strong by the strain?
> Shall I take away pity, that knits heart to heart,
>   And sacrifice high?
> Will ye lose all your heroes that lift from the fire
>   White brows to the sky?
> Shall I take away love, that redeems with a price,
>   And smiles at its loss?
> Can ye spare from your lives that would climb unto mine
>   The Christ on His Cross?'"[2]

Yes, but the problem is still there. All of these considerations may qualify it, dull its edge, and dilute its venom—but a question still pursues us. Why should there be sin, and brutality, and greed, and violence in a world which God made

[2] *Quoted in the author's "Common-sense Religion," The Macmillan Company, N. Y., p. 146.*

to be good? Where do such ungodly factors come from? How did they get here? Why do they continue to bedevil us?

There are three ways of approach to the kernel of the problem.

A. We may blithely ignore it. We may cultivate the Pollyanna attitude and turn a blind eye to all that is unpleasant. There may be good and bad elements in life, but the best way to handle the evil is to pay no attention to it. Let it dissolve in its own iniquity. Good is positive, evil is negative. If we throw our whole weight of emphasis on the good, it will thrive and gradually smother out the evil. This point of view is not all nonsense but it runs too close to self-deception. Evil cannot be dismissed as the absence of good. It is not as negative as all that. Certainly it is capable of producing some very positive harm. And there are evils which can be eradicated. They must be recognized, tagged, labeled, fought, and destroyed.

B. The existence of evil may be denied as a logical impossibility. God is good and He is the author of all things. Therefore no place is left for anything evil. Sin and sickness are figments of the human imagination, sometimes called the "mortal mind." They must be non-existent because there is no possible origin for them since God is the Source of all creation. But—such a denial answers nothing. If sin and sickness are only mistaken ideas, the question still remains— where did such ideas come from? If evil is impossible, so is the idea of evil. For God is the Source of the world of ideas as well as the world of what we commonly call hard facts. And as far as human misery is concerned, what's the difference whether it comes from evil or from the idea of evil? A man may be killed with a gun or frightened to death. We may argue the cause of his demise, but in either case we have a funeral.

C. The third course is to face the facts honestly and admit that we do not know. From time out of mind people have worried their brains over the problem of evil without arriving at any satisfactory solution. Conditions are too complex for us. Some experiences which we think to be evil turn out to be very good for us. Others are mixed to such an extent that we cannot unravel the one from the other. Our vision is limited and our judgment is faulty.

Nevertheless, when all allowances have been made, evil is still a fact which we cannot escape. For guidance we look to our Blessed Lord who offers us no answer other than His own example. He met life with all its thorns and brambles. He did not minimize the forces of evil but challenged them without compromise on Calvary. He did not tell us why they are there or where they come from. But He did subdue them and worked a victory which He invites us to share. Whatever the reason for evil may be, its power is temporary and must submit to the goodness of God eventually. In that faith we line up with Christ, waging moral and spiritual warfare in His Name, trusting God for the triumph of the right without which life becomes a quagmire of insane futility.

God is good. Our destiny is to be like Him.

XXVII

CHRISTIAN MORALITY

WHY BE moral? It is far easier to ignore moral obligations and do what we like rather than what we ought. What's the good of going out of our way and making life harder for the sake of moral standards?

Some people will reply by reiterating the old adage that "honesty is the best policy" and will pay in the end. Obviously this is a low-grade reason, actuated by a questionable appeal to personal selfishness. But, apart from that, one may well be suspicious of the practical operation of such a policy. The truth is, you see many an ungodly person flourishing in his state of ungodliness. Honest people often live their lives in penury and restricted privileges while unscrupulous persons seem to skim off the cream very handily. It is not so clear that morality really does pay in that kind of coin.

Others would exhort us to be moral for the sake of society. Our ability to live and work together depends upon common standards of right and wrong. Society can live over the delinquencies of a few people here and there, but if disregard for moral principles should become a prevailing habit, society would collapse and no one could have confidence in anybody. Certainly this is true and it is a worthy appeal as far as it goes. But have we any reason to think our society is permanent? What finally becomes of all our moral efforts for a society which will one day become extinct? There must be some reason which will still be valid when this world crumbles away in cosmic dissolution.

"What shall it profit a man if he shall gain the whole world, and lose his own soul?"[1] Eternal life is the goal and the final explanation of moral living. Here in this life we are strengthening or weakening our immortal souls for their eternal opportunities. Moral living is a contributing factor to that spiritual character which survives death. He who lives up to moral standards here is building up spiritual sinews for service in the life to come. There may be other and lesser reasons, but they are all incomplete apart from the call to eternal life.

We have purposely headed this chapter "Christian Morality" rather than "Christian Morals" because there is a distinction between the two. Morality is a constant fact. Morals change. God has established His universe upon and regulates it by certain laws. These laws are permanent, dependable, immutable. One of them is the Moral Law. The germ of it is inherent in human nature. It is expressed in sets of morals which are the applications of the Moral Law to changing conditions. Eventually morals are destined to coincide with morality (or the Moral Law), but in the meantime we fumble the best we can with human perversities, sometimes improving our morals and sometimes slipping backward. Our business is to evolve a set of working morals which will measure up to the ultimate standard of the Moral Law.

[1] *St. Mark 8:36.*

Everywhere all kinds of people have recognized some kind of difference between right and wrong. There is an innate morality and it covers a general field of moral principles. Justice, truth, courage, generosity, personal decency—these are recognized everywhere, but their application in everyday morals has undergone many fluctuations. It is quite true that we condemn some things today as morally reprehensible which were once considered correct enough. Time was when polygamy was unquestioned on moral grounds. Now we call it morally very bad. Once upon a time the law of retaliation was considered right and proper—"an eye for an eye and a tooth for a tooth." Our Lord set it aside with His higher injunction, "love your enemies." In some parts of central Africa it is still morally sanctioned to eat human beings. In our own country vegetarians question even our moral right to eat animal food. Many people say you can't tell anything about it, that the whole thing is a matter of conventionalized custom, and there is no final standard of right and wrong.

As Christians we cannot submit to any such moral surrender. We believe that God is the Source of all life and the Creator of all things. In His creative work there is an intelligent purpose which can be fulfilled only by the harmonious interaction of all parts of His creation. Man has been endowed with free will. He may or he may not coöperate with God's purpose according to his own choice. Harmony with God is eternally right, and those principles of human living which produce such harmony are the principles of right human conduct. How can we know them? The feeling for them is born within us. We learn what they are in action through our Lord Jesus Christ. He not only teaches us the way but in His own life shows us how it is done, and then offers us help to do likewise. He is the measure of the perfect life, and we are right or wrong as we approach or depart from Him. There are eternally true standards which never change. We grow in our knowledge and appreciation of them. We may change but right is always right.

In a partly Christianized society we have some customs or morals which conform to the Moral Law. We have many others which are a long way below par or are in flat opposition to it. That is why we are often confused on the whole question of Christian conduct. Current morals are a mixture of pagan and Christian. Therefore many a person may be socially respectable but spiritually immoral. We Christians have to live in a world of mixed values and we are obliged to sift them out, specializing in those which belong to Christ, and possessed of sufficient courage to repudiate the others even at some cost and inconvenience. It has always been so. Twenty centuries ago Christians lived in an overwhelmingly pagan civilization. They could not resign themselves to the low moral views of their day. Within a corrupt society they erected their own moral standards and lived above their neighbors often to their own material disadvantage. Gradually their better way of living prevailed, and Christian morals began to supersede those of inferior breed. As the Gospel was carried into non-Christian lands the same process was repeated over and over again. It is a slow business. Many of the old habits have remained. Now and then they flare up into temporary popularity. The progress has been uneven —up and down with successes and failures. In the confusion it is not always easy to pick our way with certainty. The battle is still on, and the wounds are often grievous.

At the present time we are suffering from the effects of easy living. When our pioneer ancestors were opening up new areas they expected hardships and faced them without complaint. Today, however, we have settled into a relatively luxurious mode of living wherein physical hardships irritate us as unjust and unnecessary. We call it a richer life. In a sense it is, but what has it done to our moral fiber? We are fearfully concerned about the standards of living—but what about the standard of life?

A dear old lady one day expressed to me her doleful apprehensions over the ease of modern housekeeping. She told me of her early days of homesteading in a tar-paper shack, when they were snowed in solidly during the winter, when they sometimes sliced their frozen bread with a saw and chopped their meat out of the pork barrel with an ax. She could not understand the modern housekeeper who complained bitterly if the vacuum cleaner got out of order, or if the electric current failed for an hour, or if the house temperature fell below seventy degrees. She was sure the younger generation was growing soft and flabby and needed the discipline of downright hardship.

We would smile at such a sturdy soul—and admire her without in the least agreeing with her. But can we be sure that the comparative ease of modern living has not engendered an expectation of corresponding moral ease? Our Lord once reminded His listeners how they were always watching the weather signs. If they saw a cloud in the west, they knew it meant rain. If a wind blew up from the south, they knew it would bring heat. They had learned to judge the weather —but "why even of yourselves judge ye not what is right?"[2]

They were able to estimate weather conditions by training and experience. How could they expect to judge between right and wrong unless they trained their moral faculties? It is good advice for any of us. Just as there is a trained eye, a trained hand, or a trained mind, so there is also such a thing as a trained conscience. You wouldn't expect to find a proficient bookkeeper, carpenter, or attorney who had not received training in his line. Yet we have a way of expecting people to be proficient in judging moral values who have had no moral training at all. We take it for granted that our children will grow up morally right by associating with their elders and imbibing a general atmosphere of right living. The wonder is that there are not more moral lapses. Some innate sense of decency protects us.

We are all equipped with this something which we call "conscience." It is not easy to define but we all know it. Down inside of us is a moral umpire, a moral sense which passes judgment on our own conduct. Pious people have called it the Voice of God. Psychologists may describe it in more elaborate language. In any case, it is part of our moral equipment which, like any other faculty, demands cultivation. A neglected conscience becomes dull and unresponsive and, in the end, may become quite useless. A warped conscience may be turned into a hindrance rather than a help. But a conscience which is diligently cultivated by regular attention and exercise will acquire a sensitiveness to the Moral Law and become increasingly reliable in its decisions.

[2] *St. Luke 12:57.*

So said St. Paul when he stated his case before Felix—"herein do I exercise myself, to have always a conscience void of offence toward God, and toward men."[3]

The training of a Christian conscience is accomplished by constant and steady reference to Christian morality as summarized in the Eleven Commandments. It is one of the wonders of the ages that the Ten Commandments over a period of more than three thousand years have never been outdated. Their brief, crisp enactments still retain all the vigor of their origin. Their applications may be legion, but in themselves they touch the heart of the essential Moral Law. Whatever else our Lord did to the accumulated mass of Jewish regulations, He retained in His Gospel all those Commandments in their entirety, only supplementing their negative suggestions with one positive addition—"a new commandment I give unto you, That ye love one another."[4] Christian love means, simply, fair-play. You can love people even if you don't like them.

Now there are two kinds of Christian morality—personal morality and group morality. To be sure, they dove-tail into each other, and the one is incomplete without its companion. Nevertheless they cover two fields which are often dissociated in our popular judgments.

1. Personal morality is the kind we usually consider, involving our relations as individuals with other individuals. In such cases personal responsibility is more easily recognized and the trained conscience operates with greater facility. Every person is important in the eyes of God, and we fail of

[3] *Acts 24:16.*
[4] *St. John 13:34.*

our Christian standards insofar as we treat anyone as less than a person. To elevate things above persons is immoral from a Christian point of view. Artificial distinctions which raise certain people by degrading others is immoral. Cheating, thievery, or murder in any of their forms are contrary to Christian morality because they selfishly exploit or destroy the personality of others who are at least potentially children of God. Sexual vice is immoral not for its physical consequences but because it is debasing to personality. Pride, snobbishness, malicious gossip, personal hatreds—they are all morally evil because they are deterrents to the development of personality which is man's divine heritage. Anything that makes for the enhancement of personality is morally right. This is the principle embodied in the familiar Golden Rule—"all things whatsoever ye would that men should do to you, do ye even so to them."[5] This Rule was not new with our Lord except that He stated it in positive form and authenticated it with His teaching of the Fatherhood of God which automatically makes all men brethren in the human family.

2. But when it comes to group morality the deferred issues are not so clear. It is easy for me to respect and appreciate an individual Negro, or Japanese, or Russian, as the case may be, but I may not be at all immune to supercilious contempt for Negroes, or Japanese, or Russians. My personal morality becomes lost in the fog of racial antipathy. That, of course, is the basic cause of war. We shall never achieve international peace until we have accepted workable standards of national and racial morality. A respectable citizen would

[5] *St. Matthew 7:12.*

never think of brutally mistreating the cripple who lives next door, but in a surge of mob violence he may be quite capable of participating in a lynching party which is morally on the same plane. A business man who would indignantly refuse to swindle his competitor across the street will feel no twinge of conscience in voting the same thing through a Board of Directors where his personal responsibility is submerged in corporate action. Women will wax softly sentimental over the evils of sweat-shop labor, and then rush eagerly to the bargain counter to save a few pennies on purchases which could only be possible as products of the same sweat-shops.

Individually we have really acquired some commendable morals based on Christian morality. The history of the past two thousand years is illuminated by many an example of fine Christian conduct standing out brightly in the surrounding shadows. But corporately we are still in the Dark Ages. The modern campaign for social righteousness is an encouraging sign of a concerted effort to broaden the base of Christian morals and inculcate a sense of corporate responsibility among people acting in groups which will be at least equal to the moral sense prevailing among them as individuals. The Kingdom of God can never come to pass with any such bisected morality.

We moderns are likely to look down on the Middle Ages as a period of arrested development. It was no such thing, and there was one feature of it which might well give us pause today. The code of chivalry was something that really worked. To become a knight in those days required a long preparation of testing and training. At the age of seven years the aspirant began as a page, and spent seven years learning the rudimentary rules of chivalry. At fourteen he was advanced to the position of squire, and acted as personal attendant to a knight for seven years more. Then he had to qualify for knightly honors by performing some deed of personal valor—he had to "win his spurs." The night before his admission to the order he spent in solitary vigil before the altar with his armor before him as a symbol of complete dedication. Then he took his vows of chivalry and was dubbed a knight. Religion, honor, and courtesy were the watchwords of his future conduct. At all costs he must fulfil his knightly duties. No excuses were accepted. Should he break the code, he was counted a recreant knight, unfit to associate with his fellows. He might suffer loss, he might face defeat, he might lose his life—but he must not violate the code. Some things he must do and other things he simply could not do, because he was a knight. "Noblesse oblige" was the principle which governed all his actions.

Today we have largely convinced ourselves that we need no code of conduct. We have gone in for self-expression with its attendant self-indulgence, and we discount the value of moral discipline. Yet in spite of it all there is a Christian code. Honesty, fair-play, decent living, reverence for God, respect for our fellowmen, loyalty to Jesus Christ—these are the governing principles of the Christian life. There is a Christian "noblesse oblige"—some things a Christian must do and others he must not do, just because he is a Christian. The ethical implications of Christianity are ever present. One cannot be a good Christian and a moral leper at the same time. To believe in Christ and to live like a heathen is an impossible contradiction. "Thou shalt love the Lord thy God with all thy heart, and with all thy soul, and with all thy mind. This is the first and great commandment. And the second is like unto it, Thou shalt love thy neighbour as thyself."[6]

[6] *St. Matthew 22:37–39.*

XXVIII

CHRISTIAN MISSIONS

To BE a Christian is to be a missionary. The Christian thrives spiritually when he is giving his religion away, just as the Church has always grown stronger at its base when it was expanding its frontiers.

The rector of a parish where the church had burned, leaving the congregation sadly demoralized, asked Phillips Brooks what he would do under such circumstances. The great Bishop replied—"The first thing I would do would be to take up an offering for foreign missions."

The study of Comparative Religions has been a great blessing in helping us appreciate the religious aspirations of other peoples, but it has also led many Christians to think that we should not impose our Gospel on people who already have a religion of their own. If it really were a question of imposition, there might be some merit to such a contention. But our Lord came to establish a Kingdom for all men and He left specific instructions to extend His invitation—"Go ye therefore and teach all nations,"[1] "ye shall be witnesses unto Me both in Jerusalem, and in all Judaea, and in Samaria, and unto the uttermost part of the earth."[2] If Christ is our

[1] *St. Matthew 28:19.*
[2] *Acts 1:8.*

Lord and Saviour, we cannot pass lightly over His commands. He has every right to know how the affairs of His Kingdom should be conducted.

The time-worn complaint is always arising that we have too much to do in our home communities—that we should Christianize our own people before we attempt to move out to others. The point is that religion simply doesn't work that way. No nation has ever yet been completely Christianized. No nation can be until all the others are. We may be thankful that our forefathers realized this. If they had waited until all of Europe was thoroughly Christian, we in America would be uproariously pagan today. What if the Apostles had confined their efforts to Jerusalem until that city was entirely converted to the Gospel? They would still be at it, while the rest of the world would know nothing but heathen gods and the doubtful accompaniments of pagan civilization. Would we be willing to see ourselves totally ignorant of Christ—no Gospel, no Christian altars, no Sacraments, no Easter, no Christmas, none of the fruits of Christian teaching? Obedient to our Lord's command the Apostles set no limits to their missionary activities. They did move out into Judaea, and Samaria, and on to the ends of the world as it was known in their day. They recognized that properly speaking there are no "Foreign Missions" because all people are God's children and His Kingdom knows no foreigners. Nothing has happened since that time to reverse the truth of it.

Three reasons might be cited for the necessity of Christian Missions:

1. The world today is a unit. It cannot be separated off

into water-tight compartments. In fact, it grows smaller all the time as the various parts of it are bound more closely together through the advance of modern means of communication. Everything that happens in the world affects us and *vice versa*. If a plague breaks out in India, the health of every American community is endangered, and elaborate precautions are instituted to keep the infection away. A crop failure in the United States affects the food supply of all the countries of Europe. Let one country debase its currency and the echo of it is heard in every exchange the world over. No war can really be localized. In spite of nationalistic propaganda to the contrary, no nation can be truly self-contained.

Year after year these ties are drawn more closely around a shrinking world. How can religion be torn from such a context and marked off for home consumption? Every Christian nation has been moulded by its Christian inheritance. The very fact that any considerable number of its people have accepted Christ's Gospel means that Christian principles have, to a greater or less degree, been incorporated in the national tradition and have influenced the national habits. Every time a commercial representative is sent to a foreign country he carries some of that Christianity with him because it is bred in his bones. He may misrepresent Christ but he cannot leave Christ behind him. When western civilization moves into the Orient, Christianity has got to go with it or it isn't western civilization. Western culture and Christian ideals are inextricably intertwined. To give out one without the other is like offering electric fixtures without any current. We have already done too much of that very thing to the disadvantage of all concerned.

2. We must carry the Gospel to non-Christian people because we have no right to keep it to ourselves. We are trustees—not owners. We have received the benefits of the Christian faith, not because we deserved them, but because of the generosity of other Christians. Selfishness is the supreme spiritual corrosive. Cling to Christianity and it spoils on your hands. Dam up the Church and it stagnates. The Gospel is not something to be treasured—it is to be shared. That is the very nature of it. If by clutching what you have you squeeze the life out of it, you are not only depriving others but you are despoiling yourself. This is not a matter of thin theory. It has proved itself too often to be seriously questioned.

3. We have yet much to learn of our own Gospel by what other people can teach us about it. We shall never know its full content until all races have revealed its variegated riches. Christianity means something different and better to us now than it did to those who lived it in the tenth century. (Not that the Gospel has changed, but that Christian experience has expanded. Likewise it means something different to different kinds of people today. The essence and scope of it may be the same, but every new convert teaches us more of its meaning. To us Americans Christ has His own significance, but that does not mean that everyone must become an American before he can become a Christian. We want Chinese Christians, and Japanese Christians, and Indian, and African, and Polynesian, in order that we may all know better what a Christian ought to be.

Today we speak more of the mission of the Church than

of "missions." We have learned that the old distinction between "foreign" and "domestic" missions is unreal. The mission of the Church is one and indivisible, and it is the very essence of its life. It has been said that "the Church exists by mission as fire by burning." Archbishop Ramsey of Canterbury expressed it in his observation that "the Church that lives to itself will die by itself."

We have a mission to our own community, to the people of the teeming urban areas, to farmers and ranchers and Indians, to the underprivileged poor and to the overprivileged rich. We express our sense of mission not only by the gifts that we give but by the way in which we live out our Christian convictions in home, school, office, and factory.

In foreign lands, we are increasingly learning to express the Church's mission by our cooperation with indigenous Churches and ministries, by respecting their national customs and leadership, and by recognizing that we are fellow-seekers of the truth that God has revealed to all men.

The Church does not send out missionaries to patronize those of other traditions, or to make them American Episcopalians. They go to share with others, at home or abroad, what God has entrusted to all His people, that we and they together may approach somewhat nearer to "the measure of the stature of the fulness of Christ."[3]

[3] *Ephesians 4:13.*

XXIX

CHRISTIAN WITNESS

EVERYBODY stands for something. Whoever you are, you are contributing something to the course of human events. When an issue arises you may remain silent and believe you are not committing yourself, but your very silence counts for something one way or the other. Every life sheds an influence on other lives—good or bad, positive or negative, helpful or harmful. There is no such thing as a blank personality. These cross-hatched influences flowing out of many lives make the broad pattern of modern society. No one can stay out of it even if he wants to.

Christ is an issue in modern life. Every man and woman contributes something toward what His standing shall be in the world of our time. Strictly speaking there can be no spiritual neutrality. If you support Christ, you are helping Him. If you deny Him, you are opposing Him. If you ignore Him, you are retarding Him. But you are always doing something to Christ.

It is a temptation to shuffle people about in one or another of these three groups and pigeonhole them for future reference. Actually life is too complicated for any such simplified segregation. Many people will go with Christ up to a certain point—and then become confused. They will bear a good enough witness in theory but become sadly bewildered when it comes to daily practice. For example, most of us will be mildly shocked at the idea of polytheism. We consider it an ancient evil which we have happily outgrown— or a curious hang-over in backward parts of the modern world, with no particular meaning for us. We have been reared in the spirit of monotheism—One God and Father of us all—and we would scarcely think of questioning it.

The old idea of polytheism postulated separate deities for many different activities. There was a god of the sea and a god of the land, a god of the home and a god of the state, a god of war and a god of peace—and so on. Under the pagan conception due regard had to be paid to each one of these as the occasion required. The Romans appealed to Mars, Jupiter, Venus, or Minerva depending on the circumstances of the moment. Sometimes a situation would be mixed, and it was difficult to decide in the province of which god it might properly fall. In such cases appeal would be made to several for safety's sake. To us, with our Christian background, it is all very absurd. The first Christians flatly repudiated it. We consider it fitting as well as courageous that they should have suffered and died on that issue. It was their personal witness to Christ and it wins our hearty approval and gratitude.

But what are we doing about it? On Sunday we worship Christ devoutly and sincerely. On Monday we go out into the business world and pay homage to some gilded god of commerce, often directly opposed to Christ.

We welcome the Prince of Peace on His birthday, and for

the balance of the year resign ourselves to the inevitability of international strife as though somehow it had to be right.

We sing praises to the God of love and good-will—and then do the rounds of our social circle where we make offerings to a green-eyed goddess of gossip, snobbery and ill-will.

Too much we are theoretical Christians—and practical polytheists. The modern world retains too many relics of classical paganism. It is not easy to bear the kind of Christian witness which Christ expects of us. But He does expect it. We have the examples of great Christian heroes whom we admire and love to commemorate. But most of them lived in dramatic settings with real battles to wage. If we were paraded out on the great stage of human history and put on trial for our faith, we also would prove our loyalty and glory in our opportunities. The difference is that most of our tribulations are unromantic troubles, small personal irritations with nothing at all inspiring about them. It is hard to wage war on trifles.

Perhaps for that very reason ours is the greater test of faith and loyalty. You would be willing to prove your devotion to Christ in a big way. But is your faith of sufficient quality to prove loyal in small things? You read the story of those Christians who were thrown to the wild beasts in imperial Rome and you find it vivid, interesting, thrilling, fascinating. Yet I am sure those Christians found it to be no such thing. To them it was undoubtedly sordid and disgusting. They did not know they were doing anything heroic for our edification today. They were simply being loyal to Christ in hard times.

There are three ways in which we may and should bear

our personal witness to Christ today just as truly as did any of the martyrs who redden the pages of our Church calendars.

1. By personal life. For the most part people do not judge Christ nearly so much on His own merits as they do on the behavior of His followers. Those who injure Christ most are not His open enemies. Rather it is those who speak Him fair and live Him black. Seldom will you find a person who will presume to object to our Lord. But you will find many who will pass Him by because they object to those who bear His Name.

Two men were walking down the street together. "There," said the first man, pointing across the way, "is the founder of our local atheists' club."

"Nonsense," said the second man. "I know that fellow. He is a pillar in such-and-such a Church."

"Yes," replied the first man, "I know that too. He professes his religion so loudly and lives his life so badly that he has alienated his friends from the Christian faith. In protest against his obvious insincerity they have organized an atheists' club to express their disapproval."

Every Christian carries the reputation of Christ in his hands, and his personal life commends Christ or discredits Him.

2. By personal testimony. Why are people so reluctant to talk about their religion? There is, to be sure, a commendable reticence in matters of deep spiritual moment. Most of us despise the appearance of sham. We are nauseated by pious pretensions and prove our distaste by a clam-like refusal to mention our religious convictions. There may be something

to be said for it but we are scarcely justified in hiding our re·ligion away as though we were ashamed of it. After all our Lord did declare, "Whosoever shall confess Me before men, him shall the Son of man also confess before the angels of God."[1] You don't have to argue but you can bear witness.

A Churchwoman had a friend who was a society woman and totally uninterested in anything religious. The society woman's husband died, leaving her well fixed financially but otherwise desolate. The Churchwoman wrote a note to her friend expressing sympathy and making reference to the love of God and eternal life. After the funeral the society woman asked the Churchwoman to come and call. She explained that in her bereavement she had received scores of letters of condolence, but only in that one from the Churchwoman had there been any mention of Christian comfort. (Imagine that, if you will!) "Now," she went on, "you have something that I need desperately. Tell me about it." Whereupon the Churchwoman told in very simple terms what Christ meant to her, together with the Church and the Sacraments. As a result the society woman was presently baptized, confirmed, and lived the rest of her life as a devoted communicant of the Church, finding a solace there which nothing else could supply.

Often people are wavering, ready to stumble off in one direction or the other. A simple statement of one's own faith may be enough to steady the waverer. One need not be a theologian or any other kind of religious expert, but one can always speak up for Christ with, sometimes, momentous results.

[1] *St. Luke 12:8.*

3. By personal service. Too often Church people move on the assumption that the work of the Church is the professional responsibility of the clergy. They may not realize that frequently non-professional service is more effective among those on the outside. Crowds of people remain unchurched because they think they are not wanted or that nobody cares. A little friendly effort may work wonders.

A new rector came to a parish at the beginning of Lent. The vestry told him that the Bishop usually came for Confirmation just after Easter. The rector said he would ask to have the visitation postponed until he was sufficiently acquainted with his new field to gather together a Confirmation class. The vestry objected. They asked him to announce a time for instruction and leave it to them to bring candidates. With many misgivings the rector acquiesced, announced a meeting for instruction, and came to the parish house at the appointed time. He was met by more than a hundred people, the majority of whom were communicants in the parish who had brought their friends to learn about the Church. A few weeks later a large class was presented to the Bishop for Confirmation.

It's the old story of St. Andrew—he brought his brother to Christ. It's the way the Gospel has always spread and the Church has grown, by the personal witness of Christians. No degree of powerful leadership can accomplish it. No amount of efficient organization can do it so well. Through Christians Christ becomes known. There is a priesthood of the laity.

XXX

CHRISTIANITY IN PRACTICE

W E MODERNS like to consider ourselves a practical people. We are more interested in doing things and getting them done than we are in discussing theories about them. Sometimes we race the engine of efficiency so fast that we become entangled in the machinery of our own plunging activity. Then we must stop and look things over to discover just where we are going.

In our more sober moments we know very well that any true progress consists first in the formulating of sound principles, and second, in putting those principles into practice. This is so very self-evident in most matters that it calls for little argument. But when we come to the Christian religion, it does not always seem quite so clear. Generally speaking, it is not difficult to interest people in the main principles of the Christian faith. The problem comes in nailing that faith down to a point of specific performance. Religious vagueness may be comforting, and consoling, but it gets few spiritual results. A sentimental appeal to the spirit of Christ is the cheapest possible way of avoiding the inconvenience of living like a Christian. The world is full of admirers of Christ, but it is not over-populated with His followers.

Christianity is a demanding religion. It is the height of futility to invite people into the company of Christ merely for the purpose of absorbing spiritual satisfaction. He neither wants nor does He ask for a divided allegiance. If you are to travel with Him, you must be prepared to go all the way.

It is not easy to be a Christian, and there is no justification for encouraging people to believe that it is easy. I might arise and boldly announce to you that the Gospel of Christ is God's greatest gift to the world, that the Incarnation is the supreme event in all human history, that Christianity is the most valuable factor in the life of men or of any man. Then I might appeal to you to accept it because you will find it a pleasant experience, you will be sure to enjoy it, you will see that it is easy to take. If your brains are working at all, you will promptly tell me that the two propositions do not make sense. There must be a trick in it somewhere. You would tell me that Christianity cannot be the great thing I claim it to be or, if it is, something more must be expected of us commensurate with its importance. I would be like a man trying to give away good dollars on the street corner. Nobody would accept them because free dollars are generally spurious.

The prevailing popular sin is the sin of compromise. We all have some decent instincts and, at least when we are at our best, it is difficult for any of us to be wholly deaf to the call of Christ. But the world is a distracting place in which to live, and in our bewilderment we easily follow the line of least resistance. We complacently excuse ourselves for living a pagan existence embroidered with occasional reminiscences of Christ. How often does one hear the jovial remark—

"Well, I suppose I am not much of a Christian but I do enjoy a good sermon." What does it mean? Did Christ die to provide us with a delectable vocabulary? Is the Christian religion only a social accessory, compounded out of second-rate interests, or is it a vital power of the first magnitude intended for actual use?

Every life should have a dominating motive—a supreme loyalty to which all others surrender if a decision should be called for. This does not mean a one-track life, but a life in which many diverse elements contribute to a common purpose. One of the most pathetic features of modern American life is its aimless scurrying, always rushing somewhere but never pausing long enough to answer the question—what for? Our colleges are crowded with young people who have no idea why they are there. Young men and young women marry each other because it is the accepted way for two people to live together, but with very little determination to erect a sound family unit in society. Men and women accept positions in business with no notion of making a contribution to the common good, but rather to secure the largest possible returns with which to buy themselves a few pleasures. Every day hundreds of people die as forgotten men and women because in their negative existence they have never done anything for which they will be missed.

In such a confusion of purposes, or no purpose at all, compromise becomes the breath of their nostrils. Nothing is permanent. Expediency is the watchword. Anything may be sacrificed for the impulse of the moment. Ask these people what it is they are living for and you will throw them all a-stutter. It is absurd to approach such a public and ask them to add Christ as one more item in their long list of fluctuating interests. It only encourages further compromise. It is more true to Christ and far better for the people themselves to confront them with the uncompromising claims of His divine sonship. Said our Lord "no man can serve two masters" —neither can he serve a dozen. Christ doesn't want part of you—He wants all of you. He asks not for your kind condescension but for your life. He would be the object of your supreme loyalty. William Carey, the cobbler, was once asked "what is your business?" He replied, "My business is to preach the Gospel and I cobble shoes to pay expenses."

Jesus Christ could never have won His way originally on the part-time allegiance of a host of tepid listeners. It was a small number of resolute Christians who melted down the opposing paganism of the Roman empire by the burning fervor of their invincible convictions. Nothing less than that will resolve the abounding paganism of modern America. Talking will not do it. Money will not do it. Neither will organization, publicity, nor expensive architecture. Christians will do it—Christians who have taken Christ seriously and have welcomed Him to the pre-eminent position which He seeks. And this is no summer pastime. It means an irrevocable choice. In effect He says to us, "He that is not with Me is against Me; you must make up your minds but don't do it thoughtlessly; if you accept my sovereignty, you will never be the same again; you will be marked men and marked women—marked with the sign of the cross."

In a book published shortly before his death Robert Norwood wrote, "We admit that, in a world like ours, if one wants to be comfortable, it is best to leave Jesus alone, to have nothing to do with Him. We heard of a splendid young man, teaching a group of agnostics and atheists about Jesus. He himself had been an atheist, yet one of the most spiritual young men we know. This is what he said to his group; 'Leave Jesus alone, because, if He gets hold of you, you are done for. You will never be satisfied with life as you have been living it. A long, hard road of struggle and anguish is before you. Best leave Him alone.' "[1]

Don't be afraid of it—but don't trifle with it. Approach Christ with some determination. Refuse to be satisfied with an occasional rousing of your spiritual emotions. Set up a rule for your Christian life, a certain minimum of daily spiritual practice, and make it your business to follow it. Impulsive spurts of Christian interest can never develop a Christian character. You need something specific to work on. Souls must be trained and strengthened by regular exercise if they are to stand the strain of any normal human life. Your rule need not be oppressive but it should be definite. Let it be a program of daily prayer, of regular public worship, of some steady and useful service offered to God. Admit into your life some real sense of duty, and you will discover a workable antidote to that fatty degeneration of the soul which sometimes becomes epidemic among conventional Christians. Such a rule may not always be easy to carry through—but why should it be? It will put feet on your religion and allow it to go places.

We cannot afford to spend this short life on matters nonessential. Beware of spiritual compromise. A reduced Christ

[1] *Robert Winkworth Norwood, "Increasing Christhood," Charles Scribner's Sons, N. Y., p. 41.*

can never bring God's Kingdom to pass. Don't look for the easiest Christian way. Look for the greatest Christian good, even if it costs you more.

Magnify your Christian privileges.

Exalt Christ.

Be loyal to His Church.

Christ is your One Master.

Tolerate no other.

INDEX